TEST YOUR VOCABULARY

WRITE S IF THE WORD IN THE SECOND COLUMN
IS SIMILAR IN MEANING TO THE WORD IN THE
FIRST COLUMN OR **O** IF IT IS OPPOSITE.

1. MYRIAD	A. FEW	_O_
2. PANACEA	B. CURE-ALL	___
3. OPULENT	C. SPARE	___
4. ESCHEW	D. SHUN	___
5. NEFARIOUS	E. WICKED	___
6. INCARCERATE	F. IMPRISON	_S_
7. AMELIORATE	G. MAKE WORSE	___
8. CANDOR	H. HYPOCRISY	___
9. TACITURN	I. TALKATIVE	___
10. VERBOSE	J. WORDY	_S_

FIND THE ANSWERS IN
THE RANDOM HOUSE
POWER VOCABULARY BUILDER

Published by Ballantine Books:

RANDOM HOUSE WEBSTER'S DICTIONARY
RANDOM HOUSE ROGET'S THESAURUS
THE RANDOM HOUSE GUIDE TO GOOD WRITING
RANDOM HOUSE SPANISH-ENGLISH ENGLISH-SPANISH
  DICTIONARY
RANDOM HOUSE LATIN-AMERICAN SPANISH
  DICTIONARY
THE RANDOM HOUSE POWER VOCABULARY BUILDER
RANDOM HOUSE JAPANESE-ENGLISH
  ENGLISH-JAPANESE DICTIONARY

The Random House House Power Vocabulary Builder

BALLANTINE BOOKS • NEW YORK

http://www.randomhouse.com

Library of Congress Catalog Card Number: 96-96202

ISBN: 0-345-40545-5

Manufactured in the United States of America

First Ballantine Books Edition: August 1996

10 9 8 7 6 5 4 3 2

CONTENTS

FOREWORD

Expressing oneself is a basic human action. Words, whether spoken or written, express what we are thinking and what we wish to get across. A larger vocabulary enables you to express your thoughts more vividly and precisely. Along with teaching you new words, *The Random House Power Vocabulary Builder* gives you the tools to widen your choice of words for expressing your thoughts.

The Random House Power Vocabulary Builder explains the building blocks of the English language (roots, prefixes, suffixes, imported words); offers tips for proper expression (spelling, pronunciation, usage); and takes a look at its ever-changing aspects (special words, gender-neutral language, and new words).

The English language is one of the richest in the world, with influences from all over the globe. There are, however, some core influences that reflect its largely European origins: primarily Latin, Greek, and French. A multitude of words stem from these languages, and the greater part of this book is designed to teach you these word origins, thereby helping you build a broader and more versatile vocabulary.

To further help you excel in English usage, this book provides quizzes and puzzles to reinforce what you will learn in the coming chapters. And to maintain this new knowledge, be sure to write and speak the words in complete sentences, thus incorporating and registering them in your growing, more powerful vocabulary.

1. BUILD A MORE POWERFUL VOCABULARY

Words are the building blocks of thought. They are the means by which we understand the ideas of others and express our own opinions. It is only logical that people who know how to use words concisely and accurately find it easier to achieve their aims.

In fact, formal education has less relationship to vocabulary achievement than you might expect; people *can* improve their word power on their own. This section will show you how to expand and improve your vocabulary in *just ten minutes a day!*

Each of the following lessons is designed to take ten minutes to complete. Do one lesson a day. Work from beginning to end because the lessons build on each other. Follow these three easy steps:

Step 1: Time

Begin by setting aside a block of ten minutes a day. Don't split your time into two five-minute segments—set aside one ten-minute period every day. Consider using ten minutes in the early morning before you begin your regular activities. Or you might want to use ten minutes on the bus, subway, or train or ten minutes during a work break. Maybe right after dinner is a convenient time for you. Whatever time you select, make it *your* time—carve it in granite! To make your work even easier, try to set aside the same time every day. You'll be surprised at how quickly your vocabulary builds.

Step 2: Place

Now, find a place where you can work undisturbed. If you know that you have difficulty tuning out the distractions of public transportation or the office lunchroom, try to study at home.

1

Perhaps you have the ability to completely ignore extraneous chatter or music and so can concentrate in the middle of the family room or in a crowded cafeteria. Wherever you decide to study, try to settle in the same place every day. In this way, you'll set to work more quickly, concentrate better, and succeed sooner.

Step 3: Method

Ten minutes a day is all it takes to build a powerful vocabulary. To help you get into the rhythm of working in ten-minute segments, set your alarm or kitchen timer for ten minutes. When you hear the buzzer, you'll know that you've spent ten minutes on your vocabulary. Soon you'll be able to pace yourself without the timer.

TEST YOUR VOCABULARY

How Good Is Your Vocabulary?

To see how your vocabulary measures up to that of other people, take the following quizzes. As you go through each one, put a check mark next to any word you don't know. After you complete each quiz, go back and see which of your choices proved correct. Then take a minute to study the words you missed.

Quiz 1: Grading Your Word Power

The first quiz consists of twenty-five phrases, each containing an italicized word. Circle the correct response. This quiz has no time limit.

1. a *lenient* supervisor
   a. short b. not strict c. inflexible d. shrewd
2. an *audacious* endeavor
   a. foolish b. serious c. expensive d. bold
3. a *latent* talent
   a. apparent b. valuable c. present but not apparent
   d. useless
4. a *gaudy* dress
   a. expensive b. deep green c. flattering d. showy
5. a *disheveled* person
   a. useless b. untidy c. miserable d. vicious
6. *feign* illness
   a. suffer b. pretend c. die from d. enjoy

7. an *agile* child
   a. intelligent   b. nimble   c. neglected   d. annoying
8. a *somber* night
   a. dismal   b. expensive   c. lively   d. disastrous
9. a *prosaic* event
   a. extraordinary   b. irregular   c. commonplace
   d. pretty
10. a *vivacious* person
    a. annoying   b. dismal   c. vicious   d. spirited
11. a *baffling* situation
    a. puzzling   b. obvious   c. easy   d. old
12. a *hiatus* in the schedule
    a. continuation   b. uniformity   c. gap   d. beginning
13. a *lackluster* report
    a. enthusiastic   b. praiseworthy   c. dull   d. wordy
14. a *prevalent* condition
    a. adult   b. widespread   c. previous   d. fatal
15. a *loquacious* person
    a. talkative   b. cutthroat   c. laconic   d. enthusiastic
16. an *anonymous* victim
    a. willing   b. known   c. not known or named   d. foreign
17. a *vicarious* thrill
    a. incomplete   b. triumphant   c. spoiled   d. indirect
18. a *languid* feeling
    a. nervous   b. energetic   c. fatigued   d. robust
19. *vernacular* language
    a. ordinary   b. elevated   c. formal   d. informal
20. a religious *icon*
    a. gesture   b. picture   c. ritual   d. structure
21. *inclement* weather
    a. fair   b. unexpected   c. foul   d. disturbing
22. a *cavalier* attitude
    a. pleasant   b. dramatic   c. considerate   d. arrogant
23. a *caustic* remark
    a. wise   b. biting   c. prudent   d. complimentary
24. a timely *caveat*
    a. bargain   b. purchase   c. warning   d. movement
25. an *ominous* situation
    a. pleasant   b. rigid   c. obvious   d. threatening

Refer to the following chart to score your results:

0–6	correct	Below average
7–13	correct	Average

14–20   correct   Above average
21–25   correct   Superior

The following three quizzes evaluate whether you have an average, good, or excellent vocabulary. The quizzes have no time limit.

Quiz 2: Test for an Average Vocabulary

If you have an average vocabulary, you should be able to match the two columns below correctly. Write your answer in the space provided. Nearly three quarters of the adults tested knew all these words.

1. IMMINENT AT HAND	a. cleanse	J	I
2. FLUSTER	b. flashy		C
3. RIGID	c. confuse		G
4. PURGE	d. restore		A
5. REHABILITATE	e. hinder		D
6. LATENT HIDDEN	f. pretend	I	J
7. GAUDY	g. stiff		B
8. FEIGN	h. coax		F
9. CAJOLE	i. hidden		H
10. IMPEDE	j. at hand		E

Quiz 3: Test for a Good Vocabulary

Only half the adults tested got all of the following words correct. See how well *you* can do! Write S if the word in the second column is similar in meaning to the word in the first column or O if it is opposite.

			S or O
1. myriad	few	O	O
2. PANACEA	cure-all	S	
3. OPULENT	spare	O	
4. ESCHEW	shun	S	
5. NEFARIOUS	wicked	S	
6. INCARCERATE	imprison	S	S
7. AMELIORATE	make worse	O	
8. CANDOR	hypocrisy	O	
9. TACITURN	talkative	O	
10. VERBOSE	wordy	S	S

Quiz 4: Test for an Excellent Vocabulary

Fewer than one quarter of the adults tested got all of the following words correct. In the space provided, write T if the definition is true or F if it is false.

T or F

1. *Obsequiousness* is a sign of pride. — F
2. *Parsimonious* people are extravagant. — F / T
3. Recycling is an *exigency* of the moment. — T / F
4. The hawk is a *predatory* bird. — T
5. An *aquiline* nose is straight. — F
6. A *covert* plan is out in the open. — F
7. It is hard to explain things to an *obtuse* person. — T
8. Someone with *catholic* views is narrow-minded. — F / T
9. A large debt *obviates* financial worries. — F
10. *Erudite* people are well-read. — T

ANSWERS TO TESTS IN CHAPTER 1

Answers to Quiz 1

1. b 2. d 3. c 4. d 5. b 6. b 7. b 8. a 9. c 10. d 11. a 12. c 13. c 14. b
15. a 16. c 17. d 18. c 19. a 20. b 21. c 22. d 23. b 24. c 25. d

Answers to Quiz 2

1. j 2. c 3. g 4. a 5. d 6. i 7. b 8. f 9. h 10. e

Answers to Quiz 3

1. O 2. S 3. O 4. S 5. S 6. S 7. O 8. O 9. O 10. S

Answers to Quiz 4

1. F 2. F 3. T 4. T 5. F 6. F 7. T 8. F 9. F 10. T

2. Pronunciation Tips

Obviously, knowing the meaning of a word is only half the battle: you also have to know how to pronounce it. The best way to learn how to pronounce new words is by using a dictionary. It is the best source for the words you need to get you where you want to go.

Lesson 1. Test Your Pronunciation Skills

How Good Is Your Pronunciation?

Let's see how you pronounce some fairly difficult words. As you work through each quiz, put a check mark next to any word whose pronunciation you don't know. After you finish each quiz, go back and see which of your choices were right. (Some words have alternate pronunciations.) Finally, take a few minutes to study the words you missed.

Each of the following quizzes contains twenty words. See how many you can pronounce correctly. There is no time limit.

Quiz 1: Pronunciation

1. badinage
2. salubrious
3. apocryphal
4. putsch
5. effeminacy
6. effusive
7. mandible
8. raison d'être
9. amblyopia
10. dacha
11. exegesis
12. dishabille
13. élan
14. febrile
15. gamut
16. obsequious
17. jejune
18. ribald
19. gecko
20. wizened

Answers:

To satisfy your curiosity, here are the definitions as well as the pronunciations. To rank yourself against others, refer to the chart at the end of this section.

If you are not familiar with the pronunciation symbols, refer to the pronunciation key at the end of this section.

1. **badinage** (bad'n äzh', bad'n ij) light, playful banter or raillery
2. **salubrious** (sə loo'brē əs) favorable to or promoting health; healthful
3. **apocryphal** (ə pok'rə fəl) of doubtful authenticity; false
4. **putsch** (pŏŏch) a plot to overthrow a government
5. **effeminacy** (i fem'ə nə sē) the quality of being soft or delicate to an unmanly degree in traits, tastes, habits, etc.
6. **effusive** (i fyoo'siv) unduly demonstrative; lacking reserve
7. **mandible** (man'də bəl) the bone of the lower jaw
8. **raison** d'être (rā'zōn de'trə) reason or justification for being or existing
9. **amblyopia** (am'blē ō'pē ə) dimness of sight, without an apparent organic cause
10. **dacha** (dä'chə) a Russian country house or villa
11. **exegesis** (ek'si jē'sis) a critical explanation or interpretation, especially of Scripture
12. **dishabille** (dis'ə bēl') the state of being carelessly or partly dressed; a state of disarray or disorder
13. **élan** (ā län') dash; impetuous ardor
14. **febrile** (fē'brəl, feb'rəl) feverish
15. **gamut** (gam'ət) the entire scale or range
16. **obsequious** (əb sē'kwē əs) servile, compliant, or deferential
17. **jejune** (ji joon') insipid, dull; childish; deficient or lacking in nutritive value
18. **ribald** (rib'əld) vulgar or indecent in speech; coarsely mocking
19. **gecko** (gek'ō) a harmless nocturnal lizard
20. **wizened** (wiz'ənd) withered; shriveled

Now use this chart to score your results:

0–5	correct	Below average
6–10	correct	Average
11–15	correct	Above average
16–20	correct	Superior

Want to try again? See how many of these twenty words you can pronounce correctly. The quiz has no time limit.

Quiz 2: Pronunciation

 1. vignette
 2. bailiwick
 3. juvenilia
 4. baroque
 5. flaccid
 6. cupidity
 7. ghee
 8. sententious
 9. zealous
10. ragout
11. blasé
12. cabochon
13. loath
14. quotidian
15. obdurate
16. cache
17. jocund
18. cabriolet
19. escutcheon
20. penuche

Answers:
To rank yourself against others, refer to the scoring chart at the end of this test section.

 1. **vignette** (vin yet′) a short, graceful literary sketch; a decorative design or small illustration used on the title page of a book or at the beginning or end of a chapter
 2. **bailiwick** (bā′lə wik′) a person's area of skill, knowledge, or training; the district within which a bailiff has jurisdiction
 3. **juvenilia** (jo͞o′və nil′ē ə) works, especially writings, produced in youth
 4. **baroque** (bə rōk′) extravagantly ornamented; ornate; designating a style of art or music of the 17th–18th century
 5. **flaccid** (flak′sid) soft and limp; flabby
 6. **cupidity** (kyo͞o pid′i tē) eager or inordinate desire, especially for wealth; greed or avarice
 7. **ghee** (gē) liquid butter made from the milk of cows and buffalos and clarified by boiling, used in Indian cooking
 8. **sententious** (sen ten′shəs) given to excessive moralizing; self-righteous; abounding in pithy aphorisms or maxims, as a book
 9. **zealous** (zel′əs) ardently active or devoted
10. **ragout** (ra go͞o′) a highly seasoned stew of meat or fish
11. **blasé** (blä zā′) indifferent to or bored with life or a particular activity
12. **cabochon** (kab′ə shon′) a precious stone of convex hemispherical or oval form, polished but not cut into facets

13. **loath** (lōth, lō<u>th</u>) unwilling; reluctant
14. **quotidian** (kwō tid′ē ən) daily; everyday; ordinary
15. **obdurate** (ob′dŏŏ rit, -dyŏŏ-) unmoved by persuasion, pity, or tender feelings; unyielding
16. **cache** (kash) a hiding place
17. **jocund** (jok′ənd) cheerful; merry
18. **cabriolet** (kab′rē ə lā′) a light, two-wheeled one-horse carriage
19. **escutcheon** (i skuch′ən) a shield or shieldlike surface on which a coat of arms is depicted
20. **penuche** (pə nōō′ chē) a candy made of brown sugar, butter, and milk, usually with nuts

Refer to the following chart to score your results:

0–6	correct	Below average
7–13	correct	Average
14–20	correct	Above average
21–25	correct	Superior

Lesson 2.

Here are several more pronunciation quizzes to provide you with additional practice.

Quiz 3: Pronunciation

1. dybbuk
2. hauteur
3. nacre
4. sidle
5. toque
6. viscid
7. lingua franca
8. shoji
9. guano
10. apropos
11. insouciance
12. folderol
13. cavil
14. macabre
15. elision
16. denouement
17. parvenu
18. pince-nez
19. alopecia
20. chicanery

Answers:

1. **dybbuk** (dib′ək) in Jewish folklore, a demon or the soul of a dead person that enters the body of a living person and controls him or her
2. **hauteur** (hō tûr′) a haughty manner or spirit
3. **nacre** (nā′kər) mother-of-pearl

4. **sidle** (sīd′l) to move sideways
5. **toque** (tōk) a soft, brimless, close-fitting hat for women; a chef's hat; a velvet hat with a narrow, turned-up brim, a full crown, and a plume, worn especially in the sixteenth century
6. **viscid** (vis′id) having a glutinous consistency; sticky
7. **lingua franca** (ling′gwə frang′kə) a language widely used as a means of communication among speakers of different languages
8. **shoji** (shō′jē) a light screen of translucent paper, used as a sliding door or a room divider in Japanese homes
9. **guano** (gwä′nō) a natural manure composed chiefly of the excrement of sea birds, found especially on islands near the Peruvian coast; bird lime
10. **apropos** (ap′rə pō′) appropriate; timely; to the purpose; opportunely; with reference or regard
11. **insouciance** (in sōō′sē əns) lack of care or concern; indifference
12. **folderol** (fol′də rol′) mere nonsense; foolish talk or ideas
13. **cavil** (kav′əl) to quibble; an irritating or trivial objection
14. **macabre** (mə kä′brə) gruesome; horrible; grim
15. **elision** (i lizh′ən) the omission of a vowel, consonant, or syllable in pronunciation
16. **denouement** (dā′nōō män′) the final resolution of a plot, as of a drama or novel; outcome
17. **parvenu** (pär′və nōō′, -nyōō′) a person who has suddenly acquired wealth or importance but lacks the proper social qualifications; upstart
18. **pince-nez** (pans′nā′, pins′-) a pair of eyeglasses held on the face by a spring that pinches the nose
19. **alopecia** (al′ə pē′shē ə, -sē ə) baldness
20. **chicanery** (shi kā′nə rē, chi-) trickery or deception by the use of cunning or clever tricks

Quiz 4: Pronunciation

1. façade
2. obeisance
3. gnome
4. diva
5. liaison
6. mauve
7. fiat
8. kiosk
9. chassis
10. omniscient
11. defalcation
12. contumacious
13. heinous
14. emollient

15. gibe
16. ewer
17. hirsute

18. ogle
19. ennui
20. canard

Answers:

1. **façade** (fə säd′) the front of a building, especially an imposing or decorative one; a superficial appearance or illusion of something
2. **obeisance** (ō bā′səns, ō bē′-) a movement of the body expressing deep respect or deferential courtesy, as before a superior; a deep bow
3. **gnome** (nōm) one of a legendary species of diminutive creatures, usually described as shriveled little old men, who inhabit the interior of the earth and act as guardians of its treasure; troll; dwarf
4. **diva** (dē′və, -vä) a distinguished female singer; prima donna
5. **liaison** (lē ā′zən, lē′ā zôn′, lē′ə zon′) a contact maintained between units to ensure concerted action; an illicit sexual relationship
6. **mauve** (mōv, môv) pale bluish purple
7. **fiat** (fē′ät, -at; fī′ət, -at) an authoritative decree, sanction, or order
8. **kiosk** (kē′osk, kē osk′) a kind of open pavilion or summerhouse common in Turkey and Iran; a similar structure used as a bandstand, newsstand, etc.
9. **chassis** (chas′ē, -is, shas′ē) the frame, wheels, and machinery of a motor vehicle, on which the body is supported
10. **omniscient** (om nish′ənt) having complete or infinite knowledge, awareness, or understanding; perceiving all things; all-knowing
11. **defalcation** (dē′fal kā′shən, -fôl-) the misappropriation of money held by an official, trustee, or other fiduciary
12. **contumacious** (kon′tōō mā′shəs, -tyōō-) stubbornly perverse or rebellious; obstinately disobedient
13. **heinous** (hā′nəs) hateful; odious
14. **emollient** (i mol′yənt) something that softens or soothes the skin, as a medical substance
15. **gibe** (jīb) to mock, jeer; a caustic remark
16. **ewer** (yōō′ər) a pitcher with a wide spout
17. **hirsute** (hûr′sōōt, hûr sōōt′) hairy; shaggy
18. **ogle** (ō′gəl) to look at amorously, flirtatiously, or impertinently

19. **ennui** (än wē′) weariness and discontent resulting from satiety or lack of interest; boredom
20. **canard** (kə närd′) a false story, report, or rumor, usually derogatory

WORDS OFTEN MISPRONOUNCED

The following is a list of words that are often considered difficult because their pronunciation is not obvious. You will find the correct pronunciation in parentheses next to each of these words. The pronunciation key appears at the end of the list. A great way to remember these words is by testing yourself, repeatedly uttering the correct pronunciations.

abdomen	(ab′də mən)	conduit	(kon′dwit)
aborigine	(ab′ə rij′ə nē)	consommé	(kon′sə mā′)
		corps	(kôr, kōr)
agile	(aj′əl)	corpuscle	(kôr′pə səl)
albino	(al bī′nō)	cortege	(kôr tezh′)
apropos	(ap′rə pō′)	cotillion	(kə til′yən)
avoirdupois	(av′ər də poiz′)	coup	(kōō)
balk	(bôk)	coxswain	(kok′sən)
baroque	(bə rōk′)	crosier	(krō′zhər)
bayou	(bī′ōō)	crouton	(krōō′ton)
brooch	(brōch)	cuisine	(kwi zēn′)
buoy	(bōō′ē, boi)	dachshund	(däks′-hōōnt′, -hōōnd′, dash′-)
cello	(chel′ō)		
cerebral	(sə rē′brəl, ser′ə-)		
chaise longue	(shāz′ lông′)	debris	(də brē′, dā′brē)
chamois	(sham′ē)		
chantey	(shan′tē)	debut	(dā byōō′)
chauffeur	(shō′fər, shō fûr′)	devotee	(dev′ə tē′)
		dinghy	(ding′gē)
chic	(shēk)	diphtheria	(dif thēr′ē ə)
cholera	(kol′ər ə)	diphthong	(dif′thông)
cinchona	(sing kō′nə)	discern	(di sûrn′)
clandestine	(klan des′tin)	draught	(draft)
		drought	(drout)
clapboard	(klab′ərd)	duodenum	(dōō′ə dē′nəm)
clique	(klēk)		
colonel	(kûr′nl)	dyspepsia	(dis pep′shə, -sē ə)
compote	(kom′pōt)		

edifice (ed'ə fis)

egregious (i grē'jəs)

emu (ē'myoo)

entree (än'trā)

façade (fə säd')

facile (fas'il)

fiancé (fē'än sā', fē ̄
än'sā)

frigate (frig'it)

fuchsia (fyoo'shə)

fuselage (fyoo'sə
läzh')

fusillade (fyoo'sə läd',
-läd')

gendarme (zhän'därm)

gentian (jen'shən)

gestation (jes tā'shən)

gibber (jib'ər)

gladiolus (glad'ē ō'ləs)

glazier (glā'zhər)

glower (glou'ər)

gnu (noo)

gourmet (goor mā',
goor'mā)

granary (gran'ə rē)

guerrilla (gə ril'ə)

guillotine (gil'ə tēn')

gunwale (gun'l)

habitué (hə bich'oo
ā')

harbinger (här'bin jər)

heifer (hef'ər)

heinous (hā'nəs)

hirsute (hûr'soot)

holocaust (hol'ə kôst)

hosiery (hō'zhə rē)

iguana (i gwä'nə)

imbroglio (im brōl'yō)

inchoate (in kō'it)

incognito (in'kog
nē'tō, in
kog'ni tō)

indigenous (in dij'ə nəs)

interstice (in tûr'stis)

inure (in yoor')

irascible (i ras'ə bəl)

isosceles (ī sos'ə lēz')

isthmus (is'məs)

jodhpurs (jod'pərz)

joust (joust)

khaki (kak'ē)

kohlrabi (kōl rä'bē)

labyrinth (lab'ə rinth)

lascivious (lə siv'ē əs)

legerdemain (lej'ər də
mān')

leisure (lē'zhər)

lemur (lē'mər)

liaison (lē ā'zən, lē'ə
zon')

lien (lēn)

lieu (loo)

lineage (lin'ē ij)

lingerie (län'zhə rā')

liturgy (lit'ər jē)

llama (lä'mə)

locale (lō kal')

logy (lō'gē)

lorgnette (lôrn yet')

louver (loo'vər)

lucid (loo'sid)

lucre (loo'kər)

machete (mə shet'ē)

machination (mak'ə
nā'shən)

mademoiselle (mad'ə mə
zel',
mad'mwə-)

maestro (mīs'trō)

mannequin (man'i kin)

marijuana (mar'ə
wä'nə)

marquis (mär'kwis,
mär kē')

matinée (mat'n ā')

mauve	(mōv)
meliorate	(mēl′yə rāt′)
mesa	(mā′sə)
mien	(mēn)
modiste	(mō dēst′)
motif	(mō tēf′)
murrain	(mûr′in)
myrrh	(mûr)
naïve	(nä ēv′)
naphtha	(nap′thə, naf′-)
niche	(nich)
nihilism	(nī′ə liz′əm)
nirvana	(nir vä′nə)
nom de plume	(nom′ də ploōm′)
nonpareil	(non′pə rel′)
nougat	(noō′gət)
nuance	(noō′äns, nyoō′-)
oblique	(ə blēk′)
ocher	(ō′kər)
omniscient	(om nish′ənt)
onerous	(on′ər əs)
onus	(ō′nəs)
opiate	(ō′pē it)
pachyderm	(pak′i dûrm′)
palsy	(pôl′zē)
paprika	(pa prē′kə)
parfait	(pär fā′)
parquet	(pär kā′)
paschal	(pas′kəl)
pecan	(pi kän′)
pellagra	(pə lag′rə)
petit	(pet′ē)
philistine	(fil′ə stēn′)
pimiento	(pi myen′tō)

plebeian	(plə bē′ən)
pneumatic	(noō mat′ik, nyoō-)
poignant	(poin′yənt)
posthumous	(pos′chə məs)
precipice	(pres′ə pis)
premier	(pri mēr′)
pristine	(pri stēn′)
protégé	(prō′tə zhā′)
pueblo	(pweb′lō)
purulent	(pyoōr′ə lənt)
quaff	(kwof)
qualm	(kwäm)
quay	(kē)
ragout	(ra goō′)
regime	(rā zhēm′)
renege	(ri nig′, -neg′)
reveille	(rev′ə lē)
ricochet	(rik′ə shā′)
rudiment	(roō′də mənt)
savoir-faire	(sav′wär fâr′)
short-lived	(shôrt′līvd′)
sleazy	(slē′zē)
soufflé	(soō flā′)
specious	(spē′shəs)
suave	(swäv)
subpoena	(sə pē′nə)
tarpaulin	(tär pô′lin, tär′pə lin)
thyme	(tīm)
travail	(trə vāl′)
usury	(yoō′zhə rē)
valance	(vā′ləns)
worsted	(woōs′tid)

PRONUNCIATION KEY

a	act, bat	n	now, on	v	voice, live
ā	able, cape	ng	sing, England	w	west, away
â	air, dare	o	box, hot	y	yes, young
ä	art, calm	ō	over, no	z	zeal, lazy,
b	back, rub	ô	order, bail		those
ch	chief, beach	oi	oil, joy	zh	vision,
d	do, bed	o͝o	book, put		measure
e	ebb, set	o͞o	ooze, rule	ə	occurs only in
ē	equal, bee	ou	out, loud		unaccented
f	fit, puff	p	page, stop		syllables and
g	give, beg	r	read, cry		indicates the
h	hit, hear	s	see, miss		sound of a *in*
i	if, big	sh	shoe, push		alone e *in*
ī	ice, bite	t	ten, bit		system i *in*
j	just, edge	th	thin, path		easily o *in*
k	kept, make	t͡h	that, other		gallop u *in*
l	low, all	u	up, love		circus
m	my, him	û	urge, burn		

3. IMPROVE YOUR SPELLING

An important part of improving your vocabulary is learning to spell correctly and confidently. English spellings present some difficulties because so many words are not spelled the way they sound. Most of these words come from other languages. For example, the word *bouillon,* meaning a kind of broth, came into English from French, and its common English pronunciations, (bŏŏl'yon) and (bŏŏl'yən), are very much like its pronunciation in French (bōō yôn'). English spellings can also create confusion because certain words do not sound the way they look. For example, *cough* and *though,* although spelled similarly, are pronounced quite differently. The first is pronounced (kôf), to rhyme with *off,* and the second is (ᵹh), to rhyme with *go* (see also the pronunciation guide toward the end of this chapter). But these words are exceptions, and most English spelling is not as difficult as some people would have you believe. There are ways to make it all easier, and the objective of this chapter is to remove some of the confusion and to give a clearer concept of English spelling.

The classic criticism of the difficulties of English spelling is the one made famous by George Bernard Shaw, in which he claims that our spelling is so irregular (and so absurd!) that the common word *fish* could as well be spelled in English as *ghoti.* The idea is as follows:

> *gh* in cou*gh* equals the sound of *f*
> *o* in w*o*men equals the sound of *i*
> *ti* in na*ti*on equals the sound of *sh*

The trouble with this analysis, amusing though it may be, is that it does not take into account what might be called "the rules of the game." Without denying that in the English lan-

16

guage we can have more than one sound for each spelling and more than one spelling for each sound, we can point to certain regularities regarding sound-spelling correspondences, among them rules of position. Taking these into account, we can see that Shaw's suggested spelling of *ghoti* for *fish* falls apart; *gh* NEVER equals the sound of *f* at the beginning of a word, only at the end, as in *rough, cough,* or *laugh.* The use of the letter *o* to represent the "short" *i* sound is even more restricted, appearing ONLY in the word *women.* Finally, *ti* produces the *sh* sound ONLY medially, typically in suffixes like *-tion* and *-tious.*

There are reasons for the sound-spelling irregularities in English; its history warrants them. For one thing, the number of sounds in the language is greater than the number of symbols available in our alphabet; some of these symbols must do double duty (as with "hard" and "soft" *c* and *g*) or must combine with other symbols in order to account for all the sounds. For another, English has borrowed heavily from other languages, retaining traces of their pronunciations with their spellings. In addition, spelling in general is conservative—it changes less readily than pronunciation. Modern English retains spellings that do not reflect the many changes in pronunciation that have occurred over the years, particularly during the Great Vowel Shift of the fifteenth century. Nor can any single set of spellings reflect the diversity of English dialects. English is a varied language that flourishes not only throughout North America and England, but over the entire globe. Add to this the fact that early printers were inconsistent and idiosyncratic in their spelling, and some of their misspellings have survived. All of these factors have led to the kinds of spelling irregularities that make the English language both frustrating and fascinating.

Nevertheless, for all its difficulties, English spelling is not entirely irrational. We return to "the rules of the game." If certain letter combinations occur predominantly in certain portions of words, a growing familiarity with these patterns can increase your confidence in using and working with the English language. And it can help to resolve an age-old problem:

FINDING SPELLINGS WHEN YOU KNOW THE SOUNDS

The Problem

Traditionally, there has been a fundamental difficulty with making efficient use of dictionaries and other reference books: How can you look up a word if you don't know how to spell it? Where do you look? In what part of the alphabet?

The Solution

Although no complete solution exists, a "Table of Sound-Spelling Correspondences" like the one below can help. By listing alternative spellings for each of the sounds of English, and tying these sounds and spellings together, the table allows you to relate what you already know about a word—how to SAY it—with what you are trying to find out about the word—how to SPELL it.

UNDERSTANDING THE TABLE OF SOUND-SPELLING CORRESPONDENCES

Contexts for Given Spelling Patterns

Tables showing the relationship between sounds and spellings can be found in most unabridged and desk dictionaries. The table that follows not only shows spelling patterns and the sounds they represent, but indicates which part of a word (beginning, middle, or end) is likely to contain these patterns. For example, "-ag(m)," as in "diaphragm," is shown with a preceding hyphen and with parentheses around the m, as one of the patterns representing the "short" a sound. This means that when the letters ag precede an m and the agm ends a word or syllable, ag is pronounced as a vowel, as if the g were not there. In fact, when an agm combination is split between syllables, as in the word "syn+tag+mat+ic," so that the g ends one syllable and the m starts the next one, the g is NOT silent.

From this example, you can see that parenthesized letters in the table indicate a CONTEXT for a given spelling pattern. Similarly, hyphens show where in a word or syllable that pattern is most likely to occur. A spelling pattern shown without any hyphens can occur in various parts of a word; some of these, like air, are also found as entire words.

Key-Word Patterns

For each sound shown along the left margin, the table shows a boldface **spelling,** followed by a word (or words) in which that spelling typically occurs. This key word allows you to fix the sound in your mind.

Following the bold spellings is a list of other spellings for the same sound and the words in which those spellings are used. Notice that you may pronounce some of the spellings in the lists differently from the bold spellings. Such spellings are probably repeated following the sounds more appropriate for your dialect. Tables of this sort usually include unusual sound-spelling associations: some that are simply rare, like the *u* in *busy* or *business* for the short *i* sound, and others that are derived from languages other than English. French spellings standing for the "long" *o* sound, for example, might include *-eau, -eaux,* and *-ot.* Long lists of such spelling patterns, with no indication of which ones are frequent enough to be useful, can indeed be overwhelming. To simplify our table, we have marked the common spelling patterns for each sound with an asterisk.

Note that the combination of a vowel plus an ellipsis (three dots) and an *e* stands for any spelling in which that vowel and the *e* are separated by a single consonant. As a general rule, this "discontinuous vowel" pattern represents the long sound of that vowel. (Long *i,* for example, is frequently spelled with *i...e,* as in *ice.*) But a discontinuous vowel can stand for other than long vowel sounds. In the word *have,* the *a...e* stands for a short *a* sound, and in the word *love, o...e* stands for the sound of short *u.*

TABLE OF SOUND-SPELLING CORRESPONDENCES

This table is useful for finding a word in the dictionary when you know the pronunciation but not the spelling. To find a word, first sound it out and then try various spelling equivalents. For example, the spellings of *pursue* and *persuade* (with first syllables that sound alike but are spelled differently) can be found by checking the spellings listed for the (ər) sound and then looking in the dictionary under *per-, pir-, pur-,* etc. A vowel and an *e* separated by dots (as i...e) indicate the "long" sound of that vowel, with a consonant separating the two letters (as in *ice*).

VOWELS AND DIPHTHONGS

(a) *a-, -a- as in at, hat ("short" a)		
-a'a-	ma'am	-ah-	dahlia
-ach(m)	drachm	-ai-	plaid
-ag(m)	diaphragm	-al-	half
		-au-	laugh
		-ua-	guarantor
		-ui-	guimpe

i(n)-, -i(n)-	*i*ngenue,
	l*i*ngerie
-i(m)-	t*i*mbre

(ā) *a . . . e, -a . . . e as in ate, hate ("long" a)	
-ae-	G*ae*lic
-ag(n)	champ*agn*e
*-ai-	r*ai*n
-aigh-	str*aigh*t
-aig(n)	arr*aig*n
-ao-	g*ao*l
-au-	g*au*ge
-a(g)ue	v*ague*
*-ay	r*ay*
*é-, -é	*é*tude, expos*é*
-e . . . e	su*ede*
*-ea-	st*ea*k
-ee	matin*ee*
eh	*eh*
*-ei-	v*ei*l
*-eig(n)	f*eig*n
*eigh-, -eigh-,	
-eigh	*eigh*t, w*eigh*t,
	w*eigh*
-eilles	Mars*eilles*
-er	dossi*er*
-es(ne)	dem*es*ne
-et	ber*et*
*-ey	ob*ey*

(âr) *air as in chair	
*-aire	doctrin*aire*
*-ar-	ch*ar*y
*-are	d*are*
-ayer	pr*ayer*
*-ear	w*ear*
-eer	Mynh*eer*
e'er	ne'*er*
*-eir	th*eir*
-er	mal de m*er*
*-ere	th*ere*
-ey're	th*ey're*

(ä) *ah as in hurrah ("broad" a)	
*-a-	f*a*ther
à	*à* la mode
-aa-	baz*aa*r
*-al(f)	h*a*lf
*-al(m)	c*a*lm
-as	faux p*as*
-at	écl*at*
-au-	l*au*gh
-e(r)-	s*e*rgeant
*-ea(r)-	h*ea*rth
-oi-	reserv*oi*r
-ua-	g*ua*rd
i(n)-, -i(n)-	*i*ngenue,
	l*i*ngerie

(e) *e as in ebb ("short" e)	
a-, -a-,	*a*ny, m*a*ny
ae-	*ae*sthete
-ai-	s*ai*d
-ay-	s*ay*s
*-ea-	l*ea*ther
-eg(m)	phl*eg*m
-ei-	h*ei*fer
-eo-	j*eo*pardy
-ie-	fr*ie*nd
-oe-	f*oe*tid

(ē) *ee as in keep ("long" e)	
ae-, -ae-	*Ae*sop,
	C*ae*sar
-ay	qu*ay*
*e-, -e-	*e*qual, s*e*cret
-e	stroph*e*
*ea-, -ea-, -ea	*ea*ch, t*ea*m,
	t*ea*
*-ea(g)ue	l*ea*gue
e'e-	*e'e*n
*e . . . e	prec*e*d*e*
*-ei-	rec*ei*ve
-eip(t)	rec*ei*pt

-eo-	pe*o*ple		*-(u)a-	q*ua*drant
*-ey	k*ey*		-ach-	y*a*cht
-i	ran*i*		-au-	astron*au*t
*i . . . e	mach*i*ne		-eau-	bure*au*cracy
*-ie-	f*ie*ld		-ou-	c*ou*gh
-is	debr*i*s		*ho-	*h*onor
*-i(g)ue	intr*igue*			
*-i(q)ue	ant*ique*			

(ō) *o as in lo

-oe-	am*oe*ba		*-au-	m*au*ve
-uay	q*uay*		-aut	h*au*tboy
*-y	cit*y*		-aux	f*aux* pas
			-eau	b*eau*

(i) *i as in if ("short" i)

		-eaux	Bord*eaux*
*-a-	dam*a*ge	-eo-	y*eo*man
-ae-	an*ae*sthetic	-ew	s*ew*
e-	*E*ngland	*o . . . e	r*o*te
-ee-	b*ee*n	*-oa-	r*oa*d
*-ei-	counterf*ei*t	*-oe-	t*oe*
-ia-	carr*ia*ge	oh	*oh*
-ie-	s*ie*ve	*-ol-	y*o*lk
-o-	w*o*men	-oo-	br*oo*ch
(b)u(s)-	b*u*siness	-ot	dep*o*t
-ui(l)-	b*ui*ld, g*ui*lt	*-ou-	s*ou*l
*-y-	s*y*m-	*-ow-	fl*ow*
	pathetic	*-owe	*owe*

(ī) *i . . . e as in ice ("long" i)

(ô) *-aw as in paw

*-ai-	f*ai*lle		*-a-	t*a*ll
ais-	*ai*sle		*(w)a(r)-	w*a*rrant
-ay-	ka*ya*k		-ah	Ut*ah*
aye	*aye*		*-al-	w*a*lk
*-ei-	st*ei*n		-as	Arkans*as*
-eigh-	h*eigh*t		*au-, -au-	*au*thor, v*au*lt
eye	*eye*		*-augh-	c*augh*t
*-ie	p*ie*		*-o-	alcoh*o*l
*-igh	h*igh*		*-oa-	br*oa*d
is-	*is*land		-oo-	fl*oo*r
*-uy	b*uy*		*-ough-	s*ough*t
*-y-, -y	c*y*cle, sk*y*			
*-ye	l*ye*			

(oi) *-oy as in boy

(o) *o as in box

			-awy-	law*y*er
*(w)a-	w*a*nder		-eu-	Fr*eu*d
			*-oi-	*oi*l

-ois	Iroqu*ois*
-uoy	b*uoy*

(o͞o) *-oo-* as in look

-o-	w*o*lf
*-oul-	w*oul*d
*-u-	p*u*ll

(o͞o) *oo-*, *-oo-*, *-oo* as in ooze, mood, ahchoo

-eu-	man*eu*ver
*-ew	gr*ew*
-iew	l*ieu*
-o	wh*o*
o . . . e	m*o*ve
-oe	cano*e*
-oeu-	man*oeu*vre
*-ou-	tr*ou*p
*u . . . e	r*u*le
*-ue	fl*ue*
-ug(n)	imp*ug*n
*-ui-	s*ui*t

(ou) *-ow* as in brow

au-	*Au*f Wiedersehen
-au	land*au*
*ou-, *-ou-	*ou*t, sh*ou*t
*-ough	b*ough*

(u) *u-*, *-u-* as in up, pup

o-, *-o-	*o*ther, s*o*n
-oe-	d*oe*s
*o . . . e	l*o*ve
-oo-	bl*oo*d
-ou(ble)	tr*ou*ble

(ûr) *ur-*, *-ur-* as in urn, turn

*ear-, -ear-	*ear*n, l*ear*n
*er-, -er-	*er*mine, t*er*m
err	*err*
-eur	pos*eur*

her-	*her*b
*-ir-, -ir	th*ir*sty, f*ir*
(w)or-	w*or*k
-our-	sc*our*ge
-urr	p*urr*
-yr-	m*yr*tle

(yo͞o) *u-*, *-u* as in utility, future

-eau-	b*eau*ty
-eu-	f*eu*d
*-ew	f*ew*
*hu-	*hu*man
hu . . . e	*hu*ge
-ieu	purl*ieu*
-iew	v*iew*
*u . . . e	*u*se
*-ue	c*ue*
-ueue	q*ueue*
yew	*yew*
you	*you*
yu-	*Yu*kon
yu . . . e	*yu*le

(ə) *a* as in alone

*-e-	syst*e*m
*-i-	easi*i*ly
*-o-	gall*o*p
*-u-	circ*u*s
à	tête-*à*-tête
-ai(n)	mount*ai*n
-ei(n)	mull*ei*n
-eo(n)	dung*eo*n
-ia-	parl*ia*ment
-io-	leg*io*n
-oi-	porp*oi*se
*-ou-	curi*ou*s
-y-	mart*y*r

(ər) *-er* as in father

*-ar	li*ar*
*-ir	elix*ir*

*-or	labor	pf-	pfennig
*-our	labour	*ph-, -ph-,	
*-ur	augur	-ph	physics,
*-ure	future		staph-
-yr	martyr		ylococcus,
			staph

(d) *d-, *-d-, *-d as in do, odor, red

(g) *g-, *-g-, *-g as in give, agate, fog

*-'d	we'd
*-dd-, *-dd	ladder, odd
*-de	fade
dh-	dhurrie
*-ed	pulled
*-ld	should

*-gg	egg
*gh-	ghost
*gu-	guard
*-gue	plague

(f) *f-, *-f-, as in feed, safer

(h) *h-, *-h- as in hit, ahoy

*-fe	life
*-ff-, *-ff	muffin, off
*-ft-	soften
*-gh	tough
*-lf	calf

wh-	who

(hw)*wh- as in where

(hyōō) *hu- as in huge
(j) *j- as in just

CONSONANTS

(Note that consonant spelling patterns such as -bb-, shown with hyphens on either side, are frequently part of two adjacent syllables in a word, with part of the combination in one syllable and the rest in the next.)

(b) *b-, *-b-, *-b as in bed, amber, rub

*-ti-	question
*-tu-	natural

*-bb-, *bb-	hobby, ebb
*-be	lobe
bh-	bheesty

-ch	Greenwich
*-d(u)	graduate
*-dg-	judgment
*-dge	bridge
*-di-	soldier
*-ge	sage

(ch) *ch-, -ch-, *-ch as in chief, ahchoo, rich

c-	cello
*-che	niche
*-tch-, *-tch	hatchet, catch
-te-	righteous

-gg-	exaggerate
*g(e)-, *-g(e)-	gem, agent
*g(i)-, *-g(i)-	gin, agile
-jj-	Hajji

(k) *k-, *-k- as in keep, making

*c-, *-c-	*c*ar, be*c*ome
*-cc-	a*cc*ount
-cch-	ba*cch*anal
*ch-	*ch*aracter
*-ck	ba*ck*
-cq-	a*cq*uaint
-cqu-	la*cqu*er
-cque	sa*cque*
cu-	bis*cu*it
-gh	lou*gh*
*-ke	ra*ke*
-kh	Si*kh*
-lk	wa*lk*
q-	*q*adi
-q	Ira*q*
-qu-	li*qu*or
-que	pla*que*

(l) *l-, *-l-, *-l as in live, alive, sail

*-le	mi*le*
*-ll	ca*ll*
-lle	fai*lle*
-sl-	li*s*le
-sle	ai*s*le

(m) *m-, *-m-, *-m as in more, amount, ham

-chm	dra*chm*
-gm	paradi*gm*
*-lm	ca*lm*
*-mb	li*mb*
*-me	ho*me*
mh-	*mh*o
*-mm-	ha*mm*er
-mn	hy*mn*

(n) *n-, *-n-, *-n as in not, center, can

*gn-	*gn*at
*kn-	*kn*ife
mn-	*mn*emonic
*-ne	do*ne*
*-nn-	ru*nn*er
*pn(eu)-	*pn*eumatic

(ng) *-ng-, *-ng as in ringing, ring

*-n(k)	pi*n*k
-ngg	mahjo*ngg*
-ngue	to*ngue*

(p) *p-, *-p-, *-p as in pen, super, stop

*-pe	ho*pe*
*-pp-	su*pp*er
-ppe	lagnia*ppe*

(r) *r-, *-r-, *-r as in red, arise, four

*-re	pu*re*
*rh-	*rh*ythm
*-rr-	ca*rr*ot
-rrh	cata*rrh*
*wr-	*wr*ong

(s) *s-, *-s-, *-s as in see, beside, alas

*c(e)-, *-c(e)-,	*c*enter, ra*c*er
*c(i)-, *-c(i)-	*c*ity, a*c*id
*-ce	mi*ce*
*ps-	*ps*ychology
*sc-	*sc*ene
sch-	*sch*ism
*-se	mou*se*
*-ss-, *-ss	me*ss*enger, lo*ss*

(sh) *sh-, *-sh-, *-sh as in ship, ashamed, wash

-ce-	o*c*ean
ch-, *-ch-	*ch*aise, ma*ch*ine

-chs-	fu*chs*ia
*-ci-	spe*ci*al
psh-	*psh*aw
s(u)-	*s*ugar
sch-	*sch*ist
*-sci-	con*sci*ence
-se-	nau*se*ous
*-si-	man*si*on
*-ss-	ti*ss*ue
*-ssi-	mi*ssi*on
*-ti-	cap*ti*on

(t) *t-, *-t-, *-t as in toe, atom, hat

-bt	dou*bt*
-cht	ya*cht*
ct-	*ct*enophore
*-ed	talk*ed*
*-ght	bou*ght*
phth-	*phth*isic
't-	*'t*was
*-te	bi*te*
th-	*th*yme
*-tt-	bo*tt*om
tw-	*tw*o

(th) *th-, *-th-, *-th as in thin, ether, path

chth-	*chth*onian

(th) *th-, *-th-, -th as in then, other, smooth

*-the	ba*the*

(v) *v-, *-v-, -v as in visit, over, luv

-f	o*f*
-ph-	Ste*ph*en
*-ve	ha*ve*
-vv-	fli*vv*er

(w) *w-, *-w- as in well, away

-ju-	mari*ju*ana
-o(i)-	ch*oi*r
ou(i)-	*ou*ija
(q)u-	q*u*iet
*wh-	*wh*ere

(y) *y- as in yet

*-i-	un*i*on
-j-	hallelu*j*ah
-ll-	torti*ll*a

(z) *z-, -z- as in zone, Bizet

*-s	ha*s*
-sc-	di*sc*ern
*-se	ri*se*
x-	*x*ylem
-ze	fu*ze*
*-zz-, *-zz	bu*zz*ard, fu*zz*

(zh) -zi- as in brazier (like zh)

*-ge	gara*ge*
*-s(u)-	mea*s*ure
*-si	divi*si*on
*-z(u)-	a*z*ure

RULES OF SPELLING

No spelling rule should be followed blindly, for every rule has exceptions.

1. Silent E Dropped. Silent *e* at the end of a word is usually dropped before a suffix beginning with a vowel: *abide, abiding; recite, recital.*

    Exceptions: Words ending in *ce* or *ge* retain the *e* before a suffix beginning with *a* or *o* to keep the soft sound of the consonant: *notice, noticeable; courage, courageous.*

2. Silent E Kept. A silent *e* following a consonant (or another *e*) is usually retained before a suffix beginning with a consonant: *late, lateness; spite, spiteful.*

    Exceptions: *fledgling, acknowledgment, judgment, wholly,* and a few similar words.

3. Final Consonant Doubled. A final consonant following a single vowel in one-syllable words, or in a syllable that will take the main accent when combined with a suffix, is doubled before a suffix beginning with a vowel: *begin, beginning; occur, occurred; bat, batted.*

    Exceptions: *h* and *x* in final position; *transferable, gaseous,* and a few others.

4. Final Consonant Single. A final consonant following another consonant, a double vowel or diphthong, or that is not in a stressed syllable, is not doubled before a suffix beginning with a vowel: *part, parting; remark, remarkable.*

    Exceptions: an unaccented syllable does not prevent doubling of the final consonant, especially in British usage: *traveller* for *traveler.*

5. Double Consonants Remain. Double consonants are usually retained before a suffix except when a final *l* is to be followed by *ly* or *less.* To avoid a triple *lll,* one *l* is usually dropped: *full, fully.*

    Exceptions: Usage is divided, with some preferring *skilful* over *skillful, instalment* over *installment,* etc.

6. Final Y. If the *y* follows a consonant, change *y* to *i* before all endings except *ing.* Do not change it before *ing* or if it follows a vowel: *bury, buried, burying; try, tries;* but *attorney, attorneys.*

    Exceptions: *day, daily; gay, gaily; lay, laid; say, said.*

7. Final IE to Y. Words ending in *ie* change to *y* before *ing: die, dying; lie, lying.*

8. Double and Triple E Reduced. Words ending in double *e* drop one *e* before an ending beginning in *e,* to avoid a triple *e.* Words ending in silent *e* usually drop the *e* before endings beginning in *e* to avoid forming a syllable. Other words end-

ing in a vowel sound commonly retain the letters indicating the sound. *Free + ed = freed.*

9. EI or IE. Words having the sound of *ē* are commonly spelled *ie* following all letters but *c;* with a preceding *c,* the common spelling is *ei.* Examples: *believe, achieve, besiege;* but *conceit, ceiling, receive, conceive.* When the sound is *ā* the common spelling is *ei* regardless of the preceding letter. Examples: *eight, weight, deign.*

   Exceptions: *either, neither, seize, financier;* some words in which *e* and *i* are pronounced separately, such as *notoriety.*

10. Words Ending in C. Before an ending beginning with *e, i,* or *y,* words ending in *c* commonly add *k* to keep the *c* hard: *panic, panicky.*

11. Compounds. Some compounds written as a unit bring together unusual combinations of letters. They are seldom changed on this account. *bookkeeper, roommate.*

    Exceptions: A few words are regularly clipped when compounded, such as *full* in *awful, cupful,* etc.

RULES OF WORD DIVISION

1. Do not divide a one-syllable word. This includes past tenses like *walked* and *dreamed,* which should never be split before the *-ed* ending.

2. Do not divide a word so that a single letter is left at the end of a line, as in *a⋅bout,* or so that a single letter starts the following line, as in *cit⋅y.*

3. Hyphenated compounds should preferably be divided only after the hyphen. If the first portion of the compound is a single letter, however, as in *D-day,* the word should not be divided.

4. Word segments like *-ceous, -scious, -sial, -tion, -tious* should not be divided.

5. The portion of a word left at the end of a line should not encourage a misleading pronunciation, as would be the case if *acetate,* a three-syllable word, were divided after the first *e.*

WORDS MOST OFTEN MISSPELLED

We have listed here some of the words that have traditionally proved difficult to spell. The list includes not only "exceptions," words that defy common spelling rules, but some that pose problems even while adhering to these conventions.

aberrant
abscess
absence
absorption
abundance
accede
acceptance
accessible
accidentally
accommodate
according
accordion
accumulate
accustom
achievement
acknowledge
acknowledgment
acoustics
acquaintance
acquiesce
acquire
acquittal
across
address
adequate
adherent
adjourn
admittance
adolescence
adolescent
advantageous
advertisement
affidavit
against
aggravate
aggression
aging
aisle
all right
alien
allegiance
almost
although
always
amateur

analysis
analytical
analyze
anesthetic
annual
anoint
anonymous
answer
antarctic
antecedent
anticipation
antihistamine
anxiety
aperitif
apocryphal
apostasy
apparent
appearance
appetite
appreciate
appropriate
approximate
apropos
arctic
arguing
argument
arouse
arrangement
arthritis
article
artificial
asked
assassin
assess
asthma
athlete
athletic
attorneys
author
authoritative
auxiliary

bachelor
balance
bankruptcy
barbiturate

barrette
basically
basis
beggar
beginning
belief
believable
believe
beneficial
beneficiary
benefit
benefited
blizzard
bludgeon
bologna
bookkeeping
bouillon
boundaries
breathe
brief
brilliant
broccoli
bronchial
brutality
bulletin
buoy
buoyant
bureau
bureaucracy
burglary
business

cafeteria
caffeine
calisthenics
camaraderie
camouflage
campaign
cancel
cancellation
candidate
cantaloupe
capacity
cappuccino
carburetor
career

careful
carriage
carrying
casserole
category
caterpillar
cavalry
ceiling
cellar
cemetery
census
certain
challenge
chandelier
changeable
changing
characteristic
chief
choir
choose
cinnamon
circuit
civilized
clothes
codeine
collateral
colloquial
colonel
colossal
column
coming
commemorate
commission
commitment
committed
committee
comparative
comparison
competition
competitive
complaint
concede
conceivable
conceive
condemn

condescend
conferred
confidential
congratulate
conscience
conscientious
conscious
consensus
consequently
consistent
consummate
continuous
control
controlled
controversy
convalesce
convenience
coolly
copyright
cornucopia
corollary
corporation
correlate
correspondence
correspondent
counselor
counterfeit
courageous
courteous
crisis
criticism
criticize
culinary
curiosity
curriculum
cylinder

debt
debtor
deceive
decide
decision
decisive
defendant
definite
definitely
dependent
de rigueur
descend

descendant
description
desiccate
desirable
despair
desperate
destroy
develop
development
diabetes
diaphragm
different
dilemma
dining
diocese
diphtheria
disappear
disappearance
disappoint
disastrous
discipline
disease
dissatisfied
dissident
dissipate
distinguish
divide
divine
doesn't
dormitory
duly
dumbbell
during

easier
easily
ecstasy
effervescent
efficacy
efficiency
efficient
eighth
eightieth
electrician
eligibility
eligible
eliminate
ellipsis
embarrass

encouraging
endurance
energetic
enforceable
enthusiasm
environment
equipped
erroneous
especially
esteemed
exacerbate
exaggerate
exceed
excel
excellent
except
exceptionally
excessive
executive
exercise
exhibition
exhilarate
existence
expense
experience
experiment
explanation
exquisite
extemporaneous
extraordinary
extremely

facilities
fallacy
familiar
fascinate
fascism
feasible
February
fictitious
fiend
fierce
fiftieth
finagle
finally
financial
foliage
forcible
forehead

foreign
forfeit
formally
forte
fortieth
fortunately
forty
fourth
friend
frieze
fundamental
furniture

galoshes
gauge
genealogy
generally
gnash
government
governor
graffiti
grammar
grateful
grievance
grievous
guarantee
guard
guidance

handkerchief
haphazard
harass
harebrained
hazard
height
hemorrhage
hemorrhoid
hereditary
heroes
hierarchy
hindrance
hoping
hors d'oeuvres
huge
humorous
hundredth
hydraulic
hygiene

hygienist
hypocrisy
icicle
identification
idiosyncrasy
imaginary
immediately
immense
impresario
inalienable
incident
incidentally
inconvenience
incredible
indelible
independent
indestructible
indictment
indigestible
indispensable
inevitable
inferred
influential
initial
initiative
innocuous
innuendo
inoculation
inscrutable
installation
instantaneous
intellectual
intelligence
intercede
interest
interfere
intermittent
intimate
inveigle
irrelevant
irresistible
island

jealous
jeopardize
journal
judgment
judicial

khaki
kindergarten
knowledge

laboratory
laid
larynx
leery
leisure
length
liable
liaison
libel
library
license
lieutenant
likelihood
liquefy
liqueur
literature
livelihood
loneliness
losing
lovable

magazine
maintenance
manageable
management
maneuver
manufacturer
maraschino
marital
marriage
marriageable
mathematics
mayonnaise
meant
medicine
medieval
memento
mileage
millennium
miniature
minuet
miscellaneous
mischievous
misspell
mistletoe

moccasin
molasses
molecule
monotonous
mortgage
murmur
muscle
mutual
mysterious

naive
naturally
necessarily
necessary
necessity
neighbor
neither
nickel
niece
ninetieth
ninety
ninth
noticeable
notoriety
nuptial

obbligato
occasion
occasionally
occurred
occurrence
offense
official
omission
omit
omitted
oneself
ophthalmology
opinion
opportunity
optimism
optimist
ordinarily
origin
original
outrageous

paean
pageant
paid

pamphlet
paradise
parakeet
parallel
paralysis
paralyze
paraphernalia
parimutuel
parliament
partial
participate
particularly
pasteurize
pastime
pavilion
peaceable
peasant
peculiar
penicillin
perceive
perform
performance
peril
permanent
permissible
perpendicular
perseverance
persistent
personnel
perspiration
persuade
persuasion
persuasive
petition
philosophy
physician
piccolo
plaited
plateau
plausible
playwright
pleasant
plebeian
pneumonia
poinsettia
politician
pomegranate
possess

possession
possibility
possible
practically
practice
precede
precedence
precisely
predecessor
preference
preferred
prejudice
preparatory
prescription
prevalent
primitive
prior
privilege
probability
probably
procedure
proceed
professor
proffer
pronounce
pronunciation
propagate
protégé(e)
psychiatry
psychology
pursuant
pursue
pursuit
putrefy

quantity
questionnaire
queue

rarefy
recede
receipt
receivable
receive
recipe
reciprocal
recognize
recommend
reference

referred
reign
relegate
relevant
relieve
religious
remembrance
reminisce
remiss
remittance
rendezvous
repetition
replaceable
representative
requisition
resistance
responsibility
restaurant
restaurateur
resuscitate
reticence
reveille
rhyme
rhythm
riddance
ridiculous
rococo
roommate

sacrifice
sacrilegious
safety
salary
sandwich
sarsaparilla
sassafras
satisfaction
scarcity
scene
scenery
schedule
scheme
scholarly
scissors
secede
secrecy
secretary
seize
seizure

separate
separately
sergeant
serviceable
seventieth
several
sheik
shepherd
sheriff
shining
shoulder
shrapnel
siege
sieve
significance
silhouette
similar
simultaneity
simultaneous
sincerely
sixtieth
skiing
socially
society
solemn
soliloquy
sophomore
sorority
sovereign
spaghetti
spatial
special
specifically
specimen
speech
sponsor
spontaneous
statistics
statute
stevedore
stiletto
stopped
stopping
strength
strictly
studying
stupefy
submitted

substantial
subtle
subtly
succeed
successful
succession
successive
sufficient
superintendent
supersede
supplement
suppress
surprise
surveillance
susceptible
suspicion
sustenance
syllable
symmetrical
sympathize
sympathy
synchronous
synonym
syphilis
systematically

tariff
temperament
temperature
temporarily
tendency
tentative
terrestrial
therefore
thirtieth
thorough
thought
thousandth
through
till
titillate
together
tonight
tournament
tourniquet
tragedy
tragically
transferred
transient

tries
truly
twelfth
twentieth
typical
tyranny

unanimous
undoubtedly
unique
unison
unmanageable
unnecessary
until

upholsterer
usable
usage
using
usually
utilize

vacancy
vacuum
vague
valuable
variety
vegetable
veil

vengeance
vermilion
veterinarian
vichyssoise
village
villain

warrant
Wednesday
weird
wherever
whim
wholly
whose

wield
woolen
wretched
writing
written
wrote
wrought

xylophone

yacht
yield

zealous
zucchini

4. Build Words Using Prefixes

A prefix is a letter or group of letters placed at the beginning of a word to change its meaning. Later we will show you how knowing a handful of roots can help you figure out scores of words. Prefixes are also frequently used to form new words, for example *pro-Clinton, post-contemporary, refabricate, non-Baptist, anti-Muslim.* Here we will begin by teaching you a few prefixes that can open the door to more powerful words. Here, for example, is a sampling of words that derive from the Latin prefix "circum-," meaning *around.*

Circum- Words

circumambulate	to walk around
circumference	the outer boundary of something
circumfluent	flowing around; encompassing
circumfuse	to surround, as with fluid
circumjacent	lying around; surrounding
circumlocution	a roundabout way of speaking
circumlunar	rotating about the moon
circumnavigate	to sail around
circumpolar	around or near one of the earth's poles
circumrotate	to rotate like a wheel
circumscribe	to encircle; mark off or delimit; restrict

Lesson 1. Common Latin Prefixes

Below are ten common Latin prefixes and their variations. Study the chart and examples. Then, to help you remember them, complete the quizzes that follow.

Prefix	Meaning	Variations	Examples
1. ad-	to, toward		adjoin, adverb
		a-	ascribe
		ac-	accede
		af-	affix
		ag-	aggregate
		at-	attempt
2. com-	with, together		commotion
		co-	cohabit, coworker
		col-	collaborate
		con-	concede, conduct
		cor-	correlate, correspond
3. de-	down		depress, deform
4. dis-	away, apart, opposite of		disagree, dishonest
		di-	divert
		dif-	diffuse
5. ex-	out		exchange, excavate
		e-	elongate, evaporate
		ec-	eccentric
		ef-	effluent, effuse
6. in-	in, into		inscribe, inhabit
		il-	illuminate
		im-	import, impart
		ir-	irradiate
7. in-	not		inflexible, indecent
		ig-	ignoble
		il-	illiterate, illegal

		im- immodest,
		impatient
		ir- irregular
8. pre-	before	premature
9. pro-	forward	proclaim
10. re-	again,	recover,
	back	return

Quiz 1: Applying Latin Prefixes

Each of the following phrases contains an italicized word. Based on the meaning of its prefix, select the closest synonym. Circle the correct response.

1. *adjudicate* the matter
   a. sit in judgment on   b. throw out   c. argue   d. adjust
2. an *illicit* affair
   a. public   b. external   c. unlawful   d. renewed
3. an important *confederation*
   a. visit   b. return   c. church   d. alliance
4. *prolong* a speech
   a. shorten   b. dictate   c. extend   d. preserve
5. an *accredited* school
   a. second-rate   b. authorized   c. undesirable
   d. separated
6. valuable *collateral*
   a. security   b. comments   c. opinions   d. animals
7. *ascribe* the phrase to
   a. write   b. scrawl   c. scribble   d. credit
8. *imbibe* too freely
   a. speak   b. drink   c. travel   d. laugh
9. *precursor* of greater things
   a. banner   b. detractor   c. forerunner   d. hope
10. *compress* metal
    a. help   b. coat   c. squeeze   d. buff

Quiz 2: Defining Words

Based on the meaning of its prefix, define each of the following words.

1. accord _____
2. irradiate _____
3. predestination _____

4. reincarnation _____

5. convolution _____

6. invoke _____

7. cohabit _____

8. irrelevant _____

9. irreducible _____

10. excommunicate _____

Suggested Answers: 1. agreement 2. illuminate 3. fate; destiny 4. rebirth; resurrection 5. a rolled up or coiled condition 6. to request or call forth 7. to live together as husband and wife 8. not relevant 9. incapable of being reduced 10. to exclude from communion

LESSON 2. COMMON GREEK PREFIXES

Below are five common Greek prefixes and their variations. Study the chart and examples. Then, to help you remember the prefixes, complete the quizzes that follow.

Prefix	Meaning	Variations	Examples
1. a-	not, without		atypical, asexual
		an-	anarchy
2. apo-	off, away		apology, apostrophe
3. epi-	beside, upon		epigraph, epidermis
		ep-	epoch
4. para-	beside		paragraph, paraphrase
5. syn-	together, with		synthesis, synonym
		syl-	syllable, syllogism
		sym-	symbiosis, symphony

Quiz 3: Applying Greek Prefixes

Each of the following phrases contains an italicized word. Based on the meaning of its prefix, select the closest synonym. Circle your response.

Formed from:

1. a new *synagogue*
   a. combination
   b. sentence
   c. house of worship
   d. building

   Greek "syn-" + "-agogos," *bringer, gatherer*

2. the true *apogee*
   a. limit of endurance
   b. insult
   c. closest point of an orbit
   d. farthest point of an orbit

   Greek "apo-" + "ge," *earth*

3. the fifth annual *synod*
   a. church council
   b. religious holiday
   c. house-cleaning
   d. painting

   Greek "syn-" + "hodos," *way*

4. the sad *episode*
   a. incident
   b. anecdote
   c. death
   d. accident

   Greek "epi-" + "hodos," *way*

5. the witty *epigram*
   a. television show
   b. radio broadcast
   c. saying
   d. song

   Greek "epi-" + "gramma," *something written*

6. guilty of *apostasy*
   a. murder
   b. desertion
   c. an unnamed crime
   d. abandonment of religious faith

   Greek "apo-" + "stasis," *standing*

7. *aseptic* ointment
   a. free from germs
   b. effective
   c. expensive
   d. greasy

   Greek "a-" + "septos," *rotted*

8. clear and effective *syntax*
   a. treatment
   b. word arrangement
   c. speech
   d. magazine article

   Greek "syn-" + "taxis," *order*

9. injured *epidermis*
   a. leg ligament
   b. elbow
   c. skin
   d. shinbone

   Greek "epi-" + "dermis," *skin*

10. a cutting *epithet*
    a. weapon   c. knife   Greek "epi-"
    b. funeral   d. descriptive + "theton,"
       oration   word   *placed*

Quiz 4: Matching Synonyms

Based on your knowledge of Greek prefixes, match each of the numbered words with the closest synonym. Write your answer in the space provided.

1. SYLLOGISM   a. running beside   ____
2. PARALEGAL   b. climax; highest point ____
3. ANONYMOUS   c. bottomless hole   ____
4. ANESTHETIC   d. one sent out;
                     messenger   ____
5. APOSTLE   e. logical argument   ____
6. PARALLEL   f. doubting God's
                     existence   ____
7. APOCRYPHAL   g. attorney's assistant ____
8. APOGEE   h. false; spurious   ____
9. AGNOSTIC   i. causing loss of feeling ____
10. ABYSS   j. nameless   ____

LESSON 3. OLD ENGLISH PREFIXES

Below are the five most common Old English prefixes and their variations. Study the chart and examples. Then, to help you remember the prefixes, complete the quizzes that follow.

Prefix	Meaning	Examples
a-	on, to, at, by	ablaze, afoot
be-	over, around	bespeak, besiege
mis-	wrong, badly	mistake, misspell
over-	beyond, above	overreach, overawe
un-	not	unwilling, unethical

Quiz 5: Applying Old English Prefixes

Each of the following phrases contains an italicized word. Based on the meaning of its prefix, select the closest synonym. Circle your response.

1. a *miscarriage* of justice
    a. instance b. hero c. failure d. example

2. *beseech* movingly
   a. implore   b. search   c. evoke   d. refuse
3. walking two *abreast*
   a. together   b. side by side   c. back to back   d. in tandem
4. *bestowed* on us
   a. hurled   b. smashed   c. dependent   d. presented
5. an unfortunate *misalliance*
   a. treaty   b. conversation   c. bad deal   d. improper marriage
6. an *overwrought* patient
   a. highly emotional   b. extremely ill   c. very restrained
   d. overmedicated
7. an *unkempt* look
   a. funny   b. messy   c. ugly   d. pretty
8. an embarrassing *miscue*
   a. joke   b. anecdote   c. step   d. error
9. *bedaub* with clay
   a. sculpt   b. present   c. smear   d. create
10. *bemoan* his situation
    a. celebrate   b. share   c. lament   d. hide

Quiz 6: Matching Synonyms

Based on your knowledge of Old English prefixes, match each of the numbered words with the closest synonym. Write your answer in the space provided.

1. UNFEIGNED	a. conquer	_____
2. MISBEGOTTEN	b. right on the mark	_____
3. BEGUILE	c. too fervent	_____
4. MISCARRIAGE	d. envy; resent	_____
5. BEMUSE	e. sincere; genuine	_____
6. MISHAP	f. accident	_____
7. OVERCOME	g. illegitimate	_____
8. BEGRUDGE	h. mislead	_____
9. UNERRING	i. bewilder	_____
10. OVERZEALOUS	j. spontaneous abortion	_____

ANSWERS TO QUIZZES IN CHAPTER 4

Answers to Quiz 1

1. a   **2.** c   **3.** d   **4.** c   **5.** b   **6.** a   **7.** d   **8.** b   **9.** c   **10.** c

Answers to Quiz 3

1. c 2. d 3. a 4. a 5. c 6. d 7. a 8. b 9. c 10. d

Answers to Quiz 4

1. e 2. g 3. j 4. i 5. d 6. a 7. h 8. b 9. f 10. c

Answers to Quiz 5

1. c 2. a 3. b 4. d 5. d 6. a 7. b 8. d 9. c 10. c

Answers to Quiz 6

1. e 2. g 3. h 4. j 5. i 6. f 7. a 8. d 9. b 10. c

5. GLOSSARY OF IMPORTANT PREFIXES TO KNOW

In the previous section you learned that *prefixes* are forms like *ad-*, *com-*, and *de-*, placed at the beginning of words to change their meaning: *ad-* + *join* = *adjoin*. Learning common prefixes helps you remember words and their spellings and figure out their meanings. The following alphabetical list contains the most common prefixes found in English words.

a-¹, *prefix.* from Old English, used **1.** before some nouns to make them into adverbs showing "place where"; **a-** + *shore* → *ashore* = *on (or into) the shore.* **2.** before some verbs to make them into words showing a state or process: **a-** + *sleep* → *asleep* (= *sleeping*); *a-* + *blaze* → *ablaze* (= *blazing*).

a-², *prefix.* a variant spelling of **an-**. It comes from Latin and is used before some adjectives to mean "not": *a-* + *moral* → *amoral* (= *without morals*); *a-* + *tonal* → *atonal* (= *without tone*).

ab-, *prefix.* from Latin, used before some words and roots to mean "off, away": *abnormal* (= *away from what is normal*). Compare A-².

ad-, *prefix.* from Latin, meaning "toward" and indicating direction or tendency: *ad-* + *join* → *adjoin* (= join toward, attack).

ambi-, *prefix.* from Latin, meaning "both" and "around." These meanings are found in such words as: *ambiguous, ambivalence, ambiance.*

amphi- *prefix.* from Greek, meaning "both; on two sides." This meaning is found in such words as: *amphibian, amphibious, amphitheater.*

an-, *prefix.* from Greek, used before roots or stems beginning with a vowel or *h*, meaning "not; without; lacking": *anaerobic* (= *without oxygen*); *anonymous* (= *without name*). Compare A-².

ante-, *prefix.* from Latin, used before roots, meaning **1.** "happening before": *antebellum* (= *before the war*) **2.** "located in front of": *anteroom* (= *room located in front of another*).

anti-, *prefix.* from Greek, used before nouns and adjectives, meaning **1.** against, opposed to: *anti-Semitic, antislavery.* **2.** preventing, counteracting, or working against: *anticoagulant, antifreeze.* **3.** destroying or disabling: *antiaircraft, antipersonnel.* **4.** identical to in form or function, but lacking in some important ways: *anticlimax, antihero, antiparticle*. **5.** an antagonist or rival of: *Antichrist, antipope*. **6.** situated opposite: *Anti-Lebanon*. Also, *before a vowel*, **ant-**.

apo-, *prefix.* from Greek, meaning "away, off, apart": *apo- + strophe → apostrophe* (= a turn away, digression).

aqua-, *prefix.* from Latin, meaning "water". This meaning is found in such words as: *aquaculture, aqualung, aquarium, aquatic, aqueduct, aqueous, aquifer.*

auto-, *prefix.* from Greek, meaning "self." This meaning is found in such words as: *autocrat, autograph, autonomous, autonomy, autopsy.* Also, *esp. before a vowel*, **aut-**.

baro-, *prefix.* from Greek, meaning "weight." This meaning is found in such words as: *barograph, barometer, baroreceptor.*

be-, *prefix.* from Old English, used **1.** to make verbs meaning "to make, become, treat as": *be- + cloud → becloud (= make like a cloud, hard to see); be- + friend → befriend (= treat someone as a friend)*. **2.** before adjectives and verbs ending in *-ed* to mean "covered all over; completely; all around": *be- + decked → bedecked (= decked or covered all over); be- + jeweled → bejeweled (= covered with jewels)*.

bi-, *prefix.* from Latin, meaning "twice, two." This meaning is found in such words as: *biennial, bisect, bicentennial, bigamy, biped, binoculars, bilateral, bipartisan, biweekly.* —**Usage.** In some words, especially words referring to time periods, the prefix *bi-* has two meanings: "twice a + ~" and "every two + ~-s". Thus, *biannual* means both "twice a year" and "every two years." Be careful; check many of these words.

bio-, *prefix.* from Greek, meaning "life." This meaning is found in such words as: *biodegradable, biology, biosphere.*

centi-, *prefix.* from Latin, used before roots to mean "hundredth" or "hundred": *centiliter (= one hundredth of a liter); centipede (= (creature having) one hundred feet).*

chiro-, *prefix.* from Greek, meaning "hand." This meaning is found in such words as: *chirography, chiropodist, chiropractor, chiromancy.*

circum-, *prefix.* from Latin, meaning "round, around." This meaning is found in such words as *circuit, circuitous, circumcise, circumference, circumnavigate, circumstance, circumvent, circumlocution, circus.*

co-, *prefix.* from Latin, meaning **1.** "joint, jointly, together." This meaning is found in such words as: *cochair, costar, coworker.* **2.** "auxiliary, helping." This meaning is found in such words as: *copilot.*

col-[1], var. of COM- before *l*: *collateral*.

col-[2], var. of COLO- before a vowel: *colectomy*.

com-, *prefix.* from Latin, meaning "with, together with." This meaning is found in such words as: *combine, compare, commingle.* For variants before other sounds, see CO-, COL-[1], CON-, COR-.

con-, *prefix.* a variant spelling of COM-. It comes from Latin, meaning "together, with." This meaning is found in such words as: *convene, condone, connection.*

contra-, *prefix.* from Latin, meaning "against, opposite, opposing." This meaning is found in such words as: *contraband, contraception, contradict, contrary.*

cor-, *prefix.* another form of COM- that is used before roots beginning with *r*: *correlate.*

counter-, *prefix.* from Middle English, meaning "against, counter to, opposed to." This meaning is found in such words as: *counterattack, counteroffer, counterclockwise.*

de-, *prefix.* from Latin, used to form verbs and some adjectives meaning **1.** motion or being carried down from, away, or off: *deplane (= move down or off an airplane); descend (= move or go down);* **2.** reversing or undoing the effects of an action: *deflate (= reverse the flow of air out of something); dehumanize (= reverse the positive, humanizing effects of something);* **3.** taking out or removal of a thing: *decaffeinate (= take out the caffeine from something); declaw (= remove the claws of an animal);* **4.** finishing or completeness of an action: *defunct (= completely non-functioning); despoil (= completely spoil).*

deci-, *prefix.* from Latin, meaning "ten." This meaning now appears in the names of units of measurement that are one tenth the size of the unit named by the second element of the compound: *decibel (= one tenth of a bel); deciliter (= one-tenth of a liter).* See the root -DEC-.

dem-, *prefix.* from Greek, meaning "people." This meaning is found in such words as: *demagogue, democracy, demography.*

demi-, *prefix.* from French, meaning "half." This meaning is found in such words as: *demigod, demitasse.*

demo-, *prefix.* like DEM-, from Greek, meaning "people, population." This meaning is found in such words as: *democracy, demography.*

di-, *prefix.* from Greek, meaning "two, double." This meaning is found in such words as: *diptych, dioxide.*

dia-, *prefix.* from Greek, meaning "through, across, from point to point; completely." These meanings are found in such words as: *diachronic, diagnosis, dialogue, dialysis, diameter, diaphanous, diarrhea, diathermy.*

dis-, *prefix.* from Latin, meaning "apart," It now has the following meanings: **1.** opposite of: *disagreement (= opposite of agreement).* **2.** not disapprove: *(= not to approve); dishonest (= not honest); disobey (= not obey).* **3.** reverse; remove: *disconnect (= to remove the connection of); discontinue (= to stop continuing); dissolve (= remove the solidness of; make liquid).*

dys-, *prefix.* from Greek, meaning "ill, bad." This meaning is found in such words as: *dysentery, dyslexia, dyspepsia.*

electro-, *prefix.* from New Latin, meaning "electric" or "electricity": *electro- + magnetic → electromagnetic.*

em-, *prefix.* a form of EN- used before roots beginning with *b, p,* and sometimes *m: embalm.* Compare IM-¹.

en-, *prefix.* ultimately from Latin, used before adjectives or nouns to from verbs meaning **1.** to cause (a person or thing) to be in (the place, condition, or state mentioned); to keep in or place in: *en- + rich → enrich (= to cause to be rich); en- + tomb → entomb (= to cause to be in a tomb);* **2.** to restrict on all sides, completely: *en-* + *circle* → *encircle* (= *to restrict on all sides within a circle*).

epi-, *prefix.* from Greek, meaning "on, upon, at" (*epicenter*), "outer, exterior" (*epidermis*), "accompanying, additional" (*epiphenomenon*).

eu-, *prefix.* from Greek, meaning "good, well"; it now sometimes means "true, genuine." This meaning is found in such words as: *eugenics, eulogize, eulogy, euphemism, euphoria, euthanasia.*

Euro-, *prefix.* contraction of "Europe," used with roots and means "Europe," "Western Europe," or "the European Community": *Euro-* + *-centric* → *Eurocentric* (= *centered on Europe*); *Euro-* + *-crat* → *Eurocrat* (= *bureaucrat in the European Community*). Also, *esp. before a vowel,* **Eur-**.

ex-, *prefix.* from Latin, meaning **1.** "out, out of, away, forth." It is found in such words as: *exclude, exhale, exit, export, extract.* **2.** "former; formerly having been": *ex-member* (= *former member*).

exo-, *prefix.* from Greek, meaning "outside, outer, external": *exocentric.* Also, *before a vowel,* **ex-**.

extra-, *prefix.* from Latin, meaning "outside of; beyond": *extra-* + *galactic* → *extragalactic* (= *outside the galaxy*); *extra-* + *sensory* → *extrasensory* (= *beyond the senses*).

fore-, *prefix.* from Old English, used before nouns, meaning **1.** before (in space, time, condition, etc.): *fore-* + *-cast* → *forecast* (= *prediction before weather comes*); *fore-* + *taste* → *foretaste* (= *a taste before the event takes place*); *fore-* + *warn* → *forewarn* (= *to warn ahead of time*). **2.** front: *fore-* + *head* → *forehead* (= *front of the head*). **3.** preceding: *fore-* + *father* → *forefather* (= *father that came before*). **4.** superior: *fore-* + *man* → *foreman* (= *superior to the other workers*).

hemo- (or **hema-**), *prefix.* from Greek, meaning "blood." This meaning is found in such words as: *hemoglobin, hemophilia, hemorrhage, hemorrhoid.* Also, *esp. before a vowel,* **hem-**.

hyper-, *prefix.* from Greek, used **1.** before nouns and adjectives meaning "excessive; overly; too much; unusual": *hyper-* + *critical* → *hypercritical* (= *overly critical*); *hyper-* + *inflation* → *hyperinflation* (= *inflation that is unusual or too high*). Compare SUPER-. **2.** in computer words to refer to anything not rigidly connected in a step-by-step manner: *hyper-* + *text* → *hypertext* (= *text or information that the user can gain access to in the order he or she chooses*).

hypo-, *prefix.* from Greek, used before roots, meaning "under, below": *hypo-* + *dermic* → *hypodermic* (= *under the skin*); *hypo-* + *thermia* → *hypothermia* (= *heat or temperature below what it should be*). Also, *esp. before a vowel,* **hyp-**.

il-[1], *prefix.* another form of IN-[2] that is used before roots beginning with *l*; it means "not": *il-* + *legible* → *illegible* (= *that cannot be easily read*).

il-[2], *prefix.* another form of IN-[1] that is used before roots beginning with *l*; it means "in, into": *il-* + *-luminate* (= *light*) → *illuminate* (= *shine on or into*).

im-[1], *prefix.* another form of IN-[2] that is used before roots beginning with *p, b* and *m*; it means "not": *im-* + *possible* → *impossible* (= *that is not possible*).

im-², *prefix.* another form of IN-¹ that is used before roots beginning with *p, b* and *m*; it means "in, into": *im-* + *-migrate* → *immigrate (= travel in or into).*

in-¹, *prefix.* from Old English, used before verbs and nouns and means "in; into; on": *in-* + *come* → *income (= money coming in); in-* + *corporate (= body)* → *incorporate (= make into one body); in-* + *land* → *inland (= in the land).*

in-², *prefix.* from Latin, used before adjectives, meaning "not": *in-* + *accurate* → *inaccurate (= not accurate); in-* + *capable* → *incapable (= not capable); in-* + *direct* → *indirect (= not direct).* For variants before other sounds, see IM-, IL-, IR-.

inter-, *prefix.* from Latin, meaning "between, among": *intercity (= between cities); interdepartmental (= between or among departments).*

intra-, *prefix.* from Latin, meaning "within": *intraspecies (= within species).* Compare INTRO-, INTER-.

intro-, *prefix.* from Latin, meaning "inside, within": *intro-* + *-duce (= lead)* → *introduce (= bring inside or within to meet someone); intro-* + *-version (= a turning)* → *introversion (= a turning inside or within).* Compare INTRA-.

ir-¹, *prefix.* another form of IN-¹ that is used before roots beginning with *r: ir-* + *radiate* → *irradiate.*

ir-², *prefix.* another form of IN-² that is used before roots beginning with *r: ir-* + *reducible* → *irreducible.*

iso-, *prefix.* from Greek, meaning "equal." This meaning is found in such scientific and chemical words as: *isochromatic.*

kilo-, *prefix.* from Greek, used before quantities, meaning "thousand": *kilo-* + *liter* → *kiloliter (= one thousand liters); kilo-* + *watt* → *kilowatt (= one thousand watts).*

mal-, *prefix.* from Latin, meaning "bad; wrongful; ill." This meaning is found in such words as: *maladroit, malcontent, malfunction.*

maxi-, *prefix.* contraction of the word *maximum,* meaning "very large or long in comparison with others of its kind." This meaning is found in such words as: *maxiskirt.*

mega-, *prefix.* from Greek, meaning **1.** extremely large, huge: *megalith (= extremely large stone or rock); meagstructure (= a huge structure).* **2.** one million of the units of (the base root or word): *megahertz (= one million hertz); megaton (= one million tons).* **3.** very large quantities or amounts: *megabucks (= a great deal of money); megadose (= a large dose of medicine)* **4.** things that are extraordinary examples of their kind: *megahit (= a smash movie or stage hit); megatrend (= important, very popular trend).*

meta-, *prefix.* from Greek, meaning "after, along with, beyond, among, behind." These meanings are found in such words as: *metabolism, metamorphosis, metaphor, metaphysics.*

micro-, *prefix.* from Latin, meaning **1.** small or very small in comparison with others of its kind: *micro-* + *organism* → *microorganism (= very small living creature).* **2.** restricted in scope: *micro-* + *habitat* → *microhabitat; micro-* + *economics* → *microeconomics.* **3.** containing or dealing with texts that require enlargement to be read: *micro- + film → microfilm.* **4.** one millionth: *micro- + gram → microgram.* Also, *esp. before a vowel,* **micr-.**

mid-, *prefix.* from Old English, meaning "being at or near the middle point of": *midday; mid-Victorian; mid-twentieth century.*

milli-, *prefix.* from Latin, meaning **1.** one thousand: *milli- + -pede (= foot) → millipede (= a small creature with very many legs).* **2.** (in the metric system) equal to ¹/₁₀₀₀ of the unit mentioned: *milli- + meter → millimeter (= ¹/₁₀₀₀ of a meter).*

mini-, *prefix.* contraction of the word *minimum,* meaning **1.** of a small or reduced size in comparison with others of its kind: *mini- + car → minicar; mini- + gun → minigun.* **2.** limited in scope, intensity, or duration: *mini- + boom (= economic upturn) → miniboom (= short-lived economic boom); mini- + course → minicourse (= short course of study).* **3.** (of clothing) short; not reaching the knee: *mini- + dress → minidress; mini- + skirt → miniskirt.* See -MIN-, -MICRO-.

mis-, *prefix.* from Old English, used before nouns, verbs, and adjectives meaning **1.** mistaken; wrong; wrongly; incorrectly: *mis- + trial → mistrial (= a trial conducted improperly); mis- + print → misprint (= something incorrectly printed); misfire: (= fail to fire properly).* **2.** the opposite of: *mis- + trust → mistrust (= the opposite of trust).*

mono-, *prefix.* from Greek, meaning "one, single, lone." This meaning is found in such words as: *monarch, monastery, monochrome, monocle, monogamy, monogram, monograph, monolingual, monolith, monologue, mononucleosis, monopoly, monopterous, monorail, monosyllable, monotonous.*

multi-, *prefix.* from Latin, meaning "many, much, multiple, many times, more than one, composed of many like parts, in many respects": *multi- + colored → multicolored (= having many colors); multi- + vitamin → multivitamin (= composed of many vitamins).*

neo-, *prefix.* from Greek, meaning "new." It has come to mean "new, recent, revived, changed": *neo- + colonialism → neocolonialism (= colonialism that has been revived); neo- + -lithic → neolithic (= of a recent Stone Age).* Also, *esp. before a vowel,* **ne-.**

neuro-, *prefix.* fom Greek, meaning "nerve, nerves." Its meaning now includes "nervous system," and this meaning is found in such words as: *neurology, neurosurgery.*

non-, *prefix.* from Latin, usually meaning "not," used **1.** before adjectives and adverbs and means a simple negative or absence of something: *non- + violent → nonviolent.* **2.** before a noun of action and means the failure of such action: *non- + payment → nonpayment (= failure to pay).* **3.** before a noun to suggest that the thing mentioned is not true, real, or worthy of the name, as in *nonbook, noncandidate, non-event.*

ob-, *prefix.* from Latin, used before roots, meaning "toward," "to," "on," "over," "against": *ob- + -jec- → object.*

octa-, *prefix.* from Greek, meaning "eight": *octa- + -gon → octagon (= eight-sided figure).*

omni-, *prefix.* from Latin, meaning "all": *omni- + directional → omnidirectional (= in all directions).*

ortho-, *prefix.* from Greek, meaning "straight, upright, right, correct": *ortho-* + *graph* → *orthography* (= *correct writing*); *ortho-* + *dontics* → *orthodontics* (= *dentistry dealing with straightening teeth*); *ortho-* + *pedic* → *orthopedic* (= *correction of improper bone structure from childhood*).

out-, *prefix.* from Old English, used **1.** before verbs, meaning "going beyond, surpassing, or outdoing (the action of the verb)": *out-* + *bid* → *outbid; out-* + *do* → *outdo; out-* + *last* → *outlast.* **2.** before nouns to form certain compounds meaning "outside; out": *out-* + *cast* → *outcast; out-* + *come* → *outcome; out-* + *side* → *outside.*

over-, *prefix.* from Old English, meaning **1.** the same as the adverb or adjective OVER, as in: *overboard; overcoat; overhang; overlord; overthrow.* **2.** "over the limit; to excess; too much; too": *overact* (= *to act too much*); *overcrowd* (= *to crowd too many people or things into*); *overaggressive* (= *too aggressive*); *overfull; overweight.* **3.** "outer," as when referring to an outer covering: *overskirt* (= *a skirt worn over something, such as a gown*).

pan-, *prefix.* from Greek, meaning "all." This meaning is found in such words as: *panorama; pantheism.* It is also used esp. in terms that imply or suggest the union of all branches of a group: *Pan-American; Pan-* + *hellenic* (*Greek*) → *Panhellenic* (= *all Greeks united in one group*); *Pan-Slavism* (= *all the people of Slavic background united*).

para-¹, *prefix.* from Greek, meaning **1.** "at or to one side of, beside, side by side." This meaning is found in such words as: *parabola; paragraph.* **2.** "beyond, past, by": *paradox.* **3.** "abnormal, defective": *paranoia.* **4.** (before names of jobs or occupations) "ancilliary, subsidiary, assisting." This meaning is found in such words as: *paralegal; paraprofessional.* Also, *esp. before a vowel,* **par-.**

para-², *prefix.* taken from PARACHUTE, and is used to form compounds that refer to persons or things that use parachutes or that are landed by parachute: *paratrooper.*

penta-, *prefix.* from Greek, meaning "five": *penta-* + *-gon* → *pentagon* (= *five-sided figure*).

per-, *prefix.* from Latin, used before roots, meaning "through, thoroughly, completely, very": *per-* + *-vert* → *pervert* (= *a person completely turned away from the normal*); *per-* + *-fect* → *perfect* (= *thoroughly or completely done*).

peri-, *prefix.* from Greek, used before roots, meaning **1.** "about, around": *peri-* + *meter* → *perimeter* (= *distance around an area*); *peri-* + *-scope* → *periscope* (= *instrument for looking around oneself*). **2.** "enclosing, surrounding": *peri-* + *cardium* → *pericardium* (= *a sac surrounding the heart*). **3.** "near": *peri-* + *helion* → *perihelion* (= *point of an orbit nearest to the sun*).

petro-¹, *prefix.* from Greek, meaning "rock, stone": *petro-* + *-ology* → *petrology* (= *the study of rocks or stone*).

petro-², *prefix.* taken from PETROLEUM and used to form compounds: *petro-* + *chemistry* → *petrochemistry; petro-* + *power* → *petropower* (= *power derived from petroleum*).

photo-, *prefix.* from Greek, meaning "light": *photo-* + *biology* → *photobi-*

ology; photo- + -on → photon (= elementary "particle" of light). Also means "photographic" or "photograph": *photo- + copy → photocopy.*

poly-, *prefix.* from Greek, meaning "much, many": *polyandry (= the custom of having many husbands); polyglot (= speaking many languages).*

post-, *prefix.* from Latin, meaning "after (in time), following (some event)"; "behind, at the rear or end of": *post- + industrial → postindustrial (= after the industrial age); post- + war → postwar (= after the war).*

pre-, *prefix.* from Latin, **1.** meaning "before, in front of," "prior to, in advance of," "being more than, surpassing": *pre- + -dict → predict (= say in advance of something); pre- + eminent → preeminent (= surpassing or being more than eminent); pre- + face → preface (= something written in front of a book, etc.)* **2.** used before verbs to form new verbs that refer to an activity taking place before or instead of the usual occurrence of the same activity: *pre- + board → preboard (= to board an airplane before the other passengers); pre- + cook → precook (= cook before regular cooking).* **3.** used in forming adjectives that refer to a period of time before the event, period, person, etc., mentioned in the root: *pre- + school → preschool (= before the age of starting school); pre- + war → prewar (= before the war started).*

pro-¹, *prefix.* from Latin, **1.** meaning "forward, forward movement or location; advancement": *proceed; progress; prominent; promote; propose.* **2.** used before roots and words, meaning "bringing into existence": *procreate; produce.* **3.** used before roots and words, meaning "in place of": *pronoun.* **4.** used to form adjectives, meaning "favoring the group, interests, course of action, etc., named by the noun; calling for the interests named by the noun": *pro- + choice → pro-choice (= in favor of allowing a choice to be made regarding abortions); pro- + war → prowar (= in favor of fighting a war).*

pro-², *prefix.* from Greek, meaning **1.** "before, beforehand, in front of": *prognosis; prophylactic; prothesis; proboscis.* **2.** "primitive or early form": *prodrug; prosimian.*

proto-, *prefix.* from Greek, meaning "first, foremost, earliest form of": *proto- + lithic → protolithic; protoplasm.* Also, *esp. before a vowel,* **prot-.**

pseudo-, *prefix.* from Greek, meaning **1.** "false; pretended; unreal": *pseudo- + intellectual → pseudointellectual (= a person pretending to be an intellectual).* **2.** "closely or deceptively resembling": *pseudo- + carp → pseudocarp (= a fish closely resembling a carp); pseudo- + -pod → pseudopod (= a part of an animal that closely resembles a foot).* Also, *esp. before a vowel,* **pseud-.**

psycho-, *prefix.* from Greek, meaning "soul; mind." This meaning is found in such words as: *parapsychology, psychedelic, psychiatry, psychic, psychological, psychology, psychopath, psychosis, psychotic.*

pyro-, *prefix.* from Greek, meaning "fire, heat, high temperature": *pyromaniac, pyrotechnics.*

quasi-, *prefix.* from Latin, meaning "as if, as though." It is used before adjectives and nouns and means "having some of the features but not all; resembling; almost the same as": *quasi-scientific, quasiparticle, quasi-stellar.*

radio-, *prefix.* ultimately from Latin *radius,* meaning "beam, ray." It is used before roots and nouns and means "radiant energy": *radiometer.* It is also used to mean "radio waves": *radiolocation; radiotelephone.* Other meanings are: **1.** the giving off of rays as a result of the breakup of atomic nuclei: *radioactivity; radiocarbon.* **2.** x-rays: *radiograph; radiotherapy.*

re-, *prefix.* from Latin, used **1.** before roots and sometimes words to form verbs and nouns meaning or referring to action in a backward direction: *re-* + *-cede-* → *recede* (= *fall back*); *re-* + *-vert-* → *revert* (= *turn back*). **2.** to form verbs or nouns showing action in answer to or intended to undo or reverse a situation: *rebel; remove; respond; restore; revoke.* **3.** to form verbs or nouns showing action that is done over, often with the meaning that the outcome of the original action was in some way not enough or not long lasting, or that the performance of the new action brings back an earlier state of affairs: *recapture; reoccur; repossess; resole* (= *put another sole on a shoe*); *retype.*

retro-, *prefix.* from Latin, meaning "back, backward": *retro-* + *-gress* → *retrogress* (= *proceed backward*); *retro-* + *rocket* → *retrorocket.*

self-, *prefix.* from Old English, used **1.** before nouns to refer to something that one does by oneself or to oneself: *self-control* (= *control of oneself*); *self-government; self-help; self-portrait.* **2.** before adjectives and nouns to refer to an action that is done without assistance: *self-adhesive; a self-loading gun; self-study.*

semi-, *prefix.* from Latin, meaning **1.** "half": *semiannual; semicircle.* **2.** "partially; partly; somewhat": *semiautomatic; semidetached; semiformal.* **3.** "happening or occurring twice in (a certain length of time)": *semiannual.*

sex-, *prefix.* from Latin, meaning "six": *sexpartite* (= *having six parts or divisions*).

socio-, *prefix.* from Latin, used before roots and sometimes words, meaning "social; sociological; society": *socio-* + *economic* → *socioeconomic; socio-* + *-metry* → *sociometry* (= *social statistics*). See -SOC-.

step-, *prefix.* from Old English, used before words to name a member of a family related by the remarriage of a parent and not by blood: *When my father married his second wife, she already had a son who became my stepbrother.*

sub-, *prefix.* from Latin, meaning **1.** "under, below, beneath": *subsoil; subway.* **2.** "just outside of, near": *subalpine; subtropical.* **3.** "less than, not quite": *subhuman; subteen.* **4.** "secondary, at a lower point in a hierarchy": *subcommittee; subplot.* Sometimes this prefix is spelled as *su-, suc-, suf-, sug-, sum-, sup-, sur-, sus-.*

super-, *prefix.* from Latin, meaning **1.** "above, beyond; above or over (another); situated or located over": *superimpose, superstructure, superficial.* **2.** "an individual, thing, or property that surpasses customary or normal amounts or levels, as being larger, more powerful, or having something to a great degree or to too great a degree": *superconductivity, superman, supercomputer, superhighway, superhuman, supercritical, supercool.*

supra-, *prefix.* from Latin, meaning "above, over; beyond the limits of": *supraorbital; supranational.* Compare SUPER-.

sur-, *prefix.* from French, meaning "over, above, in addition": *surcharge; surname; surrender.*

sym-, *prefix*. another form of the prefix SYN-. It appears before roots beginning with *b, p, m, symbol; symphony; symmetry.*

syn-, *prefix*. from Greek, meaning "with; together." This meaning is found in such words as: *synchronous, idiosyncrasy, photsynthesis, synagogue, synchronize, synonym, synthesis.* See SYM-.

tele-, *prefix*. **1.** from Greek, meaning "far." It is used before roots and sometimes words and means "reaching over a distance, carried out between two remote points, performed or operating through electronic transmissions": *telegraph; telekinesis; teletypewriter.* **2.** tele- is also used to mean "television:" *telegenic; telethon.* Also, *esp. before a vowel,* **tel-.**

trans-, *prefix*. from Latin, used **1.** before verb roots that refer to movement or carrying from one place to another; it means "across; through": *transfer; transmit; transplant.* **2.** to mean "complete change": *transform; transmute.* **3.** before roots to form adjectives that mean "crossing, going beyond, on the other side of (the place or thing named)": *transnational; trans-Siberian.*

tri-, *prefix*. from Latin, meaning "three": *triatomic; trilateral.*

ultra-, *prefix*. from Latin, meaning **1.** "located beyond, on the far side of": *ultraviolet.* **2.** "carrying to the furthest degree possible, on the fringe of": *ultraleft; ultramodern.* **3.** "extremely": *ultralight.* **4.** "going beyond normal or customary bounds or limits": *ultramicroscope; ultrasound; ultrastructure.*

un-[1], *prefix*. from Old English, used very freely to form adjectives and the adverbs and nouns formed from these adjectives. It means "not," and it brings negative or opposite force: *unfair, unfairly, unfairness; unfelt; unseen; unfitting; unformed; unheard-of; unrest; unemployment.*

un-[2], *prefix*. from Old English, used **1.** before verbs, meaning "a reversal of some action or state, or a removal, a taking away, or a release": *unbend; uncork; unfasten.* **2.** before some verbs to intensify the meaning: *unloose (= let loose with force).*

under-, *prefix*. from Old English, meaning **1.** "a place or situation below or beneath": *underbrush; undertow.* **2.** "lower in grade, rank or dignity": *undersheriff; understudy.* **3.** before adjectives to mean "of lesser degree, extent, or amount": *undersized.* **4.** "not showing enough; too little": *underfed.*

vice-, *prefix*. from Latin, meaning "in place of, instead of." It is used before roots and sometimes words and means "deputy"; it is used esp. in the titles of officials who serve in the absence of the official named by the base word: *viceroy (→ vice- + roy, "king"); vice-chancellor; vice-chairman.*

6. BUILD WORDS USING SUFFIXES

A suffix is a letter or group of letters placed at the end of a word to change its grammatical function, tense, or meaning. Suffixes can be used to create a verb from a noun or adjective or an adjective from a verb, for example. They can change a word's tense as well; "-ed" can make a present-tense verb into a past participle, for instance. They can even change a word's meaning; the suffix "-ette," for example, can make a word into its diminutive: "kitchen" becomes "kitchenette."

Just as recognizing a small number of prefixes can help you figure out many unfamiliar words, so knowing a few common suffixes can help you build a more powerful vocabulary.

LESSON 1. TEN POWERFUL SUFFIXES

Below are ten useful suffixes. Read through the chart and examples. To reinforce your study, complete the quizzes that follow.

Suffix	Meaning	Variations	Examples
1. -ate	to make		alienate, regulate
	marked by		passionate, affectionate
2. -en	to make		weaken, moisten
3. -ism	the quality or practice of		absolutism, baptism
4. -ation	the act or condition of		allegation, affirmation
		-ition	recognition
		-tion	commotion

5. -ty	the state of		modesty
		-ity	security
6. -er	one that does or deals with		worker, teacher
		-ar	scholar
		-ier	furrier
		-or	bettor
7. -an	one that does or deals with		comedian, historian
8. -al	resembling or pertaining to		natural, accidental
9. -ous	full of		perilous
		-ious	gracious, vicious
10. -able	capable of being		lovable, affordable
		-ible	reversible

Quiz 1: Applying Suffixes

Each of the following phrases contains an italicized word. Based on the meaning of its suffix, select the closest synonym. Circle your response.

1. *combustible* rubbish
   a. unbreakable b. able to burst c. affordable d. flammable
2. *pastoral* scenes
   a. clerical b. attractive c. rural d. homely
3. a *partisan* of the rebellion
   a. flag b. supporter c. sign d. result
4. a *palatial* home
   a. magnificent b. modest c. formal d. enjoyable
5. the *collegiate* atmosphere
   a. churchlike b. friendly c. cooperative d. academic
6. *assiduity* in studies
   a. alacrity b. cleverness c. diligence d. laziness
7. a country of *pedestrians*
   a. scholars b. walkers c. shopkeepers d. students
8. an *abstemious* eater
   a. aloof b. idle c. absent-minded d. sparing

9. *perilous* practices
   a. commonplace b. rare c. dangerous d. useless
10. *deleterious* effects
   a. good b. neutral c. bad d. delightful

Quiz 2: Matching Synonyms

Based on your knowledge of suffixes, match each of the numbered words with the closest synonym. If in doubt, refer to the root word that follows each numbered word.

1. CULPABLE
   (Root word: Latin
   "culpa," *blame*)

2. PARITY
   (Root word: Latin "par,"
   equal)

3. AMENABLE
   (Root word: French
   "amener," *to lead to*)

4. MENDACIOUS
   (Root word: Latin
   "mendax," *dishonest*)

5. SEMPITERNAL
   (Root word: Latin
   "semper," *always*)

6. NIHILISM
   (Root word: Latin "nihil,"
   nothing)

7. ATAVISM
   (Root word: Latin
   "atavus," *remote*)

8. FEALTY
   (Root word: French
   "fealté," *fidelity*)

9. CASTIGATE
   (Root word: Latin
   "castus," *chaste*)

10. NOXIOUS
    (Root word: Latin
    "noxa," *harm*)

a. blameworthy

b. injurious

c. everlasting

d. reversion to type

e. equality

f. to chastise; censure

g. willing

h. total rejection of law

i. lying; false

j. faithfulness

LESSON 2. TEN ADDITIONAL POWERFUL SUFFIXES

The following ten suffixes will help you understand countless additional words. After you read through the suffixes and their definitions, complete the two quizzes at the end of the lesson.

Suffix	*Meaning*	*Examples*
1. -esque	in the manner of; like	Lincolnesque
2. -aceous	resembling or having	carbonaceous
3. -ic	associated with	democratic
4. -age	act or process of; quantity or measure	marriage coverage; footage,
5. -itis	inflammation	tonsillitis
6. -ish	similar to; like a	foolish; babyish
7. -less	without	guiltless; helpless
8. -ship	occupation or skill; condition of being	authorship, penmanship; friendship
9. -ian	a person who is, does, or participates in	comedian
10. -ferous	bearing or conveying	odoriferous

Quiz 3: Matching Synonyms

Based on your knowledge of suffixes, match each of the numbered words with its closest synonym. Write your answer in the space provided.

1. WASPISH	a. inattentive, sloppy	_____
2. FELLOWSHIP	b. egotistic	_____
3. ANGELIC	c. distance	_____
4. MILEAGE	d. huge	_____
5. PICTURESQUE	e. eternal	_____
6. CURVACEOUS	f. irritable	_____
7. TITANIC	g. voluptuous	_____
8. CARELESS	h. companionship	_____
9. SELFISH	i. innocent	_____
10. TIMELESS	j. colorful	_____

Quiz 4: Applying Suffixes

Each of the following phrases contains an italicized word. Based on the meaning of its suffix, select the closest synonym. If in doubt, refer to the root word listed in the right-hand column. Circle your response.

Root Word

1. *auriferous* mineral
   a. containing gold   b. extremely
   hard   c. having an odor
   d. very common

   Latin
   "aurum,"
   gold

2. *conical* shape
   a. humorous; amusing   b. like a
   cone   c. spherical   d. rigid

   Greek
   "konos," *cone*

3. suffering from *carditis*
   a. eye infection   b. a tin ear
   c. inflammation of the heart
   d. stiff joints

   Greek
   "kardia,"
   heart

4. graceful *Romanesque*
   a. architectural style   b. departure   c. essay   d. apology

5. *olivaceous* color
   a. oily   b. deep green   c. faded   d. attractive

6. frightful *carnage*
   a. journey   b. slaughter
   c. scene   d. sensuality

   Latin
   "carnis," *flesh*

7. *satanic* nature
   a. evil   b. cheerful   c. shiny   d. generous

8. admirable *craftsmanship*
   a. display   b. individual   c. shop   d. artfulness

9. *veracious* remarks
   a. vivid   b. vicious   c. windy
   d. truthful

   Latin
   "verus," *true*

10. painful *appendicitis*
    a. news   b. surgery   c. inflammation of the appendix
    d. removal of the appendix

ANSWERS TO QUIZZES IN CHAPTER 6

Answers to Quiz 1

1. d 2. c 3. b 4. a 5. d 6. c 7. b 8. d 9. c 10. c

Answers to Quiz 2

1. a 2. e 3. g 4. i 5. c 6. h 7. d 8. j 9. f 10. b

Answers to Quiz 3

1. f 2. h 3. i 4. c 5. j 6. g 7. d 8. a 9. b 10. e

Answers to Quiz 4

1. a 2. b 3. c 4. a 5. b 6. b 7. a 8. d 9. d 10. c

7. GLOSSARY OF IMPORTANT SUFFIXES TO KNOW

In the previous section you learned that *suffixes* are forms like *-ate*, *-ism*, and *-ous*, placed at the end of words to change their meaning: *alien* + *-ate* = *alienate*. Learning common suffixes helps you remember words and their spellings and figure out their meanings. The following alphabetical list contains the most common suffixes found in English words.

-ability, *suffix.* ultimately from Latin, a combination of -ABLE and -ITY, used to form nouns from adjectives that end in *-able*: *capable (adjective)* → *capability (noun)*; *reliable (adjective)* → *reliability (noun)*.

-able, *suffix.* ultimately from Latin, added to verbs to form adjectives meaning "capable of, fit for, tending to": *teach* + *-able* → *teachable* (= *capable of being taught*); *photograph* + *-able* → *photographable* = (*fit for photographing*). Compare -IBLE.

-aceous, *suffix.* from Latin, meaning "having the nature of, made of." This meaning is found in such words as *herbaceous, cretaceous.*

-acious, *suffix.* from Latin, used after some roots to form adjectives meaning "tending to; abounding in": *tenacious (from ten-* "hold on" + *-acious)* = *tending to hold on; loquacious (from loq(u)-* "talk" + *-acious)* = *tending to talk.* Compare -OUS.

-acity, *suffix.* from Middle English, used after some roots to form nouns with the meaning "tendency toward; abundance in": *tenacity (from- ten-* "hold on" + *-acity)* = *tendency toward holding on.*

-age, *suffix.* ultimately from Latin, used to form noncount mass or abstract nouns **1.** from other nouns, with meanings such as "collection" (*coinage* = *a collection or group of coins*) and "quantity or measure" (*footage* = *quantity of feet in measurement*). **2.** from verbs, with meanings such as "process" (*coverage* = *the act or process of covering*), "the outcome of, the fact of" or "the physical effect or remains of" (*spoilage* = *the result of spoiling; wreckage* = *the remains of wrecking*), and "amount charged" (*towage* = *charge for towing; postage* = *amount charged for posting, that is, sending through the mail*).

-aholic, *suffix.* (originally taken from the word ALCOHOLIC) used to form new words with the general meaning "a person who is addicted to or strongly desires" the activity being shown by the initial part of the word. Thus, a *chargeaholic* is someone who uses a charge card a lot; a *foodaholic* is someone who always wants food. Compare -HOLIC.

-al¹, *suffix.* from Latin, added to nouns to form adjectives meaning "relating to, of the kind of, having the form or character of": *autumn + -al → autumnal (= relating to the season autumn); nature + -al → natural (= having the character of nature).*

-al², *suffix.* from Latin, added to verbs to form nouns meaning "the act of": *deny + -al → denial (= the act of denying); refuse + -al → refusal (= the act of refusing).*

-ally, *suffix.* form from -al¹ + -ly, used to form adverbs from certain adjectives ending in -IC: *terrific (adj.) + -ally → terrifically (adverb).*

-an, *suffix.* from Latin, meaning "of, pertaining to, having qualities of," **1.** added to names of places or people to form adjectives and nouns meaning **a.** being connected with a place: *Chicago + -an → Chicagoan;* **b.** having membership in a group of: *Episcopal + -(i)an → Episcopalian;* **2.** used to form adjectives meaning "of or like (someone); supporter or believer of": *Christ + -(i)an → Christian; Freud + -(i)an → Freudian (= supporter of or believer in the theories of Sigmund Freud).* **3.** used to form nouns from words ending in -ic or -y meaning "one who works with": *electric + -(i)an → electrician; comedy + -an → comedian.*

-ance, *suffix.* ultimately from Latin, used **1.** after some adjectives ending in -ANT to form nouns meaning "quality or state of": *brilliant + -ance → brilliance.* **2.** *after some verb roots to form nouns:* *appear + -ance → appearance; resemble + -ance → resemblance.* See -ANT, -ENCE.

-ant, *suffix.* from Latin, used **1.** after some verbs to form adjectives meaning "doing or performing (the action of the verb)": *please + -ant → pleasant (= doing the pleasing).* **2.** after some verbs to form nouns meaning "one who does or performs (the action of the verb, often a formal action)": *serve + -ant → servant (= one who serves); apply (+ ic) + -ant → applicant (= one who formally applies, as for a job).* **3.** after some verbs to form nouns meaning: "substance that does or performs (the action of the verb)": *cool (verb = "to make cool") + -ant → coolant (= substance to keep engines cool).* See -ENT.

-ar, *suffix.* from Latin, used **1.** after some nouns (many of which have an *l* before the end) to form adjectives: *circle + -ar → circular; single + -ar → singular.* **2.** after some verbs to form nouns meaning "one who does or performs an act of": *beg + -ar → beggar; lie + -ar → liar.*

-ard, *suffix.* from French, used after some verbs and nouns to form nouns that refer to persons who regularly do an activity, or who are characterized in a certain way, as indicated by the stem: *dullard (= one who is dull); drunkard (= one who is drunk).*

-arian, *suffix.* from Latin, used **1.** after some nouns and adjectives that end in -ARY to form personal nouns: *library + -arian → librarian; seminary + -arian → seminarian; veterinary + -arian → veterinarian.* **2.** after some roots to form nouns meaning "a person who supports, calls for, or practices the principles of (the root noun)": *authority* + *-arian* → *authoritarian* (= *one who believes in central authority*); *totality* + *-arian* → *totalitarian* (= *one who believes in total governmental rule*).

-art, *suffix.* variant form of -ARD, found in such words as: *braggart.*

-ary, *suffix.* from Latin, used **1.** after some nouns to form adjectives meaning: "relating to, connected with": *element* + *-ary* → *elementary; honor* + *-ary* → *honorary.* **2.** after some roots to form personal nouns, or nouns that refer to objects that hold or contain things: *secretary; -libr-* (= *root meaning* "*book*") + *-ary* → *library* (= *place for holding books*); *glossary* (= *place containing specialized words and their meanings*). **3.** after some nouns to form adjectives meaning "contributing to; for the purpose of": *inflation* + *-ary* → *inflationary* (= *contributing to inflation*); *compliment* + *-ary* → *complimentary* (= *for the purpose of complimenting*).

-ate, *suffix.* **1.** from Latin, used to form adjectives meaning "showing; full of": *passion* + *-ate* → *passionate* (= *showing passion*); *consider* + *-ate* → *considerate* (= *showing the action of considering*); *literate.* **2.** used to form verbs meaning "cause to become (like); act as": *regular* + *-ate* → *regulate* (= *make regular, act by rule*); *active* + *-ate* → *activate* (= *cause to become active*); *hyphenate; calibrate.* **3.** used to form nouns meaning **a.** a group of people: *elector* + *-ate* → *electorate* (= *group who elect*). **b.** an area ruled by: *caliph* (*a kind of ruler*) + *-ate* → *caliphate* (= *area ruled by a caliph*); *protector* + *-ate* → *protectorate* (= *area ruled by a protecting nation*). **c.** the office, institution, or function of: *consul* + *-ate* → *consulate; magistrate; potentate.*

-ation, *suffix.* from Latin, used after some verbs or adjectives (some of which end in -ATE) to form nouns meaning "state or process of": *starve* + *-ation* → *starvation* (= *condition of starving*); *separate* + *-ation* → *separation* (= *state of being separate*).

-ative, *suffix.* from Latin, used after some verbs (some of which end in -ATE) and nouns to form adjectives: *regulate* + *-ative* → *regulative* (= *with the power to regulate*); *norm* (= *rule*) + *-ative* → *normative* (= *having rules*).

-ator, *suffix.* from Latin, used after verbs ending in -ATE to form nouns meaning "person or thing that does or performs (the action of the verb)": *agitate* + *-ator* → *agitator* (= *person who agitates; machine that agitates*); *vibrate* + *-ator* → *vibrator* (= *thing that vibrates*); *narrator; generator; mediator; incubator.*

-based, *suffix.* from the word *base,* used **1.** after nouns to form adjectives. **2.** after nouns of place to form adjectives meaning "operating or working from": *ground* + *-based* → *ground-based* (= *operating from the ground*); *New York* + *-based* → *New York-based* (= *working from New York*). **3.** after nouns to form adjectives meaning "making use of": *computer* + *based* → *computer-based* (= *making use of computers; as in* "*computer-based instruction*"); *logic* + *-based* → *logic-based* (= *making use of logic*).

-burger, *suffix.* (originally taken from the word *hamburger*) used after roots and some words to form nouns that mean "the food added to, or substituted for, a basic hamburger": *cheese* + *-burger* → *cheeseburger* (= *a* *hamburger with cheese added on top); fish + -burger → fishburger (= fish substituted for the meat of a hamburger).*

-cracy, *suffix.* ultimately from Greek, meaning "power; rule; government," used after roots to form nouns meaning "rule; government": *auto-* + *-cracy → autocracy (— government by one ruler); theo- ("God") + -cracy → theocracy (— a country governed by the rule of God or a god).* Compare -CRAT.

-crat, *suffix.* ultimately from Greek, meaning "ruler; person having power," used after roots to form nouns meaning "ruler; member of a ruling body": *auto-* + *-crat → autocrat (= a ruler governing alone).* Compare -CRACY.

-cy, *suffix.* from French and Latin, used **1.** to form nouns from adjectives that have stems that end in *-t, -te, -tic,* and esp. *-nt* **a.** to form abstract nouns: *democrat + -cy → democracy; accurate + -cy → accuracy; expedient + -cy → expediency; lunatic + -cy → lunacy.* **b.** to form action nouns: *vacant + -cy → vacancy; occupant + -cy → occupancy.* **2.** *to form nouns meaning "rank or office of"*: *captain + -cy → captaincy (= rank or office of a captain); magistra(te) + -cy → magistracy (= office of a magistrate).*

-dom, *suffix.* from Old English, used after some nouns and adjectives to form nouns meaning **1.** domain or area ruled: *king + -dom → kingdom (= area a king rules).* **2.** collection of persons: *official + -dom → officialdom (= a collection of officials).* **3.** rank: *earl + -dom → earldom (= the rank or position of an earl).* **4.** general condition: *free + -dom → freedom (= general condition of being free).*

-ed, *suffix.* from Old English, **1.** added to words with the following rules of form: **a.** For most regular verbs that end in a consonant, *-ed* is added directly afterwards: *cross + -ed → crossed.* When the verb ends in *-y,* the *-y* changes to *-i-* and *-ed* is added: *ready + -ed → readied.* If the root ends in *-e,* an *e* is dropped: *save + -ed → saved.* **b.** The pronunciation of the suffix *-ed* depends on the *sound* that appears before it. After the sounds (p, k, f, th, s, sh and ch) the suffix is pronounced (t): *cross + -ed → crossed (krôst);* after the sounds (t, d) it is pronounced (id): *edit + -ed → edited (ed'i tid);* after all other sounds it is pronounced (d): *budge + -ed → budged (bujd).* **2.** carries a number of different meanings. It is used **a.** to form the past tense and past participle of regular verbs: *He crossed the river. He had crossed the river when we got there.* **b.** to form an adjective indicating a condition or quality due to action of the verb: *inflated balloons (= balloons that have been inflated).* **c.** after nouns to form adjectives meaning "possessing, having, or characterized by (whatever the noun base is)": *beard + -ed → bearded (= possessing or having a beard).*

-ee, *suffix.* from French, used **1.** after verbs that take an object to form nouns meaning "the person who is the object of the action of the verb": *address + -ee → addressee (= the person whom someone else addresses).* **2.** after verbs that do not take an object to form nouns meaning "the one doing or performing the act of the verb": *escape + -ee → escapee (= one performing the act of escaping).* **3.** after other words to form nouns meaning "the one who is or does": *absent + -ee → absentee (= one who is absent).*

-eer, *suffix.* from French, used to form nouns meaning "the person who produces, handles, or is associated with" the base word: *engine + -eer → engineer (= person handling an engine).*

-en, *suffix.* from Old English, used **1. a.** after some adjectives to form verbs meaning "to be or make": *hard + -en → harden (= to be or make hard).* **b.** after some nouns to form verbs meaning "to add to, cause to be, or have": *length + -en → lengthen (= to add length to; make long).* **2.** after some nouns that are materials or sources of something to form adjectives that describe the source or material: *gold + -en → golden (= like gold).*

-ence, *suffix.* from Latin, used **1.** after some adjectives ending in -ENT to form nouns meaning "quality or state of": *abstin(ent) + -ence → abstinence.* **2.** after some verb roots to form nouns: *depend + -ence → dependence.* See -ANCE, -ENT.

-ent, *suffix.* from Latin, used **1.** after some verbs to form adjectives meaning "doing or performing (the action of the verb)": *differ + -ent → different.* **2.** after some verbs to form nouns meaning "one who does or performs (the action)": *stud(y) + -ent → student (= one who studies).* See -ANT, -ENCE.

-er¹, *suffix.* from Old English, used **1.** after verbs to form nouns meaning "a person, animal or thing that performs the action of the verb" or "the person, animal or thing used in performing the action of the verb": *bake + -er → baker (= a person who bakes); teach + -er → teacher (= a person who teaches); fertilize + -er → fertilizer (= a thing that is used to fertilize)* **2.** after nouns to form new nouns that refer to the occupation, work or labor of the root noun: *hat + -er → hatter (= one whose work is making hats); roof + -er → roofer (= one whose occupation is repairing roofs).* **3.** after nouns to form new nouns that refer to the place of origin, or the dwelling place, of the root noun: *Iceland + -er → Icelander (= person who originally comes from Iceland); southern + -er → southerner (= a person who originally comes from, or lives in, the south).* Compare -IER, -OR.

-er², *suffix.* from Middle English, regularly used to form the comparative form of short adjectives and adverbs: *hard + -er → harder; small + -er → smaller; fast + -er → faster.*

-ery (or **-ry**), *suffix.* from French, used **1.** to form nouns that refer to **a.** things in a collection: *green + -ery → greenery (= green plants as a group); machine + -ery → machinery (= a group or collection of machines)* **b.** people in a collection: *Jew + -ry → Jewry (= Jews as a group); peasant + -ry → peasantry (= peasants as a group)* **c.** an occupation, activity, or condition: *dentist + -ry → dentistry (= occupation of a dentist); rival + -ry → rivalry (= condition of being a rival); rob + -ery → robbery (= activity of robbing or being robbed).* **2.** to form nouns that refer to a place where the activity of the root is done: *bake + -ery →bakery (= place where baking is done); wine + -ery → winery (= place where wine is made).*

-ese, *suffix.* ultimately from Latin, used **1.** after nouns that refer to place names: **a.** to form adjectives to describe things made in or relating to the place: *Japan + -ese → Japanese (= of or relating to Japan or its people); Vienna + -ese → Viennese (= of or relating to Vienna or its people)* **b.** to form nouns with the meanings "the people living in (the place)" or "the language of (the place)": *Vietnam + -ese → Vietnamese (= the people living* *in/the language spoken in Vietnam).* **2.** to form nouns that describe in an insulting or humorous way the language characteristic of or typical of the base word: *Brooklyn* + *-ese* → *Brooklynese (= the language characteristic of Brooklyn); journal* + *-ese* → *journalese (= the language typical of journalists).*

-esque, *suffix.* from French, used after nouns and proper names to form adjectives meaning "resembling," "in the style or manner of," "suggesting the work of" the person or thing denoted by the base word: *Kafka* + *-esque* → *Kafkaesque (= in the style or manner of Franz Kafka); Lincoln* + *-esque* → *Lincolnesque (= in the style of Abraham Lincoln); picture* + *-esque* → *picturesque (= resembling or suggesting a picture).*

-ess, *suffix.* from French, used to form a feminine noun: *count* + *-ess* → *countess; god* + *-ess* → *goddess; lion* + *-ess* → *lioness.* —**Usage.** *The use of words ending in* -ESS *has declined sharply in the latter half of the 20th century, but some are still current: actress (but some women prefer actor); adventuress; enchantress; governess (only in its child-care sense); heiress (largely in journalistic writing); hostess (but women who conduct radio and television programs are hosts); seamstress; seductress; temptress; and waitress.*

-est, *suffix.* from Old English, regularly used to form the superlative form of short adjectives and adverbs: *fast* + *-est* → *fastest; soon* + *-est* → *soonest; warm* + *-est* → *warmest.*

-ette, *suffix.* from French, used **1.** after nouns to form nouns that refer to a smaller version of the original noun or root: *kitchen* + *-ette* → *kitchenette (= small kitchen); novel* + *-ette* → *novelette (= smaller novel).* **2.** after nouns to form nouns that refer specifically to a female: *major* + *-ette* → *majorette (= female leader of a band, or baton twirler); usher* + *-ette* → *usherette (= female usher in a movie theater).* **3.** *after nouns to form nouns that refer to a name that is an imitation product of the root: leather* + *-ette* → *leatherette (= imitation leather product).* —**Usage.** *English nouns in which* -ETTE *signifies a feminine role or identity have been thought of as implying inferiority or unimportance and are now generally avoided. Only (drum) majorette is still widely used, usually indicating a young woman who twirls a baton with a marching band.*

-ferous, *suffix.* from the root *-fer-* + the suffix *-ous.* This suffix is found in such words as: *coniferous, pestiferous.*

-fest, *suffix.* from German, added to nouns to form nouns meaning "an assembly of people engaged in a common activity" named by the first element of the compound: *gab* + *-fest* → *gabfest (= group of people gabbing or talking a lot); song* + *-fest* → *songfest (= assembly of people singing together).*

-fold, *suffix.* from Old English, used after words that refer to a number or quantity to form adjectives meaning "having the number of kinds or parts" or "multiplied the number of times": *four* + *-fold* → *fourfold (= multiplied four times); many* + *-fold* → *manyfold (= having many parts or kinds).*

-footed, *suffix.* from the word *foot,* added to nouns to form adjectives meaning "having (the kind of, number of, etc.) a foot or feet indicated": *a four-footed animal (= an animal having four feet)*.

-free, *suffix.* from Old English, used after nouns to form adjectives meaning "not containing (the noun mentioned); without": *sugar* + *-free → sugar-free (= not containing the sugar); trouble* + *-free → trouble-free (= without trouble)*.

-ful, *suffix.* from Old English, used **1.** after nouns to form adjectives meaning "full of; characterized by": *beauty* + *-ful → beautiful (= full of beauty); care* + *-ful → careful (= characterized by care)*. **2.** after verbs to form adjectives meaning "tending to; able to": *harm* + *-ful → harmful (= tending to harm); wake* + *-ful → wakeful (= tending to stay awake)*. **3.** after nouns to form nouns meaning "as much as will fill": *spoon* + *-ful → spoonful (= as much as will fill a spoon); cup* + *-ful → cupful (= as much as will fill a cup)*.

-fy, *suffix.* ultimately from Latin, used **1.** after roots to form verbs meaning "to make; cause to be; render": *pure* + *-fy → purify (= to make pure); simple* + *-fy → simplify (= make simple); liquid* + *-fy → liquefy (= to make into a liquid)*. **2.** to mean "cause to conform to": *citify (= cause to conform to city ways)*. Compare -IFY.

-gate, *suffix.* derived from *Watergate,* originally the name of a hotel complex where officials of the Republican party were caught trying to burglarize Democratic party headquarters. *Watergate* then came to be associated with "a political cover-up and scandal." The suffix is used after some nouns to form nouns that refer to scandals resulting from concealed crime in government or business: *Iran* + *-gate → Irangate (= a scandal involving arms sales to Iran)*.

-gon, *suffix.* from Greek, meaning "side; angle." This suffix is used after roots to form nouns that refer to plane figures having the number of sides mentioned: *poly-* (= *many*) + *-gon → polygon (= a many-sided figure)*.

-gram, *suffix.* from Greek, meaning "what is written." It is used after roots to form nouns that refer to something written or drawn, either by hand or machine: *cardio-* (= *of or relating to the heart*) + *-gram → cardiogram (= a recording and diagram of a heartbeat, drawn by a machine)*. Compare -GRAPH-.

-hearted, *suffix.* from Middle English, used after adjectives to form adjectives meaning "having the character or personality of (the adjective mentioned)": *cold* + *-hearted → coldhearted (= having a cold heart; unkind or mean); light* + *-hearted → lighthearted (= feeling light and happy)*.

-holic, *suffix.* another form of -AHOLIC: *choco(late)* + *-holic → chocoholic (= person addicted to chocolate)*.

-hood, *suffix.* from Old English, used to form nouns meaning **1.** "the state or condition of": *likely* + *-hood → likelihood (= the state or condition of being likely); child* + *-hood → childhood (= the state or period of time of being a child)*. **2.** "a body or group of persons of a particular character or class": *priest* + *-hood → priesthood (= a body of priests)*.

-ian, *suffix.* from Latin, used to form nouns and adjectives with the meanings of -AN: *Orwell* + *-ian → Orwellian (= interested in, or relating to, the writing* *of George Orwell); Washington + -ian → Washingtonian (= a person who lives in Washington).*

-iatrics, *suffix.* from Greek, used after some roots to form nouns meaning "healing; the medical practice of": *ger-* (= *old people*) + *-iatrics* → *geriatrics* (= *the healing of older people*); *ped-* (= *child*) + *-iatrics* → *pediatrics* (= *medical practice involving children*).

-iatry, *suffix.* from Greek, used after some roots to form nouns meaning "healing; the medical practice of": *pod-* (= *foot*) + *-iatry* → *podiatry* (= *the healing of the foot*); *psych-* (= *the mind*) + *-iatry* → *psychiatry* (= *the medical practice dealing with the mind*).

-ibility, *suffix.* from Latin, used to form nouns from adjectives that end in *-ible*: *reducible (adjective)* → *reducibility* (= *the state or condition of being reducible, of being able to be reduced*); *flexible (adjective)* → *flexibility* (= *the state or condition of being able to move smoothly*) See -ABILITY, -ABLE, -IBLE.

-ible, *suffix.* a variant form of -ABLE, used after roots, mostly of verbs, to form adjectives meaning "capable of, fit for, tending to": *cred-* (= *believe*) + *-ible* → *credible* (= *that can be believed*); *vis-* (= *see*) + *-ible* → *visible* (= *that can be seen*); *reduce* + *-ible* → *reducible* (= *that can be reduced*). See -ABILITY, -ABLE, -IBILITY.

-ic, *suffix.* from Middle English, used after nouns to form adjectives meaning "of or relating to": *metal* + *-ic* → *metallic*; *poet* + *-ic* → *poetic*. This suffix is also used after nouns to form adjectives meaning "having some characteristics of; in the style of": *ballet* + *-ic* → *balletic*; *sophomore* + *-ic* → *sophomoric*; *Byron* + *-ic* → *Byronic* (= *in the style of the writer Byron*).

-ical, *suffix.* a combination of -IC and -AL[1], used after roots to form adjectives meaning "of or relating to": *rhetor-* + *-ical* → *rhetorical*. This suffix originally provided synonyms to adjectives that ended in -IC: *poet* + *-ic* → *poetic*; *poet* + *-ical* → *poetical*. But some of these pairs of words or formations are now different in meaning: *econom-* + *-ic* → *economic* (= *of or relating to economics*); *econom-* + *-ical* → *economical* (= *being careful in spending money*); *histor-* + *-ic* → *historic* (= *having a long history; important*); *histor-* + *-ical* → *historical* (= *happening in the past*).

-ician, *suffix.* extracted from physician, musician, etc., used after nouns or roots to form nouns meaning "the person having the occupation or work of": *beauty* + *-ician* → *beautician* (= *person who works in a beauty shop*); *mort-* (= *death*) + *-ician* → *mortician* (= *person working to prepare dead people for burial*).

-ics, *suffix.* from Latin, used after roots to form nouns meaning "a body of facts, knowledge, or principles." Such nouns usually correspond to adjectives ending in -IC or -ICAL: *eth-* (= *custom; character*) + *-ics* → *ethics* (= *the principles of good character*); *phys-* (= *body*) + *-ics* → *physics* (= *the principles of bodies in motion and at rest*).

-ier, *suffix.* from French, used after nouns or roots to form nouns meaning "person or thing that does (the action of the word mentioned); person or thing in charge of (the word mentioned)": *finance* + *-ier* → *financier* (=

person doing finance); cour- (= run) + *-ier → courier* (= *messenger*); *hotel* + *-ier → hotelier* (= *person in charge of hotels*). Compare -ER[1].

-ify, *suffix.* from French, used to form verbs meaning "cause to be in (a stated condition); to make or cause to become (a certain condition)": *intense* + *-ify → intensify* (= *cause to be intense*); *speechify* (= *make speeches*). See -FY.

-in, *suffix.* extracted from *sit-in,* used after some verbs to form nouns that refer to organized protests through, using, or in support of the named activity: *pray* + *-in → pray-in* (= *a protest in which participants engage in passive resistance and prayer*).

-ine[1], *suffix.* from Latin, used after some roots or nouns to form adjectives meaning "of, relating to, or characteristic of; of the nature of; made of": *crystal* + *-ine → crystalline* (= *of, like, or made of crystal*); *equ-* (= *horse*) + *-ine → equine* (= *of or relating to horses*).

-ine[2], *suffix.* from French, used after some roots to form nouns that name chemical substances and elements: *caffe-* (= *coffee*) + *-ine → caffeine* (= *a chemical substance found in coffee*); *chlor-* + *-ine → chlorine*.

-ing[1], *suffix.* **1.** from Old English, used after verbs to form nouns that express the action of the verb or its result, product, material, etc.: *build* + *-ing → building: the art of building; a new building.* **2.** after roots (other than verb roots) to form nouns: *off* + *-ing → offing.*

-ing[2], *suffix.* from Middle English, used after verbs to form the present participle of verbs: *walk* + *-ing → walking: Is the baby walking yet?* These participles are often used as adjectives: *war* + *-ing → warring: warring factions.* Some adjectives ending in *-ing* are formed by combining a prefix with a verb. Thus *outgoing* is formed from *out-* + the present participle form of the verb *go* (=*going*). Other examples: *uplifting, outstanding, incoming.*

-ion, *suffix.* ultimately from Latin, used after some roots to form nouns that refer to action or condition: *uni-* (= *one*) + *-ion → union* (= *condition of being one*). Compare -TION.

-ious, *suffix.* from Latin, a variant form of -OUS, used after roots to form adjectives: *hilar-* (= *cheerful*) + *-ious → hilarious* (= *very funny*).

-ise, *suffix. Chiefly British.* See -IZE.

-ish, *suffix.* from Old English, used **1.** after nouns or roots to form adjectives meaning **a.** relating to; in the same manner of; having the characteristics of: *brute* + *-ish → brutish.* **b.** of or relating to the people or language of: *Brit-* + *-ish → British; Swede* + *-ish → Swedish.* **c.** like; similar to: *baby* + *-ish → babyish; mule* + *-ish → mulish; girl* + *-ish → girlish.* **d.** addicted to; inclined or tending to: *book* + *-ish → bookish* (= *tending to read books a great deal*). **e.** near or about: *fifty* + *-ish → fiftyish* (*nearly fifty years old*). **2.** after adjectives to form adjectives meaning "somewhat, rather": *old* + *-ish → oldish* (= *somewhat old*); *red* + *-ish → reddish* (= *somewhat red*); *sweet* + *-ish → sweetish.*

-ism, *suffix.* from Greek, used **1.** after verb roots to form action nouns: *baptize* + *-ism → baptism.* **2.** to form nouns showing action or practice: *adventure* + *-ism → adventurism* (= *the action or practice of taking risks in intervening in international affairs*). **3.** used to form nouns showing state or condition: *alcoholism (= disease or condition in which alcohol is involved)*. **4.** after roots to form nouns showing the names of principles or doctrines: *Darwinism (= principles of Darwin's theory of evolution); despotism*. **5.** to form nouns showing an example of a use: *witticism (= example of something witty); Africanism (= word from Africa or from an African language)*. Compare -IST, -IZE.

-ist, *suffix.* from French and Latin, forms nouns usually corresponding to verbs ending in *-ize* and nouns ending in *-ism,* and referring to a person who practices or is concerned with something: *novel + -ist → novelist (= someone writing a novel); terrorist (= one who practices terrorism, one who terrorizes)*.

-ite, *suffix.* from Latin, used after nouns and roots to form nouns meaning: **1.** a person associated with or living in a place; a person connected with a tribe, leader, set of beliefs, system, etc.: *Manhattan + -ite → Manhattanite; Israel + -ite → Israelite; Labor + -ite → Laborite (= someone following the Labor Party)*. **2.** mineral or fossil; explosive; chemical compound or drug product: *anthracite; cordite; dynamite; sulfite*.

-itis, *suffix.* ultimately from Greek, used **1.** after roots that refer to an inflammation or disease affecting a certain part of the body: *appendix + -itis → appendicitis; bronchi (= part of the lungs) + -itis → bronchitis*. **2.** to form nouns made up for a particular occasion to refer to something comparable in a funny way to a disease: *The teenagers seem to be suffering from telephonitis (= excessive use of the telephone, as if using it were a disease)*.

-ive, *suffix.* from French and Latin, used after roots or nouns to form adjectives meaning "having a tendency or connection with; like": *act(ion) + -ive → active (= tending to be full of action or activity); sport + -ive → sportive (= like sports)*.

-ize, *suffix.* ultimately from Greek, used to form verbs meaning **1.** "to make; cause to become": *fossil + -ize → fossilize (= to make something into a fossil); sterile + -ize → sterilize (= to make something sterile)*. **2.** "to convert into, give a specified character or form to; change to a state of": *computer + -ize → computerize (= make an office use computers); dramat- + -ize → dramatize (= give the form of a drama to some other piece of work); American + -ize → Americanize (= convert to an American character)*. **3.** "to subject to; cause to undergo or suffer from (an emotion or a process, sometimes named after its originator)": *hospital + -ize → hospitalize (= cause to undergo treatment in a hospital); terror + -ize → terrorize (= cause to suffer terror); galvan- + -ize → galvanize (= to coat metal or stimulate electrically, as by the experiments of L. Galvani, Italian physicist)*. Also, *chiefly British.* **-ise.**

-less, *suffix.* from Old English, used **1.** after nouns to form adjectives meaning "without, not having (the thing or quality named by the noun)": *care + -less → careless; shame + -less → shameless* **2.** after verbs to form adjectives meaning "that cannot be" plus the *-edlen* form of the verb; or "that never" plus the *-s* form of the verb: *tire + -less → tireless (= that never tires); count + -less → countless (= that cannot be counted)*.

-let, *suffix.* from Middle English, used **1.** after a noun to form a noun that is a smaller version of the original noun or root: *book + -let → booklet (= a smaller book); pig + -let → piglet (= a smaller pig).* **2.** after a noun to form a noun that is a band, ornament, or article of clothing worn on the part of the body mentioned: *ankle + -let → anklet (= piece of clothing like a sock worn on the ankle); wrist + -let → wristlet (= ornament like a bracelet worn on the wrist).*

-like, *suffix.* from Middle English, used after nouns to form adjectives meaning "of or resembling (the noun base)": *child + -like → childlike; life + -like → lifelike.*

-ling, *suffix.* from Old English, used **1.** to form a noun that indicates a feeling of distaste or disgust for the person or thing named: *hire + -ling → hireling (= someone hired to do menial or distasteful tasks); under + -ling → underling.* **2.** to form a noun that is a smaller version or example of the base word: *prince + -ling; duck + -ling → duckling.*

-logy, *suffix.* from Greek, meaning "word." It is used after roots to form nouns meaning "field of study, discipline; list of": *astro- (= star) + -logy → astrology (= study of the influence of stars or events); bio- (= life) + -logy → biology (= study of living things).* See -LOG-.

-ly, *suffix.* from Middle English, used **1.** after adjectives to form adverbs: *glad + -ly → gladly; gradual + -ly → gradually.* **2.** after nouns that refer to units of time, to form adjectives and adverbs meaning "at or for every (such unit of time)": *hour + -ly → hourly (= at every hour); day + -ly → daily (= on or for every day).* **3.** after nouns to form adjectives meaning "like (the noun mentioned):" *saint + -ly → saintly; coward + -ly → cowardly.*

-man, *suffix.* from Old English, used to form nouns meaning "person, or man, who is or does (something connected with the noun base)": *mail + -man → mailman (= person who delivers mail).*

-mania, *suffix.* from Greek, used after roots to form nouns meaning "great or strong enthusiasm for (the element of the root)": *biblio- (= book) + -mania → bibliomania (= excessive or strong interest or enthusiasm for books).*

-ment, *suffix.* from French and Latin, used **1.** after verbs to form nouns that refer to the action of the verb: *govern + -ment → government.* **2.** after verbs to form nouns that refer to a state or condition resulting from the action of a verb: *refresh + -ment → refreshment.* **3.** after verbs to form nouns that refer to a product resulting from the action of a verb: *frag- + -ment → fragment (= a piece resulting from the breaking off of something).*

-ness, *suffix.* from Old English, used after adjectives and verbs ending in *-ing* or *-edl-en* to form nouns that refer to the quality or state of the adjective or verb: *dark + -ness → darkness; prepared + -ness → preparedness (= a state of being prepared).*

-o, *suffix.* derived from Romance nouns ending in -o, used **1.** as the final element in certain nouns that are shortened from longer nouns: *ammo* (from "ammunition"); *combo* (from "combination"); *promo* (from "promotion"). **2.** after certain adjectives and nouns to form nouns that have an unfavorable or insulting meaning: *weird + -o → weirdo (= a very weird person); wine + -o → wino (= someone who drinks too much wine).* **3.** after certain nouns and adjectives to form informal nouns or adjectives; these are often used when speaking directly to another: *kid + -o → kiddo (= a kid or person); neat + -o → neato (= an informal use of "neat"); right + -o → righto (= an informal use of "right")*.

-off, *suffix.* from Old English, used to form nouns that name or refer to a competition or contest, esp. between finalists or to break a tie: *cook + -off → cookoff (= a cooking contest); runoff (= a deciding final contest)*.

-oid, *suffix.* from Greek, used to form adjectives and nouns meaning "resembling, like," with the suggestion of an incomplete or imperfect similarity to the root element: *human + -oid → humanoid (= resembling a human, but not quite the same)*.

-onym, *suffix.* from Greek, meaning "word, name." This meaning is found in such words as: *pseudonym, homonym*.

-or, *suffix.* from French, used to form nouns that are agents, or that do or perform a function: *debtor; tailor; traitor; projector; repressor; sensor; tractor*.

-ory¹, *suffix.* **1.** from Middle English, used after nouns and verbs that end in *-e* to form adjectives meaning "of or relating to (the noun or verb mentioned)": *excrete + -ory → excretory (= of or relating to excreting); sense + -ory → sensory (= of or relating to the senses)*. **2.** after certain roots to form adjectives meaning "providing or giving": *satisfact- + -ory → satisfactory (= giving satisfaction)*.

-ory², *suffix.* from Latin, used after roots to form nouns that refer to places or things that hold (the root), or places that are used for (the root): *cremat- + -ory → crematory (= a place where bodies are cremated); observat(ion) + -ory → observatory (= place where observations of the heavens are made)*.

-ose¹, *suffix.* from Latin, used after roots to form adjectives meaning "full of, abounding in, given to, or like (the root)": *verb- (= word) + -ose → verbose (= full of words); bellic- (= war) + -ose → bellicose (= eager for fighting or war)*.

-ose², *suffix.* extracted from *glucose,* used after roots to form nouns that name sugars, carbohydrates, and substances that are formed from proteins: *fruct- + -ose → fructose (= a fruit sugar); lact- + -ose → lactose (= a milk sugar); prote- + ose → proteose (= a compound made from protein)*.

-ous, *suffix.* from French, used **1.** after roots to form adjectives meaning "possessing, full of (a given quality)": *glory + -ous → glorious; wonder + ous → wondrous; covet + -ous → covetous; nerve + -ous → nervous*. **2.** after roots to form adjectives referring to the names of chemical elements: *stannous chloride,* $SnCl^2$.

-person, *suffix.* from Latin, used to replace some paired, sex-specific suffixes such as -MAN and -WOMAN or -ER¹ and -ESS: *salesman/saleswoman* are replaced by *sales + -person → salesperson; waiter/waitress* are replaced by *wait + -person → waitperson*.

-phile, *suffix.* from Greek, used **1.** after roots and sometimes words to form nouns meaning "lover of, enthusiast for (a given object)": *biblio- + -phile → bibliophile (= lover of books); Franco- + -phile → Francophile (= lover of France or French things)*. **2.** after roots to form nouns meaning "a person sexually attracted to or overly interested in (a given object)": *pedo- +*

-phile → *pedophile (= someone with a sexual attraction for children)*. See -PHIL-.

-phobe, *suffix.* from Greek, used after roots and sometimes words to form nouns that refer to persons who have a fear of something named by the root or preceding word: *Anglo- + phobe → Anglophobe (= fear of English-speakers or of England).*

-phobia, *suffix.* from Greek, used after roots and sometimes words to form nouns with the meaning "dread of, unreasonable hatred toward (a given object)": *agora- (= open space) + phobia → agoraphobia (= fear of open spaces); xeno- (= foreign) + -phobia → xenophobia (= hatred toward foreigners).*

-phobic, *suffix.* from Greek, used after roots and words to form adjectives or nouns meaning "(a person) having a continuous, irrational fear or hatred toward" the object named in the root or preceding word: *xeno- (= foreign) + -phobic → xenophobic (= (a person) having a fear or hatred of foreigners).*

-proof, *suffix.* ultimately from Latin, used to form adjectives meaning "resistant; not allowing through" the word mentioned: *child + -proof → childproof (= resistant to a child opening it); water + proof → waterproof (= not allowing water through).*

-ry, *suffix.* See -ERY.

-s¹ (or **-es**), (s, z, iz), *suffix.* from Old English, used after the root form of verbs and marks the third person singular present indicative form, agreeing with a subject that is singular: *He walks. She runs. The wind rushes through the trees.*

-s² (or **-es**), *suffix.* from Old English, used after count nouns and marks the plural form: *weeks; days; bushes; taxes; ladies; pianos; potatoes.*

-ship, *suffix.* from Old English, used to form nouns meaning **1.** "state or condition of": *friend + - ship → friendship; kin + -ship → kinship.* **2.** "the skill or ability of": *statesman + -ship → statesmanship; apprentice + -ship → apprenticeship.* **3.** "the relation of": *fellow + -ship → fellowship.*

-sick, *suffix.* from Old English, used to form adjectives meaning "sick or ill of or from (the noun of the root)": *car + -sick → carsick (= sick from traveling in a car); air + -sick → airsick (= sick from flying in a plane).*

-some¹, *suffix.* from Old English, used to form adjectives meaning "like; tending to": *burden + -some → burdensome (= like a burden); quarrel + -some → quarrelsome (= tending to quarrel).*

-some², *suffix.* from Old English, used to form nouns meaning "a collection (of the number mentioned) of objects": *threesome (= a group of three).*

-speak, *suffix.* from Old English, used after the ends of words and sometimes roots to form compound nouns that name the style or vocabulary of a certain field of work, interest, time period, etc. that is mentioned in the first word or root: *ad(vertising) + -speak → adspeak (= the jargon of advertising); art + -speak → artspeak (= the language used in discussing art); future + -speak → futurespeak.*

-ster, *suffix.* from Old English, used at the ends of words to form nouns, often implying a bad or negative sense, and referring esp. to one's occupation, habit, or association: *game* + *-ster* → *gamester* (= *one greatly interested in games*); *trick* + *-ster* → *trickster* (= *one who uses or enjoys dishonest tricks*).

-th, *suffix.* ultimately from Greek, used after words that refer to numbers to form adjectives referring to the number mentioned: *(four* + *-th* →) *fourth; tenth.*

-tion, *suffix.* from Latin, used after verbs to form nouns that refer to actions or states of the verb: *relate* + *-tion* → *relation; sect-* + *-tion* → *section; ab-breviate* + *-tion* → *abbreviation.* Compare -ION.

-tious, *suffix.* from Latin, used after roots to form adjectives, some of which are related to nouns: *fiction: fictitious; ambition: ambitious; caution: cautious; rambunctious, propitious.*

-tude, *suffix.* from Latin, used after roots, especially adjectives, to form nouns that refer to abstract ideas: *exact* + *-tude* → *exactitude; apt* + *-tude* → *aptitude; gratitude; altitude.*

-ty, *suffix.* from French, used after adjectives to form nouns that name or refer to a state or condition: *able* + *-ty* → *ability; certain* + *-ty* → *certainty; chaste* + *-ty* → *chastity.*

-ure, *suffix.* from French, used after roots and verbs to form abstract nouns that refer to action, result, and instrument or use: *press-* + *-ure* → *pressure; legislate* + *-ure* → *legislature; fract-* + *ure* → *fracture.*

-ville, *suffix.* from French, used **1.** in place names, where it meant "city, town": *Charlottesville.* **2.** after roots or words to form informal words, not all of them long-lasting, that characterize a condition, place, person, group, or situation: *dulls* + *-ville* (= *a dull, boring situation*); *gloomsville.*

-ward, *suffix.* from Old English, used to form adjectives or adverbs meaning "in or toward a certain direction in space or time": *backward.* Also, **-wards.**

-ways, *suffix.* from Middle English, used to form adjectives or adverbs meaning "in a certain direction, manner, or position": *sideways.*

-wide, *suffix.* from Old English, used to form adjectives meaning "extending or applying throughout a certain, given space," as mentioned by the noun: *community* + *-wide* → *communitywide* (= *applying to or throughout the community*); *countrywide; worldwide.*

-wise, *suffix.* from Old English, used **1.** to form adjectives and adverbs meaning "in a particular manner, position, or direction": *clockwise* (= *moving in a direction like the hands of a clock*). **2.** to form adverbs meaning "with reference to": *Timewise we can finish the work, but qualitywise, I'm not so sure.*

-woman, *suffix.* from Middle English, used to form nouns meaning "involving a woman; a woman in the role of": *chairwoman; spokeswoman.*

-worthy, *suffix.* from Old English, used to form adjectives meaning **1.** "deserving of, fit for": *news* + *-worthy* → *newsworthy* (= *fit for the news*); *trust* + *-worthy* → *trustworthy.* **2.** "capable of travel in or on": *road* + *-worthy* → *roadworthy* (= *capable of traveling on the road*); *seaworthy.*

-y¹, *suffix.* from Old English, used to form adjectives meaning "having, showing, or similar to (the substance or action of the word or stem)": *blood* + *-y* → *bloody; cloud* + *-y* → *cloudy; sexy; squeaky.*

-y[2] (or **-ie**), *suffix.* from Middle English, used **1.a.** to form nouns that bring or add a meaning of dearness or familiarity to the noun or adjective root, such as proper names, names of pets, or in baby talk: *Bill* + *-y* → *Billy; Susan* + *-ie* → *Susie; bird* + *-ie* → *birdie; sweetie.* **b.** to form nouns that are informal, new, or intended to be new; sometimes these have slightly unpleasant meanings or associations: *boondocks* → *boon-* + *-ies* → *boonies; group* + *-ie* → *groupie; Okie (a person from Oklahoma); preemie (= a premature baby); rookie.* **2.** after adjectives to form nouns, often with the meaning that the noun is an extreme (good or bad) example of the adjective or quality: *bad* + *-ie* → *baddie; big* + *-ie* → *biggie; toughie; sharpie; sickie; whitey.* Compare -o.

-y,[3] *suffix.* from Latin, used after verbs to form nouns of action, and certain other abstract nouns: *inquire* + *-y* → *inquiry; in* + *fame* + *-y* → *infamy.*

8. ROOTS OF A MORE POWERFUL VOCABULARY

Latin and Greek Roots

One of the quickest and most effective ways to improve your vocabulary is by learning to recognize the most common Latin and Greek roots, since any one of them can help you define a number of English words. Whenever you come upon an unfamiliar word, first check to see if it has a recognizable root. If you know that the Latin root "ami," for example, means *like* or *love,* you can easily figure out that "amiable" means *pleasant or friendly* and "amorous" means *loving.* Even if you cannot define a word exactly, recognizing the root will still give you a general idea of the word's meaning. Remembering that the Greek root "geo" means *earth* would certainly help you define "geophysics" as *the physics of the earth,* but it also might help you figure out that "geocentric" has to do with the center of the earth or with the earth as a center. Begin by studying the following lists of common Latin and Greek roots and representative words. Then tackle the quizzes.

LESSON 1. COMMON LATIN ROOTS

Root	Meaning	Example	Definition
ag	act	agent	representative
cad, cas	fall	cadence	rhythmic flow
cap, cept	take, hold	receptacle	container
ced, cess	go	recessive	tending to go back
cid, cis	kill, cut	incision	cut, gash
clud, clus	shut	seclusion	separation from others

cred	believe	credible	believable
cur(r), curs	run	concur	agree (i.e., run together)
fer	bear	odoriferous	yielding an odor
her, hes	cling	adhere	cling, stick
ject	throw	projection	jutting out, protrusion
leg, lect	read	legible	easily readable
pel(l), puls	drive	repulse	repel (i.e., drive back)
pon, posit	put	postpone	defer
port	carry	portable	movable
rupt	break	abrupt	sudden, quick
scrib, script	write	inscription	engraving, writing
sect	cut	dissect	cut apart
sent, sens	feel	sensitive	tender
sequ, secut	follow	sequel	result
spect	look	prospect	outlook, expectation
sta, stat	stand	stable	fixed, firm
tang, tact	touch	tactile	tangible
termin	end	terminate	abolish, end
tract	pull, draw	tractor	vehicle that pulls
ven, vent	come	convene	assemble (i.e., come together)
vert, vers	turn	invert	overturn
vid, vis	see	provident	having foresight
vinc, vict	conquer	invincible	unconquerable
volv, volut	roll, turn	evolve	develop

Quiz 1: Applying Roots

Each of the following phrases contains an italicized word. Based on the meaning of the root, select the closest synonym. Circle your response.

1. a *captive* animal
   a. confined   b. wild   c. charming   d. domestic
2. an *inverted* glass
   a. broken   b. upside-down   c. returned   d. drunk from
3. an *abrupt* stop
   a. slow   b. bad   c. sudden   d. harmful
4. a disappointing *sequel*
   a. television show   b. beginning   c. movie   d. follow-up
5. *terminate* the relationship
   a. doubt   b. intensify   c. begin   d. finish
6. an *incredible* story
   a. outlandish   b. unbelievable   c. foolish   d. upsetting
7. a *recessive* trait
   a. dominant   b. receding   c. hurtful   d. missing
8. *illegible* writing
   a. unreadable   b. graceful   c. distinct   d. large
9. a thorough *dissection*
   a. cutting apart   b. conference   c. discussion   d. putting together
10. an *unstable* relationship
    a. new   b. unsteady   c. one-sided   d. unreliable
11. an *odoriferous* cheese
    a. commonplace   b. brightly colored   c. malodorous   d. faded
12. an *invincible* warrior
    a. huge   b. foreign   c. defeated   d. unbeatable
13. the *advent* of summer
    a. departure   b. middle   c. arrival   d. complaint
14. a *provident* move
    a. prosperous   b. injudicious   c. prudent   d. hurtful
15. the top-secret *projectile*
    a. missile   b. project   c. plan   d. meeting

Quiz 2: True/False

In the space provided, write T if the definition of the numbered word is true or F if it is false.

		T or F
1. ADHERE	cling	_____
2. CADAVER	cavort	_____
3. EVOLVE	develop	_____
4. INCISION	cut	_____
5. CONCURRENT	disjointed	_____

6. RECLUSE	vivacious person	_____
7. INSCRIPTION	story	_____
8. AGENT	deputy	_____
9. TACTILE	tangible	_____
10. REPULSE	repel	_____

LESSON 2. COMMON GREEK ROOTS

Root	Meaning	Example	Definition
aster, astro	star	asterisk	star-shaped mark
chrom	color	chromatic	pertaining to color
chron, chrono	time	synchronize	occur simultaneously
cosmo	world	cosmopolitan	citizen of the world
dem	people	democracy	government by the people
meter	measure	thermometer	instrument that measures temperature
onym	name, word	pseudonym	a fictitious name
path	feeling	apathy	absence of feeling
phob	fear	claustrophobia	fear of enclosed places
phon	sound	cacophony	harsh, discordant sound
psycho	mind	psychology	science of the mind
soph	wisdom	sophistry	subtle, tricky reasoning

Quiz 3: True/False

In the space provided, write T if the definition of the numbered word is true or F if it is false.

			T or F
1.	EPIDEMIC	plague	_____
2.	HOMONYM	same-sounding name	_____
3.	CLAUSTROPHOBIA	fear of dogs	_____
4.	CACOPHONY	dissonance	_____
5.	APATHY	enthusiasm	_____
6.	ACCELEROMETER	instrument for measuring acceleration	_____
7.	SYNCHRONIZE	squabble	_____
8.	COSMOPOLITAN	international	_____
9.	SOPHISM	specious argument	_____
10.	CHROMATIC	crisp	_____

Quiz 4: Applying Greek Roots

Based on the meaning of its root, define each of the following words. If in doubt, check the suggested answers.

1. asteroid _____
2. chromatics _____
3. cosmos _____
4. anonymous _____
5. Anglophobia _____
6. cosmography _____
7. synchronous _____
8. pathetic _____
9. pedometer _____
10. democracy _____
11. phonograph _____
12. demographics _____
13. psychotic _____
14. sophisticated _____
15. cognition _____

Suggested Answers: 1. a small mass that orbits the sun 2. the science of colors 3. universe 4. without any name acknowledged 5. fear of things English 6. the study of the structure of the universe 7. coinciding in time 8. evoking feelings of pity 9. an instrument that measures distance covered in walking 10. government by the people 11. a sound-reproducing machine 12. the statistical data of a population 13. a person who is mentally ill 14. worldly-wise 15. act or fact of knowing

LESSON 3. "OTHER PLACES, OTHER FACES": *AL, ALL, ALTER*

An "alibi" is a defense by an accused person who claims to have been elsewhere at the time the offense was committed. The word comes from the Latin root "al," meaning *other*. Outside of law, an alibi often means an excuse, especially to avoid blame.

The Latin roots "al" and "alter," as well as the related Greek root "all" or "allo," all mean *other* or *another,* and form the basis of a number of English words. Below are ten such words. After you study the definitions and practice the pronunciations, complete the quizzes.

1. **alien** (āl′yən, ā′lē ən) a person born in and owing allegiance to a country other than the one in which he or she lives; a nonterrestrial being; foreign or strange.

    Although my neighbor is not an American citizen, he has lived in this country so long he no longer thinks of himself as an alien.

2. **allegory** (al′ə gôr′ē) a representation of an abstract meaning through concrete or material forms; figurative treatment of one subject under the guise of another.

    Nathaniel Hawthorne's short story "Young Goodman Brown" can be read as an allegory of an average person's encounter with sin and temptation.

3. **alias** (ā′lē əs) a false or assumed name, especially as used by a criminal. From the Latin word meaning *otherwise.*

    Many criminals use an alias with the same initials as their real name; Clyde Griffith, for example, took as his alias "Chester Gillett."

4. **alienate** (āl′yə nāt′, ā′lē ə-) to make indifferent or hostile. From Latin "alienare," *to make another.*

    Unkempt yards alienate prospective home buyers.

5. **altruism** (al′trōō iz′əm) unselfish concern for the welfare of others.

    Devotion to the poor, sick, and unfortunate of the world shows a person's altruism.

6. **altercation** (ôl′tər kā′shən) a heated or angry dispute;

noisy argument or controversy. From Latin "altercari," *to quarrel with another.*

The collision resulted in an altercation between the two drivers.

7. **inalienable** (in āl′yə nə bəl, -ā′lē ə-) not transferable to another; incapable of being repudiated.

Freedom of speech is the inalienable right of every American citizen.

8. **allograft** (al′ə graft′) tissue grafted or transplanted to another member of the same species.

Allografts of vital organs have saved many lives.

9. **allogamy** (ə log′ə mē) cross-fertilization in plants. From "allo-," *other* + "-gamy," *pollination.*

To ensure allogamy, the farmer set out many different plants close together.

10. **alter ego** (ôl′tər ē′gō) another self; an inseparable friend.

Superman's alter ego, the mild-mannered Clark Kent, is a reporter for the *Daily Planet.*

Quiz 5: Matching Synonyms

Match each of the numbered words with its closest synonym. Write your answer in the space provided.

1. ALIEN	a. absolute	_____
2. ALIAS	b. cross-fertilization	_____
3. ALTER EGO	c. selflessness, kindness	_____
4. ALLOGAMY	d. best friend	_____
5. ALLEGORY	e. another name	_____
6. INALIENABLE	f. transplant	_____
7. ALTRUISM	g. contention, quarrel	_____
8. ALIENATE	h. symbolic narrative	_____
9. ALLOGRAFT	i. stranger, outcast	_____
10. ALTERCATION	j. turn away, estrange	_____

Quiz 6: True/False

In the space provided, write T if the definition of the numbered word is true or F if it is false.

		T or F
1. ALIEN	foreign	_____
2. ALIAS	excuse	_____
3. ALTER EGO	egotist	_____
4. ALLOGAMY	multiple marriage	_____

5. ALLEGORY	moral story	_____
6. INALIENABLE	without basis in fact	_____
7. ALTRUISM	unselfishness	_____
8. ALIENATE	estrange	_____
9. ALLOGRAFT	illegal money	_____
10. ALTERCATION	dispute	_____

LESSON 4. "THE BREATH OF LIFE": *ANIMA*

Ancient peoples connected the soul with the breath. They saw that when people died they stopped breathing, and they believed that the soul left the body at the same time. They also believed that when someone sneezed, the soul left the body for a moment, so they muttered a hasty blessing to ensure that the soul would return quickly to its rightful place. The Latin root for air or breath, "anima," also means *soul, spirit,* or *mind,* reflecting this belief in a connection between life and breathing. Many English words come from this root.

Below are ten words linked to "anima." After you study the definitions and practice the pronunciations, complete the quizzes.

1. **animation** (an′ə mā′shən) liveliness or vivacity; the act or an instance of animating or enlivening. From Latin "animare," *to give life to.*

   In speech class we learned how to talk with animation to make our presentations more interesting.

2. **animadversion** (an′ə mad vûr′zhən, -shən) criticism; censure. From Latin "animus," *mind, spirit* + "adversio," *attention, warning.*

   The critic's animadversion on the subject of TV shows revealed his bias against popular culture.

3. **animus** (an′ə məs) hostile feeling or attitude.

   The jury's animus toward the defendant was obvious from the jurors' stony faces and stiff posture.

4. **pusillanimous** (pyōō′sə lan′ə məs) lacking courage or resolution; cowardly. From Latin "pusillus," *very small* + "animus," *spirit.*

   He was so pusillanimous that he wouldn't even run away from a bully.

5. **unanimity** (yōō′nə nim′i tē) the state or quality of being in

complete agreement; undivided opinion or a consensus. From Latin "unus," *one* + "animus," *mind, spirit.*

The school board's unanimity on the controversial issue of sex education was all the more surprising in light of their well-known individual differences.

6. **animate** (an'ə māt') to give life or liveliness to; alive.
   Her presence animated the otherwise dull party.

7. **animalcule** (an'ə mal'kyōōl) a minute or microscopic organism. From Latin "animalis," *living, animal* + "-culum," *tiny thing.*
   The animalcule could not be seen with the naked eye.

8. **magnanimous** (mag nan'ə məs) generous in forgiving an insult or injury; free from petty resentfulness. From Latin "magnus," *large, great* + "animus," *soul.*
   The governor's magnanimous pardon of the offender showed his liberal nature.

9. **inanimate** (in an'ə mit) not alive or lively; lifeless.
   Pinocchio was inanimate, a puppet carved from a block of wood.

10. **animism** (an'ə miz'əm) the belief that natural objects, natural phenomena, and the universe itself possess souls or consciousness.
    Their belief in animism drew them to the woods, where they felt more in touch with nature's spirit.

Quiz 7: Matching Synonyms

Match each of the numbered words with the closest synonym. Write your answer in the space provided.

1. ANIMADVERSION	a. enliven	_____
2. ANIMUS	b. harmony	_____
3. PUSILLANIMOUS	c. generous	_____
4. UNANIMITY	d. cowardly	_____
5. ANIMATE	e. hostility	_____
6. ANIMALCULE	f. spirit, zest	_____
7. MAGNANIMOUS	g. a censorious remark	_____
8. INANIMATE	h. a belief in spirits	_____
9. ANIMATION	i. a minute organism	_____
10. ANIMISM	j. inert	_____

Quiz 8: True/False

In the space provided, write T if the definition of the numbered word is true or F if it is false.

T or F

1.	ANIMADVERSION	praise	____
2.	ANIMUS	hostility	____
3.	PUSILLANIMOUS	cowardly	____
4.	UNANIMITY	total agreement	____
5.	ANIMATE	deaden	____
6.	ANIMALCULE	small soul	____
7.	MAGNANIMOUS	generous	____
8.	INANIMATE	living	____
9.	ANIMATION	liveliness	____
10.	ANIMISM	love of animals	____

LESSON 5. "THE YEAR OF WONDERS": *ANN, ENN*

While certain years are celebrated for great wonders, the first year that was actually designated "The Year of Wonders," *Annus Mirabilis,* was 1666. The English poet, dramatist, and critic John Dryden (1631–1700) enshrined that year as "Annus Mirabilis" in his poem of the same name, which commemorated the English victory over the Dutch and the Great Fire of London. "Annus," meaning *year,* comes from the Latin root "ann," a source of many useful English words. The same root is also written "enn" in the middle of a word.

Below are ten words drawn from this root. After you look over the definitions and practice the pronunciations, complete the quizzes that follow.

1. **per annum** (pər an′əm) by the year; yearly.
   The firm promised to bill the additional interest charges per annum, the invoice to arrive every January.
2. **annual** (an′ yōō əl) of, for, or pertaining to a year; yearly.
   The annual enrollment in the high school has increased sharply since the new housing was built.
3. **anniversary** (an′ə vûr′sə rē) the yearly recurrence of the date of a past event, especially the date of a wedding. From Latin "ann(i)," *year* + "vers(us)," *turned* + adjectival suffix "-ary."
   For their twenty-fifth wedding anniversary, the happy couple decided to have dinner at the restaurant where they first met.
4. **biennial** (bī en′ē əl) happening every two years; lasting for

two years. From Latin "bi-," *two* + root "enn" + adjectival suffix "-ial."

My flowering fig tree has a biennial cycle; it blooms every two years.

5. **triennial** (trī en′ē əl) occurring every three years; lasting three years. From Latin "tri-," *three* + root "enn" + adjectival suffix "-ial."

The university has set up a triennial cycle of promotions to review candidates for advancement.

6. **decennial** (di sen′ē əl) of or for ten years; occurring every ten years. From Latin "dec(em)," *ten* + root "enn" + adjectival suffix "-ial."

Every ten years, the PTA holds its decennial meeting in the state capital.

7. **centennial** (sen ten′ē əl) of or pertaining to a period of one hundred years; recurring once every hundred years. From Latin "cent(um)," *hundred* + root "enn" + adjectival suffix "-ial."

To celebrate the railroad's centennial anniversary, the town's historical society restored the run-down station so it looked exactly as it did when it was built a hundred years ago.

8. **bicentennial** (bī′sen ten′ē əl) pertaining to or in honor of a two-hundredth anniversary; consisting of or lasting two hundred years.

To advertise its bicentennial festivities next year, the town has adopted the slogan "Celebrating Two Hundred Years of Progress."

9. **millennium** (mi len′ē əm) a period of one thousand years. From Latin "mille," *thousand* + root "enn" + noun suffix "-ium."

Technology advances so rapidly now that we can scarcely imagine what life will be like in the next millennium.

10. **annuity** (ə nōō′ i tē, ə nyōō′-) a specified income payable each year or at stated intervals in consideration of a premium paid. From Latin "ann(uus)," *yearly* + noun suffix "-ity."

The annuity from her late husband's life-insurance policy was barely adequate for the poor widow's needs.

Quiz 9: Matching Synonyms

Select the best definition for each numbered word. Write your answer in the space provided.

1. BICENTENNIAL	a. every ten years	_____
2. ANNIVERSARY	b. every two years	_____
3. DECENNIAL	c. every two hundred years	_____
4. MILLENNIUM	d. every three years	_____
5. PER ANNUM	e. one thousand years	_____
6. CENTENNIAL	f. fixed payment	_____
7. ANNUITY	g. yearly recurrence of a date	_____
8. TRIENNIAL	h. every hundred years	_____
9. BIENNIAL	i. by the year	_____
10. ANNUAL	j. yearly	_____

Quiz 10: True/False

In the space provided, write T if the definition of the numbered word is true or F if it is false.

		T or F
1. ANNUITY	every two hundred years	_____
2. BICENTENNIAL	every other year	_____
3. MILLENNIUM	one thousand years	_____
4. ANNUAL	fixed amount of money	_____
5. CENTENNIAL	every hundred years	_____
6. TRIENNIAL	every three years	_____
7. PER ANNUM	by order	_____
8. BIENNIAL	every third year	_____
9. DECENNIAL	every thousand years	_____
10. ANNIVERSARY	yearly event	_____

LESSON 6. "MAN OF THE WORLD": *ANTHROPO*

In the early twentieth century, Rudolph Steiner developed an esoteric system of knowledge he called "anthroposophy." Steiner developed the word from the Greek roots "anthropo," meaning *man* or *human,* and "soph," meaning *wisdom*. He defined his philosophy as "the knowledge of the spiritual human being . . . and of everything which the spirit man can perceive in the spiritual world."

We've taken several more words from "anthropo"; below are six of them. After you look over the definitions and practice the pronunciations, complete the quizzes that follow.

1. **anthropoid** (an'thrə poid') resembling humans.

   The child was fascinated by the anthropoid ape on display in the natural history museum.

2. **anthropomorphism** (an'thrə pə môr'fizəm) the ascription of human form or attributes to a being or thing not human, such as a deity.

   To speak of the "cruel, crawling foam" is an example of anthropomorphism, for the sea is not cruel.

3. **misanthrope** (mis'ən thrōp', miz'-) a hater of humankind. From Greek "mis(o)," *hate* + "anthropos," *man.*

   In *Gulliver's Travels,* the great misanthrope Jonathan Swift depicts human beings as monstrous savages.

4. **philanthropy** (fi lan'thrə pē) good works; affection for humankind, especially as manifested in donations, as of money, to needy persons or to socially useful purposes. From Greek "phil(o)," *loving* + "anthropos," *man.*

   Thanks to the philanthropy of a wealthy patron, the new hospital wing was fully stocked with the latest equipment.

5. **anthropology** (an'thrə pol'ə jē) the science that deals with the origins, physical and cultural development, racial characteristics, and social customs and beliefs of humankind.

   After the student completed the anthropology course, she visited some of the exotic cultures she had read about.

6. **anthropocentric** (an'thrə pō sen'trik) regarding humans as the central fact of the universe.

   Philosophy that views and interprets the universe in terms of human experience and values is anthropocentric.

Quiz 11: Matching Synonyms

Select the best definition for each numbered word. Write your answer in the space provided.

1. ANTHROPOLOGY   a. believing that humans are the center of the universe   _____

2. PHILANTHROPY   b. one who dislikes people   _____

3. ANTHROPOCENTRIC   c. science of
humankind's origins,
beliefs, and customs   _____

4. ANTHROPOID   d. personification of
inanimate things   _____

5. ANTHROPOMORPHISM   e. doing good for people   _____

6. MISANTHROPE   f. humanlike   _____

Quiz 12: True/False

In the space provided, write T if the definition of the numbered
word is true or F if it is false.

T or F

1. MISANTHROPE   cynic   _____
2. PHILANTHROPY   goodwill to
humankind   _____
3. ANTHROPOMORPHISM   insecurity   _____
4. ANTHROPOCENTRIC   unselfish   _____
5. ANTHROPOLOGY   science of flowers   _____
6. ANTHROPOID   resembling humans   _____

LESSON 7. "KNOW THYSELF": *GNO*

One of the fascinating things about the study of words is the dis-
covery of close relationships between seemingly unrelated
words. Because English draws its vocabulary from many
sources, it often appropriates foreign words that ultimately derive from the same source as a native English word. A good example is our word "know," which has its exact equivalent in the
Latin and Greek root "gno." Here are eight words from this
root. First read through the pronunciations, definitions, and examples. Then complete the quizzes that follow.

1. **cognizant** (kog′nə zənt, kon′ə-) aware. From Latin "cognoscere," *to come to know* ("co-," *together* + "gnoscere,"
to know).
   He was fully cognizant of the difficulty of the mission.
2. **incognito** (in′kog nē′tō, in kog′ni tō′) with one's identity
concealed, as under an assumed name. From Latin "incog-
nitus," *not known* ("in-," *not* + "cognitus," *known*).
   The officer from naval intelligence always traveled incognito to avoid any problems with security.
3. **prognosticate** (prog nos′ti kāt′) to forecast from present

indications. From Greek "prognostikos," *knowing before-hand* ("pro-," *before* + "(gi)gno(skein)," *to know*).

The fortuneteller was able to prognosticate with the help of her tea leaves, crystal ball, and a good deal of inside information about her client.

4. **diagnostician** (diˈəg no stishˈən) an expert in determining the nature of diseases. From Greek "diagnosis," *determination* (of a disease) ("dia-," *through* + "(gi)gno(skein)," *to know*).

The diagnostician was able to allay her patient's fears after the x-ray showed that he had suffered only a sprain, not a break.

5. **cognoscenti** (konˈyə shenˈtē, kogˈnə-) well-informed persons, especially in a particular field, as in the arts. From Italian, ultimately derived from Latin "co-," *together* + "gnoscere," *to know.*

Although the exhibit had only been open one week, the cognoscenti were already proclaiming it the show of the decade.

6. **gnostic** (nosˈtik) pertaining to knowledge, especially to the esoteric knowledge taught by an early Christian mystical sect. From Greek "gnostikos," *knowing,* from the root of "(gi)gno(skein)," *to know.*

The gnostic view that everything is knowable is opposed by the agnostic view.

7. **ignoramus** (igˈnə rāˈməs, -ramˈəs) an extremely uninformed person. From the Latin word meaning *we don't know,* derived from "ignorare," *to not know* ("i(-n-)," *not* + the root of "gno(scere)," *to come to know*).

Only an ignoramus would insist that the earth is flat.

8. **cognition** (kog nishˈən) the act or process of knowing; perception. From Latin "cognitio," derived from "cognoscere," *to come to know* ("co-," *together* + "gnoscere," *to know*).

Cognition is impaired by narcotic drugs.

Quiz 13: True/False

In the space provided, write T if the definition of the numbered word is true or F if it is false.

		T or F
1. GNOSTIC	knowing	___
2. INCOGNITO	disguised	___

3. PROGNOSTICATE	curse	_____
4. IGNORAMUS	ignorant person	_____
5. COGNOSCENTI	aromatic herb	_____
6. COGNITION	perception	_____
7. DIAGNOSTICIAN	expert mechanic	_____
8. COGNIZANT	conscious	_____

Quiz 14: Defining Words

Define each of the following words.

1. ignoramus _____
2. cognoscenti _____
3. cognition _____
4. incognito _____
5. gnostic _____
6. prognosticate _____
7. diagnostician _____
8. cognizant _____

Suggested Answers: 1. unschooled person 2. those who have a superior knowledge 3. the act or process of knowing; perception 4. with one's identity concealed 5. pertaining to knowledge 6. to forecast 7. an expert in making diagnoses 8. aware

LESSON 8. "RULERS AND LEADERS": *ARCH*

In Christian theology, Michael is given the title of "archangel," principal angel and primary opponent of Satan and his horde. The Greek root "arch," meaning *chief, first; rule* or *ruler,* is the basis of a number of important and useful words.

Below are ten words drawn from this root. Read the definitions and practice the pronunciations. Then study the sample sentences and see if you can use the words in sentences of your own.

1. **archenemy** (ärch′en′ə mē) a chief enemy; Satan.
    In Christian theology, Satan is the archenemy.
2. **patriarch** (pā′trē ärk′) the male head of a family or tribe.
    From Greek "patria," *family* + "-arches," *head, chief.*
    When we gathered for Thanksgiving dinner, our great-grandfather, the family patriarch, always sat at the head of the table.
3. **anarchy** (an′ər kē) society without rule or government;

lawlessness; disorder; confusion; chaos. From Greek "an-," *not* + "arch(os)," *rule, ruler.*

The king's assassination led to anarchy throughout the country.

4. **hierarchy** (hī′ə rär′kē, hī′rär-) any system of persons or things ranked one above another; formerly, rule by church leaders, especially a high priest. From Greek "hieros," *sacred* + "arch(os)," *rule, ruler.*

The new office hierarchy ranks assistant vice presidents over directors.

5. **monarchy** (mon′ər kē) rule or government by a king, queen, emperor, or empress. From Greek "mon(o)-," *one* + "arch(os)," *rule, ruler.*

The French Revolution ended with the overthrow of the monarchy.

6. **oligarchy** (ol′i gär′kē) rule or government by a few persons. From Greek "oligos," *few* + "arch(os)," *rule, ruler.*

After the revolution, an oligarchy of army officers ruled the newly liberated country.

7. **archbishop** (ärch′bish′əp) a bishop of the highest rank; chief bishop.

The archbishop meets with the bishops from his area once a month to discuss their concerns.

8. **matriarch** (mā′trē ärk′) the female head of a family or tribe. From Greek "matri-," *mother* + "-arches," *head, chief.*

The younger members of the clan usually seek out Grandma Josie, the family matriarch, for advice.

9. **archetype** (är′ki tīp′) the original pattern or model after which a thing is made; prototype. From Greek "arch(e)-," *first, original* + "typos," *mold, type.*

Odysseus is the archetype for James Joyce's Leopold Bloom in his novel *Ulysses.*

10. **archaic** (är kā′ik) marked by the characteristics of an earlier period; antiquated. From Greek "arch(aios)," *old, early, first.*

With the advent of the pocket calculator, the slide rule has become archaic.

Quiz 15: Matching Synonyms

Select the best synonym for each of the italicized words. Circle your response.

1. the *archbishop* of Canterbury
   a. oldest bishop   b. youngest bishop   c. highest-ranking bishop   d. recently appointed bishop
2. a strong *monarchy*
   a. government by a president   b. government by a consortium   c. government by the proletariat   d. government by a king or queen
3. an *archaic* device
   a. old-fashioned   b. complicated   c. expensive   d. useful
4. a wise *patriarch*
   a. old woman   b. general   c. revolutionary   d. male family head
5. the literary and social *archetype*
   a. concern   b. exhibition   c. prototype   d. major problem
6. a state of *anarchy*
   a. hopefulness   b. lawlessness   c. strict order d. female control
7. a brutal *archenemy*
   a. less powerful enemy   b. chief enemy   c. strict enemy   d. Gabriel
8. the iron-handed *oligarchy*
   a. government by few   b. communist state   c. democracy   d. unstable government
9. a highly respected *matriarch*
   a. confidant   b. duke   c. male leader   d. female family head
10. the strict governmental *hierarchy*
    a. leadership   b. promotions   c. system of ranking   d. discipline

Quiz 16: True/False

In the space provided, write T if the synonym or definition of the numbered word is true or F if it is false.

		T or F
1. PATRIARCH	male family head	_____
2. ARCHETYPE	model	_____
3. ARCHENEMY	chief enemy	_____
4. MONARCHY	royal government	_____
5. OLIGARCHY	chaos	_____
6. ARCHBISHOP	church deacon	_____
7. MATRIARCH	wife and mother	_____

8. ANARCHY	political lawlessness	_____
9. HIERARCHY	higher orders	_____
10. ARCHAIC	old-fashioned	_____

LESSON 9. "TO LIFE!": *BIO*

In 1763 the Scottish writer James Boswell was first introduced to the acclaimed English poet, playwright, and dictionary-maker Samuel Johnson, setting the stage for the birth of modern biography. From 1772 until Johnson's death in 1784, the two men were closely associated, and Boswell devoted much of his time to compiling detailed records of Johnson's activities and conversations. Seven years after Johnson's death, Boswell published his masterpiece, the *Life of Samuel Johnson.* The word "biography," *a written account of another person's life,* comes from the Greek root "bio," meaning *life,* and "graphy," meaning *writing.* Besides *life,* "bio" can also mean *living, living thing,* or *biological.*

A number of other important words come from "bio." Here's a list of eight of them. Read through the definitions and practice the pronunciations, then go on to the quizzes.

1. **biodegradable** (bī′ō di grā′də bəl) capable of being decomposed by living organisms, as paper and kitchen scraps are, as opposed to metals, glass, and plastics, which do not decay.

     After a long campaign, the local residents persuaded the supermarkets to use biodegradable paper bags rather than nondegradable plastic.

2. **biofeedback** (bī′ō fēd′bak′) a method of learning to modify one's own bodily or physiological functions with the aid of a visual or auditory display of one's brain waves, blood pressure, or muscle tension.

     Desperate to quit smoking, she made an appointment to try biofeedback.

3. **bioengineering** (bī′ō en′jə nēr′ing) the application of engineering principles and techniques to problems in medicine and biology.

     In the last few decades, bioengineering has made important progress in the design of artificial limbs.

4. **biological clock** (bī′ə loj′i kəl klok′) an innate system in people, animals, and organisms that causes regular cycles of function or behavior.

Recently the term "biological clock" has been used in reference to women in their late thirties and early forties who are concerned about having children before they are no longer able to reproduce.

5. **bionic** (bī on'ik) utilizing electronic devices and mechanical parts to assist humans in performing tasks, as by supplementing or duplicating parts of the body. Formed from "bio-" + "(electr)onic."

The scientist used a bionic arm to examine the radioactive material.

6. **biopsy** (bī'op sē) the excision for diagnostic study of a piece of tissue from a living body. From "bio-" + Greek "opsis," *sight, view.*

The doctor took a biopsy from the patient's lung to determine the nature of the infection.

7. **biota** (bī ō'tə) the plant and animal life of a region or period. From Greek "biote," *life,* from the root "bio."

The biota from the cliffside proved more useful for conservation than the biologists had initially suspected.

8. **biohazard** (bī'ō haz'ərd) a disease-causing agent or organism, especially one produced by biological research; the health risk caused by such an agent or organism.

Will new technology like gene splicing produce heretofore unknown biohazards to threaten the world's population?

Quiz 17: Definitions

Select the word that best fits the definition. Write your answer in the space provided.

_____ 1. the excision for diagnostic study of a piece of tissue from a living body.
a. biopsy   b. bioengineering   c. incision

_____ 2. utilizing electronic devices and mechanical parts to assist humans in performing tasks.
a. biota   b. bioengineering   c. bionic

_____ 3. capable of decaying and being absorbed by the environment.
a. biogenic   b. biodegradable   c. bionic

_____ 4. a method of learning to modify one's own bodily or physiological functions.
a. autobiography   b. biofeedback   c. biota

_____ 5. the application of engineering principles and techniques to problems in medicine and biology.
       a. bioengineering b. autobiography c. biometry

_____ 6. an innate system in people, animals, and organisms that causes regular cycles of function.
       a. biota b. bionic c. biological clock

_____ 7. the plant and animal life of a region.
       a. biota b. autobiography c. biometry

_____ 8. an agent or organism that causes a health risk.
       a. biopsy b. biohazard c. biota

Quiz 18: True/False

In the space provided, write T if the definition of the numbered word is true or F if it is false.

		T or F
1. BIOPSY	tissue sample	_____
2. BIOTA	plants and animals	_____
3. BIOLOGICAL CLOCK	perpetual clock	_____
4. BIOHAZARD	health risk	_____
5. BIODEGRADABLE	capable of decomposing	_____
6. BIONIC	superhero	_____
7. BIOFEEDBACK	culinary expertise	_____
8. BIOENGINEERING	railroad supervision	_____

LESSON 10. "SPEAK!": *DICT, DIC*

The earliest known dictionaries were found in the library of the Assyrian king at Nineveh. These clay tablets, inscribed with cuneiform writing dating from the seventh century B.C., provide important clues to our understanding of Mesopotamian culture. The first English dictionary did not appear until 1440. Compiled by the Dominican monk Galfridus Grammaticus, the *Storehouse for Children or Clerics,* as the title translates, consists of Latin definitions of 10,000 English words. The word "dictionary" was first used in English in 1526, in reference to a Latin dictionary by Peter Berchorius. This was followed by a Latin-English dictionary published by Sir Thomas Elyot in 1538. All these early efforts confined themselves to uncommon words and phrases not generally known or understood, because the daily language was not supposed to require explanation.

Today we understand the word "dictionary" to mean *a book containing a selection of the words of a language, usually arranged alphabetically, giving information about their meanings, pronunciations, etymologies, etc.; a lexicon.* The word comes from the Latin root "dictio," taken from "dicere," meaning *to say, state, declare, speak.* This root has given us scores of important English words. Below are eight for you to examine. After you read through their pronunciations and definitions, complete the quizzes.

1. **malediction** (mal'i dik'shən) a curse or the utterance of a curse. From Latin "male-," *evil* + "dictio," *speech, word.*
   After the witch delivered her malediction, the princess fell into a swoon.

2. **abdication** (ab'di kā'shən) the renunciation or relinquishment of something such as a throne, right, power, or claim, especially when formal.
   Following the abdication of Edward VIII for the woman he loved, his brother George VI assumed the throne of England.

3. **benediction** (ben'i dik'shən) the invocation of a blessing. From Latin "bene-," *well, good* + "dictio," *speech, word.*
   The chaplain delivered a benediction at the end of the service.

4. **edict** (ē'dikt) a decree issued by a sovereign or other authority; an authoritative proclamation or command
   Herod's edict ordered the massacre of male infants throughout his realm.

5. **predicate** (pred'i kāt') to proclaim, declare, or affirm; base or found.
   Your acceptance into the training program is predicated upon a successful personal interview.

6. **jurisdiction** (jŏŏr'is dik'shən) the right, power, or authority to administer justice.
   The mayor's jurisdiction extends only to the area of the village itself; outside its limits, the jurisdiction passes to the town board.

7. **dictum** (dik'təm) an authoritative pronouncement; saying or maxim.
   The firm issued a dictum stating that smoking was forbidden on the premises.

8. **predictive** (pri dik'tiv) indicating the future or future conditions; predicting.

Although the day was clear and balmy, the brisk wind was predictive of the approaching cold snap.

Quiz 19: Matching Synonyms

Match each of the following numbered words with its closest synonym. Write your answer in the space provided.

1. PREDICTIVE	a. assert	_____
2. EDICT	b. maxim	_____
3. PREDICATE	c. indicating the future	_____
4. BENEDICTION	d. authority	_____
5. ABDICATION	e. decree	_____
6. MALEDICTION	f. imprecation, curse	_____
7. DICTUM	g. blessing	_____
8. JURISDICTION	h. renunciation	_____

Quiz 20: True/False

In the space provided, write T if the definition of the numbered word is true or F if it is false.

		T or F
1. PREDICTIVE	indicative of the future	_____
2. PREDICATE	declare	_____
3. EDICT	decree	_____
4. JURISDICTION	authority	_____
5. DICTUM	blessing	_____
6. ABDICATION	assumption	_____
7. MALEDICTION	machismo	_____
8. BENEDICTION	opening services	_____

LESSON 11. "LEAD ON, MACDUFF!": *DUC, DUCT*

Aqueducts, artificial channels built to transport water, were used in ancient Mesopotamia, but the ones used to supply water to ancient Rome are the most famous. Nine aqueducts were built in all; eventually they provided Rome with about thirty-eight million gallons of water daily. Parts of several are still in use, supplying water to fountains in Rome. The word "aqueduct" comes from the Latin "aqua," meaning *water,* and "ductus," meaning *a leading* or *drawing off.*

A great number of powerful words are derived from the "duc, duct" root. Here are nine such words. Read through the definitions and practice the pronunciations. Try to use each word in a sentence of your own. Finally, work through the two quizzes at the end of the lesson to help fix the words in your memory.

1. **induce** (in dōōs′, -dyōōs′) to influence or persuade, as to some action.
   Try to induce her to stay at least a few hours longer.
2. **misconduct** (mis kon′dukt) improper conduct or behavior.
   Such repeated misconduct will result in a reprimand, if not an outright dismissal.
3. **abduct** (ab dukt′) to carry (a person) off or lead (a person) away illegally; kidnap.
   Jason's mother was so fearful that he might be abducted by a stranger that she refused even to let him walk to school alone.
4. **deduce** (di dōōs′, -dyōōs′) to derive as a conclusion from something known or assumed.
   The detective was able to deduce from the facts gathered thus far that the murder took place in the early hours of the morning.
5. **viaduct** (vī′ə dukt′) a bridge for carrying a road or railroad over a valley, gorge, or the like, consisting of a number of short spans; overpass.
   The city government commissioned a firm of civil engineers to explore the possibility of building a viaduct over the river.
6. **reductive** (ri duk′tiv) pertaining to or producing a smaller size. From Latin "reduct-, reducere," *to lead back*.
   The new electronic copier had reductive and enlargement capabilities.
7. **seduce** (si dōōs′, -dyōōs′) to lead astray, as from duty or rectitude.
   He was seduced by the prospect of gain.
8. **traduce** (trə dōōs′, -dyōōs′) to speak maliciously and falsely of; slander. From Latin "traducere," *to transfer, lead across*.
   To traduce someone's character can do permanent harm to his or her reputation.
9. **ductile** (duk′til) pliable or yielding.
   The new plastic is very ductile and can be molded into many forms.

Quiz 21: Matching Synonyms

Match each of the numbered words with the closest synonym. Write your answer in the space provided.

1. SEDUCE	a. overpass	_____
2. VIADUCT	b. shrinking	_____
3. INDUCE	c. kidnap	_____
4. REDUCTIVE	d. bad behavior	_____
5. TRADUCE	e. infer	_____
6. ABDUCT	f. entice	_____
7. MISCONDUCT	g. pliable	_____
8. DEDUCE	h. defame	_____
9. DUCTILE	i. persuade	_____

Quiz 22: True/False

In the space provided, write T if the definition of the numbered word is true or F if it is false.

		T or F
1. DEDUCE	infer	_____
2. DUCTILE	pliable	_____
3. SEDUCE	lead astray	_____
4. REDUCTIVE	magnifying	_____
5. TRADUCE	malign	_____
6. VIADUCT	overpass	_____
7. ABDUCT	restore	_____
8. MISCONDUCT	improper behavior	_____
9. INDUCE	persuade	_____

LESSON 12. "JUST THE FACTS, MA'AM": *FAC, FACT, FECT*

We have formed a great many important and useful words from the Latin "facere," *to make* or *do.* A "facsimile," for example, derives from the Latin phrase "fac simile," meaning *to make similar,* and has come to mean *an exact copy.* Since facsimile copiers and transmitters have become very common, "facsimile" is now generally shortened and changed in spelling to "fax."

Many potent words are derived from the "fac, fact, fect" root. Eight such words follow. Learn them by completing this lesson; then try to use the root to help you figure out other "fac, fact" words you encounter.

1. **factious** (fak′shəs) given to or marked by discord; dissenting. From Latin "factio," *act of doing or of making connections; group* or *clique,* derived from "facere," *to do* or *make.*

    Factious groups threatened to break up the alliance.

2. **factotum** (fak tō′təm) a person employed to do all kinds of work, as a personal secretary or the chief servant of a household.

    Jeeves was the model of a gentleman's gentleman—the indispensable factotum of the frivolous Bertie Wooster.

3. **factitious** (fak tish′əs) made artificially; contrived.

    The report was merely a factitious account, not factual at all.

4. **facile** (fas′il) moving or acting with ease; fluent. From Latin "facilis," *easy to do,* derived from "facere," *to do.*

    With his facile mind, he often thought of startlingly original solutions to old problems.

5. **artifact** (är′tə fakt′) any object made by human skill or art. From the Latin phrase "arte factum," *(something) made with skill.*

    The archaeologists dug up many artifacts from the ancient Indian culture.

6. **facsimile** (fak sim′ə lē) an exact copy, as of a book, painting, or manuscript; a method of transmitting typed or printed material by means of radio or telegraph.

    If they could not obtain a facsimile of the document by noon, the deal would fall through.

7. **putrefaction** (pyōō′trə fak′shən) the decomposition of organic matter by bacteria and fungi. From Latin "putrere," *to rot* + "factio," *act of doing.*

    Once the putrefaction of the compost pile was complete, the gardener used the rotted material to enrich the soil.

8. **prefect** (prē′fekt) a person appointed to any of various positions of command, authority, or superintendence. From Latin "praefectus," formed from "prae," *ahead, surpassing* + "fectus," *doing* (from "facere," *to do*).

    The prefect was appointed to a term of three years.

Quiz 23: Definitions

Select the word that best fits the definition. Write your answer in the space provided.

_____ 1. the decomposition of organic matter by bacteria and fungi
  a. chemical analysis   b. hypothermia
  c. putrefaction

_____ 2. not natural; artificial
  a. factious   b. facile   c. factitious

_____ 3. an exact copy, as of a book, painting, or manuscript
  a. factoid   b. facsimile   c. putrefaction

_____ 4. given to dissension or strife
  a. facile   b. factious   c. obsequious

_____ 5. an object made by humans
  a. artifact   b. factotum   c. factious

_____ 6. a person employed to do all kinds of work
  a. facile   b. factotum   c. faculty

_____ 7. moving or acting easily
  a. putrefaction   b. prefect   c. facile

_____ 8. someone appointed to any of various positions of command, authority, or superintendence
  a. prefect   b. facile   c. factotum

Quiz 24: True/False

In the space provided, write T if the definition of the numbered word is true or F if it is false.

		T or F
1. FACTITIOUS	contrived	_____
2. FACTOTUM	carrier	_____
3. PUTREFACTION	rotting	_____
4. ARTIFACT	machinery	_____
5. FACSIMILE	instant transmission	_____
6. PREFECT	administrator	_____
7. FACTIOUS	dissenting	_____
8. FACILE	fluent	_____

LESSON 13. "ALWAYS FAITHFUL": *FEDER, FID, FIDE*

"Semper fidelis" is Latin for *always faithful.* The phrase is the motto of the United States Marine Corps and the title of an 1888 march by John Philip Sousa. This phrase, as with a number of useful words, comes from the Latin root "fid, fide," meaning *trust, faith.*

Below are seven words derived from this root. Read through

the meanings, practice the pronunciations, and complete the quizzes that follow to help fix the words in your memory.

1. **fidelity** (fi del'i tē) faithfulness; loyalty.
   Dogs are legendary for their fidelity to their masters.

2. **fiduciary** (fi doō'shē er'ē, -dyoō'-) a person to whom property or power is entrusted for the benefit of another; trustee. From Latin "fiducia," *trust,* related to "fidere," *to trust.*
   The bank's fiduciary administers the children's trust funds.

3. **infidel** (in'fi dl, -del') a person who does not accept a particular religious faith. From Latin "in," *not* + "fidelis," *faithful* (from "fide," *faith*).
   The ayatollah condemned Salman Rushdie as an infidel.

4. **perfidious** (pər fid'ē əs) deliberately faithless; treacherous. From Latin "perfidia" ("per-," *through* + "fide," *faith*).
   The perfidious lover missed no opportunity to be unfaithful.

5. **confide** (kən fīd') to entrust one's secrets to another. From Latin "confidere" ("con-," *with* + "fidere," *to trust*).
   The two sisters confided in each other.

6. **bona fide** (bō'nə fīd', bon'ə) genuine; real; in good faith.
   To their great astonishment, the offer of a free vacation was bona fide.

7. **affidavit** (af'i dā'vit) a written declaration upon oath made before an authorized official. From a Medieval Latin word meaning *(he) has declared on oath,* from Latin "affidare," *to pledge on faith.*
   In the affidavit, they swore they had not been involved in the accident.

Quiz 25: Matching Synonyms

Match each of the following numbered words with its closest synonym. Write your answer in the space provided.

1. CONFIDE	a. faithfulness	_____
2. FIDELITY	b. heathen	_____
3. BONA FIDE	c. declaration	_____
4. INFIDEL	d. entrust	_____
5. AFFIDAVIT	e. trustee	_____
6. PERFIDIOUS	f. genuine	_____
7. FIDUCIARY	g. faithless	_____

Quiz 26: Matching Synonyms

Select the best synonym for each numbered word. Write your answer in the space provided.

_____ 1. bona fide
a. unauthorized   b. deboned   c. real
d. well-trained

_____ 2. perfidious
a. irreligious   b. content   c. loyal   d. treacherous

_____ 3. fidelity
a. loyalty   b. alliance   c. great affection
d. random motion

_____ 4. fiduciary
a. bank teller   b. trustee   c. insurance   d. default

_____ 5. infidel
a. warrior   b. intransigent   c. heathen
d. outsider

_____ 6. affidavit
a. affright   b. declaration   c. loyalty
d. betrothal

_____ 7. confide
a. combine   b. recline   c. entrust   d. convert

LESSON 14. "FLOW GENTLY, SWEET AFTON": *FLU*

In 1991, the upper fifth of working Americans took home more money than the other four-fifths put together—the highest proportion of wealthy people since the end of World War II. One word to describe such wealthy people is "affluent," *prosperous.* The word comes from the Latin root "fluere," meaning *to flow.* As a river would flow freely, so the money of the affluent flows easily.

Seven of the most useful and important words formed from the "flu" root follow. Study the definitions and read through the pronunciations. Then do the quizzes.

1. **flume** (floom) a deep, narrow channel containing a mountain stream or torrent; an amusement-park ride through a water-filled chute or slide.
    The adults steadfastly refused to try the log flume ride, but the children enjoyed it thoroughly.
2. **confluence** (kon′floo əns) a flowing together of two or more streams; their place of junction.

The confluence of the rivers is marked by a strong current.
3. **fluent** (flōo′ənt) spoken or written effortlessly; easy; graceful; flowing.

Jennifer was such a fluent speaker that she was in great demand as a lecturer.
4. **fluctuation** (fluk′chōo ā′shən) continual change from one course, condition, etc., to another.

The fluctuation in temperature was astonishing, considering it was still only February.
5. **fluvial** (flōo′vē əl) of or pertaining to a river; produced by or found in a river.

The contours of the riverbank were altered over the years by fluvial deposits.
6. **influx** (in′fluks′) a flowing in.

The unexpected influx of refugees severely strained the community's resources.
7. **flux** (fluks) a flowing or flow; continuous change.

His political views are in constant flux.

Quiz 27: True/False
In the space provided, write T if the definition of the numbered word is true or F if it is false.

		T or F
1. FLUCTUATION	change	_____
2. FLUVIAL	deep crevasse	_____
3. FLUENT	flowing	_____
4. FLUX	flow	_____
5. INFLUX	egress	_____
6. CONFLUENCE	diversion	_____
7. FLUME	feather	_____

Quiz 28: Matching Synonyms
Select the best definition for each numbered word. Write your answer in the space provided.

1. FLUX	a. gorge	_____
2. CONFLUENCE	b. flowing easily	_____
3. FLUME	c. continual shift	_____
4. FLUCTUATION	d. an inflow	_____
5. FLUENT	e. a flow	_____
6. INFLUX	f. riverine	_____
7. FLUVIAL	g. convergence	_____

LESSON 15. "IN THE BEGINNING": *GEN*

Genesis, the first book of the Old Testament, tells of the beginning of the world. The English word "genesis" is taken from the Greek word for *origin* or *source.* From the root "gen," meaning *beget, bear, kind,* or *race,* a number of powerful vocabulary builders has evolved.

Here are ten "gen" words. Study the definitions and practice the pronunciations to help you learn the words. To accustom yourself to using these new terms in your daily speech and writing, work through the two quizzes at the end of the lesson.

1. **gene** (jēn) the unit of heredity in the chromosomes that controls the development of inherited traits. From Greek "-genes," *born, begotten.*
   The gene for color blindness is linked to the Y chromosome.
2. **engender** (en jen′dər) to produce, cause, or give rise to.
   Hatred engenders violence.
3. **gentility** (jen til′i tē) good breeding or refinement.
   Her obvious gentility marked her as a member of polite society.
4. **gentry** (jen′trē) wellborn and well-bred people; in England, the class under the nobility.
   In former times, the gentry lived on large estates with grand houses, lush grounds, and many servants.
5. **genus** (jē′nəs) the major subdivision of a family or subfamily in the classification of plants and animals, usually consisting of more than one species.
   The biologist assigned the newly discovered plant to the appropriate genus.
6. **genial** (jēn′yəl, jē′nē əl) cordial; favorable for life, growth, or comfort.
   Under the genial conditions in the greenhouse, the plants grew and flourished.
7. **congenital** (kən jen′i tl) existing at or from one's birth.
   The child's congenital defect was easily corrected by surgery.
8. **eugenics** (yo͞o jen′iks) the science of improving the qualities of a breed or species, especially the human race, by the careful selection of parents.
   Through eugenics, scientists hope to engineer a superior race of human beings.

9. **genealogy** (jē′nē ol′ə jē) a record or account of the ancestry and descent of a person, family, group, etc.; the study of family ancestries.

   Genealogy shows that Franklin Delano Roosevelt was a cousin of Winston Churchill.

10. **congenial** (kən jēn′yəl) agreeable or pleasant; suited or adapted in disposition; compatible.

   The student enjoyed the congenial atmosphere of the library.

Quiz 29: Definitions

Select the word that best fits the definition. Write your answer in the space provided.

_____ 1. the major subdivision of a family or subfamily in the classification of plants and animals.
   a. gene b. genus c. genial d. gentry

_____ 2. suited or adapted in disposition; agreeable.
   a. genial b. congenital c. genealogy
   d. congenial

_____ 3. wellborn and well-bred people.
   a. gene b. gentry c. nobility d. gentility

_____ 4. the science of improving the qualities of a breed or species.
   a. genetics b. gentry c. genealogy d. eugenics

_____ 5. the unit of heredity transmitted in the chromosome.
   a. ancestry b. DNA c. gene d. genus

_____ 6. cordial; favorable for life, growth, or comfort.
   a. genial b. gentry c. eugenics d. hospitality

_____ 7. to produce, cause, or give rise to.
   a. gentility b. engender c. genealogy d. genial

_____ 8. a record or account of the ancestry of a person, family, group, etc.
   a. gene b. genealogy c. glibness d. gentry

_____ 9. good breeding or refinement.
   a. reductive b. genus c. gentility d. eugenics

_____ 10. existing at or from one's birth.
   a. congenital b. genus c. congenial d. gene

Quiz 30: True/False

In the space provided, write T if the definition of the numbered word is true or F if it is false.

T or F

1. GENTRY   peasants   _____
2. CONGENITAL   incurable   _____
3. GENIAL   debased   _____
4. GENE   genetic material   _____
5. EUGENICS   matricide   _____
6. GENTILITY   viciousness   _____
7. GENEALOGY   family history   _____
8. CONGENIAL   pleasant   _____
9. GENUS   subdivision   _____
10. ENGENDER   cease   _____

ANSWERS TO QUIZ IN CHAPTER 8

Answers to Quiz 1

1. a 2. b 3. c 4. d 5. d 6. b 7. b 8. a 9. a 10. b 11. c 12. d 13. c 14. c
15. a

Answers to Quiz 2

1. T 2. F 3. T 4. T 5. F 6. F 7. F 8. T 9. T 10. T

Answers to Quiz 3

1. T 2. T 3. F 4. T 5. F 6. T 7. F 8. T 9. T 10. F

Answers to Quiz 5

1. i 2. e 3. d 4. b 5. h 6. a 7. c 8. j 9. f 10. g

Answers to Quiz 6

1. T 2. F 3. F 4. F 5. T 6. F 7. T 8. T 9. F 10. T

Answers to Quiz 7

1. g 2. e 3. d 4. b 5. a 6. i 7. c 8. j 9. f 10. h

Answers to Quiz 8

1. F 2. T 3. T 4. T 5. F 6. F 7. T 8. F 9. T 10. F

Answers to Quiz 9

1. c 2. g 3. a 4. e 5. i 6. h 7. f 8. d 9. b 10. j

Answers to Quiz 10

1. F 2. F 3. T 4. F 5. T 6. T 7. F 8. F 9. F 10. T

Answers to Quiz 11

1. c 2. e 3. a 4. f 5. d 6. b

Answers to Quiz 12

1. F 2. T 3. F 4. F 5. F 6. T

Answers to Quiz 13

1. F 2. T 3. F 4. T 5. F 6. T 7. F 8. T

Answers to Quiz 15

1. c 2. d 3. a 4. d 5. c 6. b 7. b 8. a 9. d 10. c

Answers to Quiz 16

1. T 2. T 3. T 4. T 5. F 6. F 7. F 8. T 9. F 10. T

Answers to Quiz 17

1. a 2. c 3. b 4. b 5. a 6. c 7. a 8. b

Answers to Quiz 18

1. T 2. T 3. F 4. T 5. T 6. F 7. F 8. F

Answers to Quiz 19

1. c 2. e 3. a 4. g 5. h 6. f 7. b 8. d

Answers to Quiz 20

1. T 2. T 3. T 4. T 5. F 6. F 7. F 8. F

Answers to Quiz 21

1. f 2. a 3. i 4. b 5. h 6. c 7. d 8. e 9. g

Answers to Quiz 22

1. T 2. T 3. T 4. F 5. T 6. T 7. F 8. T 9. T

Answers to Quiz 23

1. c 2. c 3. b 4. b 5. a 6. b 7. c 8. a

Answers to Quiz 24

1. T 2. F 3. T 4. F 5. F 6. T 7. T 8. T

Answers to Quiz 25

1. d 2. a 3. f 4. b 5. c 6. g 7. e

Answers to Quiz 26

1. c 2. d 3. a 4. b 5. c 6. b 7. c

Answers to Quiz 27

1. T 2. F 3. T 4. T 5. F 6. F 7. F

Answers to Quiz 28

1. e 2. g 3. a 4. c 5. b 6. d 7. f

Answers to Quiz 29

1. b 2. d 3. b 4. d 5. c 6. a 7. b 8. b 9. c 10. a

Answers to Quiz 30

1. F 2. F 3. F 4. T 5. F 6. F 7. T 8. T 9. T 10. F

9. MORE ROOT POWER

LESSON 1. "THIS WAY TO THE EGRESS": *GRAD, GRES, GRESS*

P. T. Barnum was a nineteenth-century American showman whose greatest undertaking was the circus he called "The Greatest Show on Earth." The circus, which included a menagerie that exhibited Jumbo the elephant and a museum of freaks, was famous all over the country. After its merger in 1881 with James Anthony Bailey's circus, the enterprise gained international renown. When Barnum's customers took too long to leave his famous exhibits, he posted a sign: "This way to the egress." Following the arrow in eager anticipation of a new oddity, the visitors were ushered through the egress—the exit.

Knowing that the root "grad, gres, gress" means *step, degree,* or *walk* might have given these suckers a few more minutes to enjoy the exhibits, and it can certainly help you figure out a number of powerful words. Here are nine words that use this Latin root. Study the definitions, practice the pronunciations, and work through the two quizzes.

1. **digress** (di gres′, dī-) to wander away from the main topic. From Latin "digressus, digredi," *to walk away* ("di-," *away, apart* + "gressus, gredi," *to walk, step*).

    The manager cautioned her salespeople that they would fare better if they did not digress from their prepared sales talks.

2. **transgress** (trans gres′, tranz-) to break or violate a law, command, moral code, etc. From Latin "transgressus, transgredi," *to step across.*

    Those who transgress the laws of their ancestors often feel guilty.

3. **retrograde** (re′ trə grād′) moving backward; having backward motion.

   Most of the townspeople regarded the new ordinance as a prime example of retrograde legislation.

4. **regression** (ri gresh′ən) the act of going or fact of having gone back to an earlier place or state.

   The child's regression could be seen in his thumbsucking.

5. **degrade** (di grād′) to reduce the dignity of (someone); deprive (someone) of office, rank, or title; lower (someone or something) in quality or character.

   He felt they were degrading him by making him wash the dishes.

6. **Congress** (kong′gris) the national legislative body of the United States, consisting of the Senate and the House of Representatives; *(lower case)* encounter; meeting.

   Congress held a special session to discuss the situation in the Middle East.

7. **gradation** (grā dā′shən) any process or change taking place through a series of stages, by degrees, or gradually. From Latin "gradatio," *series of steps,* derived from "gradus," *step, degree.*

   He decided to change his hair color by gradation rather than all at once.

8. **gradient** (grā′dē ənt) the degree of inclination, or the rate of ascent or descent, in a highway, railroad, etc.

   Although they liked the house very much, they were afraid that the driveway's steep gradient would make it hard to park a car there in the winter.

9. **progressive** (prə gres′iv) characterized by progress or reform; innovative; going forward; gradually increasing.

   The progressive legislation wiped out years of social inequity.

Quiz 1: Matching Synonyms

Match each of the following numbered words with its closest synonym. Write your answer in the space provided.

1. CONGRESS	a. backward moving	____
2. REGRESSION	b. depart from a subject	____
3. GRADIENT	c. disobey	____
4. PROGRESSIVE	d. meeting	____
5. DIGRESS	e. stage, degree	____

6. GRADATION   f. reversion   _____
7. RETROGRADE   g. humiliate   _____
8. DEGRADE   h. innovative   _____
9. TRANSGRESS   i. incline   _____

Quiz 2: Defining Words

Define each of the following words.

1. gradient _____
2. Congress _____
3. progressive _____
4. regression _____
5. retrograde _____
6. degrade _____
7. digress _____
8. gradation _____
9. transgress _____

Suggested Answers: 1. the degree of inclination, or the rate of ascent or descent, in a highway, etc. 2. the national legislative body of the United States; a meeting or assembly 3. characterized by reform; increasing gradually 4. the act of going back to an earlier place or state 5. moving backward; having backward motion 6. to reduce (someone) to a lower rank; deprive of office, rank, or title; to lower in quality or character 7. to wander away from the main topic 8. any process or change taking place through a series of stages, by degrees, or gradually 9. to break or violate a law, command, moral code, etc.

LESSON 2. "SPLISH, SPLASH, I WAS TAKING A BATH": _HYDRO, HYDR_

According to mythology, the ancient Greeks were menaced by a monstrous nine-headed serpent with fatally poisonous breath. Killing it was no easy matter: When you lopped off one head, it grew two in its place, and the central head was immortal. Hercules, sent to destroy the serpent as the second of his twelve labors, was triumphant when he burned off the eight peripheral heads and buried the ninth under a huge rock. From its residence, the watery marsh, came the monster's name, "Hydra," from the Greek root "hydr(o)," meaning _water_.

Quite a few words are formed from the "hydro" or "hydr" root. Here are ten of them. Read through the definitions, practice the pronunciations, and then work through the two quizzes that follow.

1. **hydrostat** (hī′drə stat′) an electrical device for detecting the presence of water, as from an overflow or a leak.

    The plumber used a hydrostat to locate the source of the leak in the bathroom.

2. **dehydrate** (dē hī′drāt) to deprive of water; dry out.

    Aside from being tasty and nutritious, dehydrated fruits and vegetables are easy to store and carry.

3. **hydrophobia** (hī′drə fō′bē ə) rabies; fear of water.

    Sufferers from hydrophobia are unable to swallow water.

4. **hydroplane** (hī′drə plān′) a light, high-powered boat, especially one with hydrofoils or a stepped bottom, designed to travel at very high speeds.

    The shore police acquired a new hydroplane to help them apprehend boaters who misuse the waterways.

5. **hydroponics** (hī′drə pon′iks) the cultivation of plants by placing the roots in liquid nutrients rather than soil.

    Some scientists predict that in the future, as arable land becomes increasingly more scarce, most of our vegetables will be grown through hydroponics.

6. **hydropower** (hī′drə pou′ər) electricity generated by falling water or another hydraulic source.

    Hydropower is efficient, clean, and economical.

7. **hydrate** (hī′drāt) to combine with water.

    Lime is hydrated for use in plaster, mortar, and cement.

8. **hydrangea** (hī drān′jə) a showy shrub cultivated for its large white, pink, or blue flower clusters. From Greek "hydr-," *water* + "angeion," *vessel.*

    Hydrangeas require a great deal of water to flourish.

9. **hydrotherapy** (hī′drə ther′əpē) the treatment of disease by the scientific application of water both internally and externally.

    To alleviate strained muscles, physical therapists often prescribe hydrotherapy.

10. **hydrosphere** (hī′drə sfēr′) the water on or surrounding the surface of the planet Earth, including the water of the oceans and the water in the atmosphere.

    Scientists are investigating whether the greenhouse effect is influencing the hydrosphere.

Quiz 3: Definitions

Select the word that best fits the definition. Write your answer in the space provided.

_____ 1. electricity generated by water
   a. hydropower   b. hydrangea
   c. hydrotherapy   d. electrolysis

_____ 2. the treatment of disease by the scientific application of water both internally and externally
   a. hydrate   b. electrolysis   c. hydrotherapy
   d. hydroponics

_____ 3. a light, high-powered boat, especially one with hydrofoils or a stepped bottom
   a. hydropower   b. hydroplane
   c. hydroelectric   d. hydroship

_____ 4. rabies; fear of water
   a. hydrate   b. hydrotherapy   c. hydroponics
   d. hydrophobia

_____ 5. the water on or surrounding the surface of the globe, including the water of the oceans and the water in the atmosphere
   a. hydrosphere   b. hydrate   c. hydrofoil
   d. hydrangea

_____ 6. to deprive of water
   a. a. hydrate   b. dehydrate   c. hydrolyze
   d. hydrotherapy

_____ 7. a showy shrub with large white, pink, or blue flower clusters
   a. hydrate   b. hydrangea   c. hydroponics
   d. hydrofoil

_____ 8. the cultivation of plants by placing the roots in liquid nutrient solutions rather than soil
   a. hydrotherapy   b. hydrangea
   c. hydroponics   d. hydrolyze

_____ 9. to combine with water
   a. hydrostat   b. hydrosphere   c. hydrangea
   d. hydrate

_____ 10. an electrical device for detecting the presence of water, as from an overflow or a leak
   a. hydrosphere   b. hydrangea
   c. hydroponics   d. hydrostat

Quiz 4: True/False

In the space provided, write T if the definition of the numbered word is true or F if it is false.

		T or F
1. HYDROPOWER	hydroelectric power	_____
2. HYDROPLANE	boat	_____
3. HYDROPONICS	gardening in water	_____
4. HYDROSTAT	water power	_____
5. HYDRANGEA	flowering plant	_____
6. HYDROTHERAPY	water cure	_____
7. HYDRATE	lose water	_____
8. HYDROSPHERE	bubble	_____
9. DEHYDRATE	wash thoroughly	_____
10. HYDROPHOBIA	pneumonia	_____

LESSON 3. "AFTER ME, THE DELUGE": *LAV, LU*

The failure of Louis XV (1710–74) to provide strong leadership and badly needed reforms contributed to the crisis that brought about the French Revolution. Louis took only nominal interest in ruling his country and was frequently influenced by his mistresses. In the last years of his reign, he did cooperate with his chancellor to try to reform the government's unequal and inefficient system of taxation, but it was too late. His reported deathbed prophecy, "After me, the deluge," was fulfilled in the overthrow of the monarchy less than twenty years later. The word "deluge," meaning *flood,* comes from the Latin root "lu," *to wash.* As a flood, a deluge would indeed wash things clean.

A number of words were formed from the "lav, lu" root. Here are several examples. Study the definitions and practice the pronunciations. To help you remember the words, complete the two quizzes at the end of the lesson.

1. **dilute** (di lо̄ōt′, dī-) to make thinner or weaker by adding water; to reduce the strength or effectiveness of (something). From Latin "dilutus, diluere," *to wash away.*
   The wine was too strong and had to be diluted.
2. **lavabo** (lə vā′bō, -vä′-) the ritual washing of the celebrant's hands after the offertory in the Mass; the passage

recited with the ritual. From the Latin word meaning *I shall wash,* with which the passage begins.

The priest intoned the Latin words of the lavabo.

3. **lavage** (lə väzh′) a washing, especially the cleansing of an organ, as the stomach, by irrigation.

Lavage is a preferred method of preventing infection.

4. **diluvial** (di lo͞o′vē əl) pertaining to or caused by a flood or deluge.

The diluvial aftermath was a bitter harvest of smashed gardens, stained siding, and missing yard furniture.

5. **alluvium** (ə lo͞o′vē əm) a deposit of sand, mud, etc., formed by flowing water.

Geologists study alluvium for clues to the earth's history.

6. **ablution** (ə blo͞o′shən) a cleansing with water or other liquid, especially as a religious ritual; a washing of the hands, body, etc.

He performed his morning ablutions with vigor.

Quiz 5: Matching Synonyms

Select the best or closest synonym for each numbered word. Write your answer in the space provided.

_____ 1. lavage
a. molten rock   b. sewage   c. washing
d. religious ritual

_____ 2. alluvium
a. great heat   b. rain   c. flood   d. deposit of sand

_____ 3. lavabo
a. religious cleansing   b. volcano   c. flooding
d. lavatory

_____ 4. ablution
a. cleansing with water   b. absence
c. sacrifice   d. small font

_____ 5. dilute
a. wash   b. weaken   c. cleanse   d. liquefy

_____ 6. diluvial
a. before the flood   b. antedate   c. monarchy
d. of a flood

Quiz 6: True/False

In the space provided, write T if the definition of the numbered word is true or F if it is false.

		T or F
1. DILUTE	reduce strength	_____
2. DILUVIAL	two-lipped	_____
3. LAVAGE	security	_____
4. ALLUVIUM	molten rock	_____
5. ABLUTION	washing	_____
6. LAVABO	religious ritual	_____

LESSON 4. "SILVER TONGUE": *LOQUI, LOQU, LOCU*

For many years, ventriloquist Edgar Bergen amused audiences as he tried to outwit his monocled wooden dummy, Charlie McCarthy. Among the most popular entertainers of his age, Bergen astonished audiences with his mastery of ventriloquism, the art of speaking so that projected sound seems to originate elsewhere, as from a hand-manipulated dummy. This ancient skill sounds easier than it is, since it requires modifying the voice through slow exhalation, minimizing movement of the tongue and lips, and maintaining an impassive expression to help shift viewers' attention to the illusory source of the voice.

The word "ventriloquism" comes from Latin "ventri-," *abdomen, stomach,* and the root "loqui," *to speak* (because it was believed that the ventriloquist produced sounds from his stomach). Many useful and important words were formed from the "loqui, loqu" root. Below are seven you should find especially helpful. Study the definitions and practice the pronunciations. To reinforce your learning, work through the two quizzes.

1. **obloquy** (ob′lə kwē) blame, censure, or abusive language.
   The vicious obloquy surprised even those who knew of the enmity between the political rivals.
2. **colloquial** (kə lō′kwē əl) characteristic of or appropriate to ordinary or familiar conversation rather than formal speech or writing.
   In standard American English, "He hasn't got any" is colloquial, while "He has none" is formal.
3. **soliloquy** (sə lil′ə kwē) the act of talking while or as if alone.
   A soliloquy is often used as a device in a drama to disclose a character's innermost thoughts.
4. **eloquent** (el′ə kwənt) having or exercising the power of fluent, forceful, and appropriate speech; movingly expressive.

William Jennings Bryan was an eloquent orator famous for his "Cross of Gold" speech.

5. **interlocution** (in'tər lō kyoo'shən) conversation; dialogue.

The interlocutions disclosed at the Watergate hearings riveted the American public to their TV sets.

6. **loquacious** (lō kwā'shəs) talking much or freely; talkative; wordy.

After the sherry, the dinner guests became loquacious.

7. **elocution** (el'ə kyoo'shən) a person's manner of speaking or reading aloud; the study and practice of public speaking.

After completing the course in public speaking, the pupils were skilled at elocution.

Quiz 7: Matching Synonyms

Match each of the numbered words with its closest synonym. Write your answer in the space provided.

1. LOQUACIOUS	a. censure	_____
2. INTERLOCUTION	b. informal	_____
3. ELOCUTION	c. monologue	_____
4. COLLOQUIAL	d. talkative	_____
5. SOLILOQUY	e. conversation	_____
6. OBLOQUY	f. fluent	_____
7. ELOQUENT	g. public speaking	_____

Quiz 8: Definitions

Select the word that best fits the definition. Write your answer in the space provided.

_____ 1. a person's manner of speaking or reading aloud; the study and practice of public speaking
  a. obloquy b. soliloquy c. prologue
  d. elocution

_____ 2. conversation; dialogue
  a. colloquial b. interlocution c. monologue
  d. elocution

_____ 3. tending to talk; garrulous
  a. eloquent b. colloquial c. loquacious
  d. elocutionary

_____ 4. characteristic of or appropriate to ordinary or fa-

miliar conversation rather than formal speech or writing
  a. colloquial b. eloquent c. prologue
  d. dialogue

_____ 5. the act of talking while or as if alone
  a. circumlocution b. dialogue c. soliloquy
  d. obloquy

_____ 6. having or exercising the power of fluent, forceful, and appropriate speech; movingly expressive
  a. interlocution b. eloquent c. colloquial
  d. loquacious

_____ 7. censure; abusive language
  a. interlocution b. soliloquy c. obloquy
  d. dialogue

LESSON 5. "STAR LIGHT, STAR BRIGHT": *LUC, LUX, LUM*

Before he was driven out of heaven because of his pride, Satan was called "Lucifer," which translates as *bringer of light*. In his epic retelling of the Bible, *Paradise Lost*, John Milton used the name "Lucifer" for the demon of sinful pride, and we call the planet Venus "Lucifer" when it appears as the morning star. "Lucifer" comes from the root "luc, lux" meaning *light*.

A number of powerful words derive from "luc" and its variations. We trust that you'll find the following seven *light* words "enlightening"! Study the definitions and practice the pronunciations. Then complete the two quizzes at the end of the lesson.

1. **pellucid** (pə loo′ sid) allowing the maximum passage of light; clear.
  The pellucid waters of the Caribbean allowed us to see the tropical fish clearly.
2. **lucid** (loo′sid) shining or bright; clearly understood.
  Stephen Hawking's lucid explanation of astrophysics became a bestseller.
3. **translucent** (trans loo′ sənt, tranz-) permitting light to pass through but diffusing it so that persons, objects, etc., on the opposite side are not clearly visible.
  Frosted window glass is translucent.
4. **elucidate** (i loo′si dāt′) to make light or clear; explain.
  Once my math teacher elucidated the mysteries of geometry, I had no further difficulty solving the problems.

5. **lucubrate** (lōō′kyŏŏ brāt′) to work, write, or study laboriously, especially at night. From Latin "lucubrare," *to work by artificial light.*

   The scholar lucubrated for many long nights in an attempt to complete his thesis.

6. **luminary** (lōō′mə ner′ē) an eminent person; an object that gives light.

   Certain that the elegant woman emerging from the limousine had to be a theatrical luminary, the crowd surged forward to get a closer look.

7. **luminous** (lōō′ mə nəs) radiating or emitting light; brilliant.

   The luminous paint emitted an eerie glow, not at all what the designer had envisioned.

Quiz 9: True/False

In the space provided, write T if the definition of the numbered word is true or F if it is false.

		T or F
1. LUCID	comprehensible	_____
2. ELUCIDATE	explain	_____
3. LUCUBRATE	lubricate	_____
4. PELLUCID	limpid, clear	_____
5. LUMINOUS	reflective	_____
6. LUMINARY	lightning	_____
7. TRANSLUCENT	opaque	_____

Quiz 10: Matching Synonyms

Select the best definition for each numbered word. Write your answer in the space provided.

1. LUMINOUS	a. study hard	_____
2. ELUCIDATE	b. prominent person	_____
3. PELLUCID	c. brilliant	_____
4. LUCUBRATE	d. permitting but diffusing light	_____
5. LUCID	e. clearly understood	_____
6. LUMINARY	f. allowing the passage of maximum light	_____
7. TRANSLUCENT	g. clarify	_____

LESSON 6. "EVIL BE TO HIM WHO DOES EVIL.": *MALE, MAL*

"Malnutrition" is defined as *a lack of the proper type and amount of nutrients required for good health*. It is estimated that more than ten million American children suffer from malnutrition; the World Health Organization reports that over 600 million people suffer from malnutrition in the emerging countries alone. Malnourished people endure a variety of side effects, including a failure to grow, increased susceptibility to infection, anemia, diarrhea, and lethargy.

The root "mal" in the word "malnourished" means *bad, evil*, and words formed around this root invariably carry negative overtones. In Latin, the root is spelled "male"; in French, it's "mal," but regardless of the spelling, the root means *evil*. Study the definitions and pronunciations of the following "mal" words until you become comfortable with them. Then work through the two quizzes.

1. **maladjusted** (mal'ə jus'tid) badly adjusted.
   Despite attempts by the psychologist to ease him into his environment, the child remained maladjusted.
2. **malefactor** (mal'ə fak'tər) a person who violates the law; a criminal.
   The police issued an all-points bulletin for the apprehension of the malefactor.
3. **maladroit** (mal'ə droit') unskillful; awkward; clumsy.
   With his large hands and thick fingers, the young man was maladroit at fine needlework.
4. **malevolent** (mə lev'ə lənt) wishing evil to another or others; showing ill will.
   Her malevolent uncle robbed the heiress of her estate and made her a virtual prisoner.
5. **malapropism** (mal'ə prop iz'əm) a confused use of words, especially one in which one word is replaced by another of similar sound but ludicrously inappropriate meaning; an instance of such a use. The word comes from Mrs. Malaprop, a character in Sheridan's comedy *The Rivals* (1775), noted for her misapplication of words. Sheridan coined the character's name from the English word "malapropos," meaning *inappropriate*, derived from the French phrase "mal à propos," *badly (suited) to the purpose*.
   "Lead the way and we'll precede" is a malapropism.

6. **malicious** (mə lish′əs) full of or characterized by evil intention.

    The malicious gossip hurt the young couple's reputation.

7. **malfeasance** (mal fē′zəns) the performance by a public official of an act that is legally unjustified, harmful, or contrary to law.

    Convicted of malfeasance, the mayor was sentenced to six months in jail.

8. **malignant** (mə lig′nənt) disposed to cause harm, suffering, or distress; tending to produce death, as a disease or tumor.

    The patient was greatly relieved when the pathologist reported that the tumor was not malignant.

9. **malign** (mə līn′) to speak harmful untruths about; slander.

    "If you malign me again," the actor threatened the tabloid reporter, "I will not hesitate to sue."

Quiz 11: Matching Synonyms

Match each of the numbered words with its closest synonym. Write your answer in the space provided.

1. MALADROIT	a. wishing others evil	_____
2. MALICIOUS	b. harmful; fatal	_____
3. MALAPROPISM	c. official misconduct	_____
4. MALFEASANCE	d. bungling, tactless	_____
5. MALIGN	e. badly adjusted	_____
6. MALIGNANT	f. spiteful	_____
7. MALEFACTOR	g. criminal	_____
8. MALEVOLENT	h. revile, defame	_____
9. MALADJUSTED	i. confused use of words	_____

Quiz 12: True/False

In the space provided, write T if the definition of the numbered word is true or F if it is false.

		T or F
1. MALEFACTOR	ranger	_____
2. MALAPROPISM	faulty stage equipment	_____
3. MALFEASANCE	food poisoning	_____
4. MALICIOUS	spiteful	_____
5. MALADJUSTED	poorly adjusted	_____

6. MALIGNANT	benign	____
7. MALADROIT	clumsy	____
8. MALEVOLENT	bad winds	____
9. MALIGN	defame	____

LESSON 7. "I Do!": *MATER, MATR*

The word "matrimony," meaning *marriage,* derives from the Latin root "mater," *mother,* because the union of a couple was established through motherhood. Most of us accept without question the idea of matrimony based on romantic love, but this is a relatively new belief. Only recently, following the rise of the middle class and the growth of democracy, has there been a tolerance of romantic marriages based on the free choice of the partners involved. Arranged marriages, accepted almost everywhere throughout history, eventually ceased to prevail in the West, although they persist in aristocratic circles to the present. The most extreme application of the custom of arranged marriages occurred in prerevolutionary China, where the bride and groom often met for the first time only on their wedding day.

We've inherited and created a number of significant words from the "mater, matr" root. Below are eight such words to help make your vocabulary more powerful and precise. Study the definitions and pronunciations; then complete the two quizzes.

1. **maternal** (mə tûr′nl) having the qualities of a mother; related through a mother.
    On his maternal side, he is related to Abigail and John Adams.
2. **matron** (mā′trən) a married woman, especially one with children, or one who has an established social position.
    The matrons got together every Thursday to play bridge or mahjong.
3. **mater** (mā′tər) informal or humorous British usage for "mother."
    "Mater is off to London again," said Giles, snidely.
4. **matrix** (mā′triks) that which gives origin or form to a thing, or which serves to enclose it.
    Rome was the matrix of Western civilization.

5. **alma mater** (äl′mə mä′tər, al′-) a school, college, or university where a person has studied, and, usually, from which he or she has graduated. From the Latin phrase meaning *nourishing mother.*

   Ellen's alma mater was Queens College.

6. **matrilineal** (ma′trə lin′ē əl, mā′-) inheriting or determining descent through the female line.

   In a matrilineal culture, the children are usually part of the mother's family.

7. **matronymic** (ma′trə nim′ik) derived from the name of the mother or another female ancestor; named after one's mother. The word is also spelled "metronymic" (mē′trə nim′ik, me′-).

   Some men have matronymic middle names.

8. **matriculate** (mə trik′yə lāt′) to enroll or cause to enroll as a student, especially in a college or university.

   She intends to matriculate at City College in the fall.

Quiz 13: Definitions

Select the word that best fits the definition. Write your answer in the space provided.

_____ 1. that which gives origin or form to a thing, or which serves to enclose it
   a. matrix   b. matrimonial   c. mater   d. alma mater

_____ 2. a school, college, or university at which a person has studied, and, usually, from which he or she has graduated
   a. maternal   b. alma mater   c. maternity   d. matrimony

_____ 3. inheriting or determining descent through the female line
   a. femaleness   b. matrix   c. matrilineal   d. lineage

_____ 4. derived from the name of the mother or another female ancestor; named after one's mother
   a. matriarch   b. matrilocal   c. alma mater   d. matronymic

_____ 5. having the qualities of a mother
   a. alma mater   b. matrilineal   c. maternal   d. matrix

_____ 6. a married woman, especially one with children, or one who has an established social position
   a. matrix   b. matron   c. alma mater
   d. homemaker

_____ 7. to enroll or cause to enroll as a student, especially in a college or university
   a. matriculate   b. graduate   c. matrix   d. alma mater

_____ 8. informal British usage for "mother"
   a. mater   b. matriarch   c. matron   d. ma

Quiz 14: True/False

In the space provided, write T if the definition of the numbered word is true or F if it is false.

		T or F
1. MATRIX	outer edges	_____
2. ALMA MATER	stepmother	_____
3. MATRILINEAL	grandmotherly	_____
4. MATRICULATE	study for a degree	_____
5. MATER	mother	_____
6. MATERNAL	motherly	_____
7. MATRONYMIC	from the mother's name	_____
8. MATRON	single woman	_____

LESSON 8. "BIRTH AND REBIRTH": *NASC, NAT*

The Renaissance (also spelled Renascence) occurred between 1300 and 1600, when the feudal society of the Middle Ages became an increasingly urban, commercial economy with a central political institution. The term "Renaissance," or *rebirth,* was first applied in the mid-nineteenth century by a French historian to what has been characterized as nothing less than the birth of modern humanity and consciousness. The word goes back to Latin "renasci," *to be reborn,* from "re-," *again* + "nasci," *to be born.*

Many significant words evolved from the "nasc, nat" root. Here are eight such words for your consideration. First, read through the pronunciations, definitions, and sentences. Then, to reinforce your reading, complete the two quizzes.

1. **natal** (nāt′l) of or pertaining to one's birth.
   The astrologer cast a natal chart for his client.
2. **nativity** (nə tiv′i tē, nā-) birth; the birth of Christ.
   The wanderer returned to the place of his nativity.
3. **nativism** (nā′ti viz′əm) the policy of protecting the interests of native inhabitants against those of immigrants.
   The supporters of nativism staged a protest to draw attention to their demands for protection against the new-
   comers.
4. **innate** (i nāt′) existing from birth; inborn.
   The art lessons brought out her innate talent.
5. **nascent** (nas′ənt, nā′sənt) beginning to exist or develop.
   The nascent republic petitioned for membership in the
   United Nations.
6. **nationalism** (nash′ə nl iz′əm, nash′nə liz′-) national spirit
   or aspirations; devotion to the interests of one's own nation. From Latin "natio," *nation, race,* derived from
   "nasci," *to be born.*
   Many Americans feel a stirring of nationalism when
   they see the flag or hear the national anthem.
7. **naturalize** (nach′ər ə līz′, nach′rə-) to invest (an alien)
   with the rights and privileges of a citizen. From Latin
   "natura," *birth, nature,* derived from "nasci," *to be born.*
   To become naturalized American citizens, immigrants
   have to study the Constitution of their adopted country.
8. **nee** (nā) born. The word is placed after the name of a married woman to introduce her maiden name. From French
   "née," going back to Latin "nata," *born,* from "nasci," *to
   be born.*
   Madame de Staël, nee Necker, was the central figure in a
   brilliant salon.

Quiz 15: True/False

In the space provided, write T if the definition of the numbered
word is true or F if it is false.

			T or F
1.	NATIVISM	protectionism	_____
2.	NATURALIZE	admit to citizenship	_____
3.	NEE	foreign wife	_____
4.	NATAL	pertaining to birth	_____
5.	NATIONALISM	immigration	_____
6.	NATIVITY	rebirth	_____

7. NASCENT   native-born   _____
8. INNATE   inborn   _____

Quiz 16: Matching Synonyms

Select the best definition for each numbered word. Write your answer in the space provided.

1. INNATE   a. admit to citizenship   _____
2. NATIONALISM   b. relating to birth   _____
3. NATURALIZE   c. beginning to exist   _____
4. NEE   d. birth   _____
5. NATAL   e. protection of native
                             inhabitants   _____
6. NASCENT   f. inborn   _____
7. NATIVISM   g. indicating maiden
                             name   _____
8. NATIVITY   h. patriotism   _____

LESSON 9. "A ROSE BY ANY OTHER NAME": *NOMIN, NOMEN*

The differences between the nominative and objective cases have baffled countless generations of English-speaking students. Is it I or me? Who or whom? The nominative case is so named because it *names* the subject, the doer of the action, whereas the objective case refers to the object, as of a verb or preposition. Here are eight words that use the root "nomin, nomen," *name*.

1. **nominee** (nom′ə nē′) a person named, as to run for elective office or to fill a particular post.
    In order to qualify for consideration, the nominee was required to present a petition with three hundred verifiable signatures.
2. **misnomer** (mis nō′mər) a misapplied name or designation; an error in naming a person or thing.
    "Expert" was a misnomer; "genius" was a far more accurate description of the young chess player.
3. **nomenclature** (nō′mən klā′chər) a set or system of names or terms, as those used in a particular science or art.
    The scientific nomenclature devised by Linnaeus was a great innovation.
4. **ignominious** (ig′nə min′ē əs) disgracing one's name; humiliating; discreditable; contemptible.
    The army suffered an ignominious defeat.

5. **nominal** (nom′ə nl) being such in name only; so-called.
   The silent partner is the nominal head of the firm.
6. **nominate** (nom′ə nāt′) to name (someone) for appointment or election to office.
   The delegate from Vermont was pleased to nominate a favorite son for President at the Democratic convention.

Quiz 17: True/False

In the space provided, write T if the definition of the numbered word is true or F if it is false.

		T or F
1. IGNOMINIOUS	foolish, ignorant	_____
2. NOMINATE	name as a candidate	_____
3. NOMENCLATURE	clamp	_____
4. NOMINEE	candidate	_____
5. NOMINAL	so-called	_____
6. MISNOMER	faux pas	_____

Quiz 18: Synonyms

Select the best synonym for each numbered word. Write your answer in the space provided.

_____ 1. ignominious
   a. ignorant   b. enormous   c. disgraceful
   d. successful

_____ 2. nomenclature
   a. biology   b. classification   c. torture device
   d. international transport

_____ 3. nominee
   a. elected official   b. hereditary title
   c. candidate   d. assumed name

_____ 4. misnomer
   a. misapplied name   b. married name   c. wrong
   road   d. misapplied remedy

_____ 5. nominal
   a. a lot   b. allot   c. so-called   d. summons

_____ 6. nominate
   a. apply   b. designate   c. reject   d. elect

LESSON 10. "DADDY DEAREST": *PATER, PATR*

To sociologists and anthropologists, patriarchy is a system of social organization in which descent is traced through the male line and all offspring have the father's name or belong to his people. Often, the system is connected to inheritance and social prerogatives, as in primogeniture, in which the eldest son is the sole heir. The ancient Greeks and Hebrews were a patriarchal society, as were the Europeans during the Middle Ages. While many aspects of patriarchy, such as the inheritance of the family name through the male line, persist in Western society, the exclusive male inheritance of property and other patriarchal customs are dying out.

From the "pater, patr" root, meaning *father,* we have formed many useful words. Eight of them follow. Go through the pronunciations, definitions, and sentences to help you make the words part of your daily speech and writing. Then complete the two quizzes.

1. **patrician** (pə trish′ən) a member of the original senatorial aristocracy in ancient Rome; any person of noble or high rank.

    You could tell she was a patrician from her elegant manner.

2. **expatriate** (*v.* eks pā′trē āt′; *n.* eks pā′trē it) to banish (a person) from his or her native country; one who has left his or her native country.

    Among the most famous American expatriates in the 1920s were the writers F. Scott Fitzgerald, Ernest Hemingway, and Gertrude Stein.

3. **patronage** (pā′trə nij, pa′-) the financial support or business afforded to a store, hotel, or the like, by customers, clients, or paying guests; the encouragement or support of an artist by a patron; the control of appointments to government jobs, especially on a basis other than merit alone. From Latin "patronus," *patron, protector, advocate,* derived from "pater," father.

    To show its appreciation for its clients' patronage, the beauty shop offered a half-price haircut to all regular customers for the month of January.

4. **paternalism** (pə tûr′nl iz′əm) the system, principle, or practice of managing or governing individuals, businesses, nations, etc., in the manner of a father dealing benevolently and often intrusively with his children.

    The employees chafed under their manager's paternalism.

5. **paternoster** (pā′tər nos′tər, pä′-, pat′ər-) the Lord's

Prayer, especially in the Latin form. The term is often capitalized.

The term "paternoster" is a translation of the first two words of the prayer in the Vulgate version, "our Father."

6. **paterfamilias** (pā′tər fə mil′ē əs, pä′-, pat′ər-) the male head of a household or family.

The paterfamilias gathered his children about him.

7. **patronymic** (pa′trə nim′ik) (a name) derived from the name of a father or ancestor, especially by the addition of a suffix or prefix indicating descent; family name or surname.

Their patronymic was Williamson, meaning "son of William."

8. **patrimony** (pa′trə mō′nē) an estate inherited from one's father or ancestors; heritage.

For his share of the patrimony, John inherited the family mansion at Newport.

Quiz 19: Definitions

Select the word that best fits the definition. Write your answer in the space provided.

_____ 1. the Lord's Prayer
    a. patrician b. paternoster c. paternalism
    d. expatriate

_____ 2. derived from the name of a father or ancestor; family name or surname
    a. paterfamilias b. patronage c. pater
    d. patronymic

_____ 3. the male head of a household or family
    a. paterfamilias b. patronymic c. patrician
    d. patrimony

_____ 4. any person of noble or high rank
    a. patricide b. patrician c. expatriate
    d. patriot

_____ 5. the system, principle, or practice of managing or governing in the manner of a father dealing with his children
    a. paterfamilias b. expatriate c. paternalism
    d. patronymic

_____ 6. to banish someone from his or her native country; one who has left his or her native country
    a. repatriate b. patronize c. paternalize
    d. expatriate

_____ 7. an estate inherited from one's father or ancestors; heritage
   a. patrimony   b. patricide   c. paternoster
   d. patronage

_____ 8. the financial support or business afforded to a store by its clients; the support of a patron; control of appointments to government jobs
   a. patronymic   b. pater   c. patronage
   d. paterfamilias

Quiz 20: Matching Synonyms

Match each of the numbered words with its closest synonym. Write your answer in the space provided.

1. PATERNOSTER	a. financial backing	_____
2. PATRONYMIC	b. exile	_____
3. PATERFAMILIAS	c. male head of a family	_____
4. PATRIMONY	d. fatherly management	_____
5. PATRONAGE	e. the Lord's Prayer	_____
6. PATERNALISM	f. aristocrat	_____
7. PATRICIAN	g. surname	_____
8. EXPATRIATE	h. inheritance	_____

LESSON 11. "KEEP ON TRUCKIN' ": *PED, POD*

From the Latin root "ped" and the related Greek root "pod," both meaning *foot,* we have derived many words relating to movement by foot. The English word "foot" is itself a Germanic cousin of the Latin and Greek forms. One curious aberration is "peddler" (also spelled "pedlar," "pedler"), for it is *not* from the root "ped," as we would expect. The word may be derived from "pedde," a Middle English word for a lidless hamper or basket in which fish and other items were carried as they were sold in the streets, though it is generally thought to be of unknown origin.

   The following eight words, however, all come from the "ped, pod" roots. Practice the pronunciations, study the definitions, and read the sentences. Then, to help set the words in your mind, complete the two quizzes that follow.

1. **quadruped** (kwod′roo ped′) any animal, especially a mammal, having four feet.
   Horses, dogs, and cats are all classified as quadrupeds.

2. **podiatrist** (pə dī'ə trist) a person who treats foot disorders. From Greek "pod-," *foot* + "-iatros," *physician*.
   Podiatrists were formerly known as chiropodists.

3. **chiropodist** (ki rop'ə dist, kī-) a podiatrist. From Greek "cheir," *hand* + "podos," *foot*.
   A chiropodist treats minor problems of the feet, including corns and bunions.

4. **biped** (bī'ped) a two-footed animal.
   Humans are bipeds.

5. **expedient** (ik spē'dē ənt) tending to promote some desired object; fit or suitable under the circumstances. From Latin "expedire," *to make ready,* literally *to free the feet.*
   It was expedient for them to prepare all the envelopes at the same time.

6. **pseudopod** (soo'də pod') an organ of propulsion on a protozoan.
   Amebas use pseudopods, literally "false feet," as a means of locomotion.

7. **pedigree** (ped'i grē') an ancestral line; lineage. From the French phrase "pied de grue," *foot of a crane* (from the claw-shaped mark used in family trees to show lineage); "pied," *foot,* going back to the Latin root "ped."
   The dog's pedigree could be traced six generations.

8. **pedometer** (pə dom'i tər) an instrument that measures distance covered in walking by recording the number of steps taken.
   The race walker used a pedometer to keep track of how much distance she could cover in an hour.

Quiz 21: Definitions

Select the best definition for each numbered word. Write your answer in the space provided.

_____ 1. pedigree
   a. dog training   b. lineage   c. horse racing
   d. nature walking

_____ 2. biped
   a. false feet   b. horses   c. two-footed animal
   d. winged creature

_____ 3. pedometer
   a. race walking   b. jogger's injury   c. foot
   care   d. measuring device

_____ 4. expedient
    a. advantageous b. extra careful
    c. unnecessary d. walking swiftly

_____ 5. quadruped
    a. four-footed animal b. four-wheeled vehicle
    c. racehorse d. four animals

_____ 6. chiropodist
    a. orthopedic surgeon b. chiropractor
    c. podiatrist d. physician's assistant

_____ 7. podiatrist
    a. children's doctor b. foot doctor
    c. chiropractor d. skin doctor

_____ 8. pseudopod
    a. false seed pod b. widow's peak c. bad
    seed d. organ of propulsion

Quiz 22: True/False

In the space provided, write T if the definition of the numbered word is true or F if it is false.

		T or F
1. CHIROPODIST	foot doctor	_____
2. PEDIGREE	lineage	_____
3. EXPEDIENT	advantageous	_____
4. PODIATRIST	foot doctor	_____
5. QUADRUPED	four-footed animal	_____
6. PEDOMETER	scale	_____
7. PSEUDOPOD	cocoon	_____
8. BIPED	stereo	_____

LESSON 12. "IT'S MY PLEASURE": *PLAC*

"S'il vous plaît," say the French to be polite. "Plaît" derives from "plaire," *to please,* which goes back to the Latin "placere." Thus the "plac" root, meaning *please,* forms the basis of the French expression for *if you please.* Many other words, including adjectives, nouns, and verbs, also derive from this root. Below are six "pleasing" words to add to your vocabulary. Look over the pronunciations, definitions, and sentences. Then to reinforce your study, complete the two quizzes.

1. **placid** (plas′id) pleasantly peaceful or calm.
    The placid lake shimmered in the early morning sun.

2. **complacent** (kəm plā′sənt) pleased, especially with oneself or one's merits, advantages, situation, etc., often without awareness of some potential danger, defect, or the like.

   She stopped being so complacent after she lost her job.

3. **placebo** (plə sē′bō) a substance having no pharmacological effect but given to a patient or subject of an experiment who supposes it to be a medicine. From the Latin word meaning *I shall please.*

   In the pharmaceutical company's latest study, one group was given the medicine; the other, a placebo.

4. **placate** (plā′kāt) to appease or pacify.

   To placate an outraged citizenry, the Board of Education decided to schedule a special meeting.

5. **implacable** (im plak′ə bəl, -plā′kə-) incapable of being appeased or pacified; inexorable.

   Despite concessions made by the allies, the dictator was implacable.

6. **complaisant** (kəm plā′sənt, -zənt, kom′plə zant′) inclined or disposed to please; obliging; gracious. From the French word for *pleasing,* derived ultimately from Latin "complacere," *to be very pleasing.*

   Jill's complaisant manner belied her reputation as a martinet.

Quiz 23: Synonyms

Select the best synonym for each numbered word. Write your answer in the space provided.

_____ 1. complaisant
    a. self-satisfied   b. fake   c. agreeable
    d. successful

_____ 2. implacable
    a. obliging   b. foolish   c. calm   d. inexorable

_____ 3. placid
    a. lake   b. tranquil   c. wintery   d. nature-loving

_____ 4. complacent
    a. smug   b. wretched   c. contemplative
    d. obsessively neat

_____ 5. placebo
    a. strong medicine   b. harmless drug   c. sugar
    cube   d. cure

_____ 6. placate
    a. offend   b. advertise   c. cause   d. appease

Quiz 24: Matching Synonyms

Match each of the numbered words with its closest synonym. Write your answer in the space provided.

1. PLACEBO	a. self-satisfied		_____
2. COMPLAISANT	b. serene		_____
3. IMPLACABLE	c. harmless substance		_____
4. COMPLACENT	d. incapable of being appeased		_____
5. PLACATE	e. pacify		_____
6. PLACID	f. obliging		_____

LESSON 13. "THE CITY OF BROTHERLY LOVE": *PHIL, PHILO*

The site of the future city of Philadelphia was settled in the mid-seventeenth century by Swedish immigrants. Later the prominent English Quaker William Penn (1644–1718) determined to establish a New World colony where religious and political freedom would be guaranteed. He first obtained from Charles II a charter for Pennsylvania (named by the king). In 1682 he surveyed the land and laid out the plan for the "City of Brotherly Love," Philadelphia. The settlement flourished from the time of its foundation, growing into a thriving center of trade and manufacturing.

The Greek root "phil, philo," meaning *love,* has given us many other words besides "Philadelphia." Here are ten of them to add to your vocabulary.

1. **philanthropy** (fi lan′thrə pē) affection for humankind, especially as manifested in donations of money, property, or work to needy persons or for socially useful purposes. From Greek "philanthropia," *love of humanity.*

   Millions of people have benefited from Andrew Carnegie's works of philanthropy.

2. **philanderer** (fi lan′dər ər) a man who makes love without serious intentions, especially one who carries on flirtations.

   When she discovered that her husband was a philanderer, she sued for divorce.

3. **bibliophile** (bib′lē ə fīl′, -fil) a person who loves or collects books, especially as examples of fine or unusual printing, binding, or the like. From Greek "biblion," *book* + "philos," *loving.*

The bibliophile was excited by the prospect of acquiring a first edition of Mark Twain's *Life on the Mississippi.*

4. **philharmonic** (fil'här mon'ik) a symphony orchestra.

   The philharmonic is presenting a concert this week.

5. **philately** (fi lat'l ē) the collection and study of postage stamps. From Greek "phil-," *loving* + "ateleia," *exemption from charges* (due to a sender's prepayment shown by a postage stamp).

   To pursue his hobby of philately, the collector attended stamp exhibitions as often as possible.

6. **philhellene** (fil hel'ēn) a friend and supporter of the Greeks.

   George was a philhellene whose greatest passion was ancient Greek sculpture.

7. **philter** (fil'tər) a potion or drug that is supposed to induce a person to fall in love with someone.

   He so desperately wanted her love that he resorted to dropping a philter into her drink.

8. **Anglophile** (ang'glə fīl', -fil) a person who greatly admires England or anything English.

   A devoted Anglophile, Barry visits England at least twice a year.

9. **philodendron** (fil'ə den'drən) an ornamental tropical plant.

   The word "philodendron" originally meant *fond of trees,* but now we use it to refer to a plant.

10. **philology** (fi lol'ə jē) the study of written records, their authenticity and original form, and the determination of their meaning; in earlier use, linguistics. From Greek "philo-," *loving* + "logos," *word, speech, reason.*

    The subject of philology, in its broadest sense, is culture and literature.

Quiz 25: Definitions

Select the word that best fits the definition. Write your answer in the space provided.

_____ 1. a person who greatly admires England or anything English
        a. Anglophile   b. philhellene   c. bibliophile
        d. philanderer

_____ 2. an ornamental tropical plant
    a. philanthropy   b. philodendron
    c. philately   d. Anglophile

_____ 3. a love potion
    a. philhellene   b. philology   c. philter
    d. bibliophile

_____ 4. the collection and study of stamps
    a. philanthropy   b. philology
    c. philharmonic   d. philately

_____ 5. a symphony orchestra
    a. philodendron   b. philter   c. philharmonic
    d. philately

_____ 6. a friend and supporter of the Greeks
    a. philanderer   b. philhellene   c. Anglophile
    d. bibliophile

_____ 7. linguistics
    a. philter   b. philately   c. philosophy
    d. philology

_____ 8. a person who loves books
    a. philanderer   b. philter   c. Anglophile
    d. bibliophile

_____ 9. concern for humanity
    a. philanthropy   b. philodendron
    c. philology   d. philter

_____ 10. a man who makes love without serious intentions,
    especially one who carries on flirtations
    a. bibliographer   b. philanderer
    c. bibliophile   d. Anglophile

Quiz 26: True/False

In the space provided, write T if the definition of the numbered
word is true or F if it is false.

		T or F
1. PHILATELY	fondness for stamps	_____
2. PHILHELLENE	supporter of Greek culture	_____
3. BIBLIOPHILE	lover of books	_____
4. PHILANDERER	womanizer	_____
5. PHILODENDRON	plant	_____
6. PHILOLOGY	study of geography	_____
7. PHILTER	filtration	_____
8. PHILANTHROPY	stinginess	_____

9. PHILHARMONIC   fond of books   _____
10. ANGLOPHILE   stamp collector   _____

LESSON 14. "HANG IN THERE, BABY!": *PEND*

The word "appendix" has two meanings. First, it is an organ located in the lower right side of the abdomen. A vestigial organ, it has no function in humans. Second, it refers to the supplementary material found at the back of a book. The two meanings can be surmised from their root, "pend," *to hang* or *weigh.* The appendix (vermiform appendix, strictly speaking) "hangs" in the abdomen, as the appendix "hangs" at the end of a text.

Knowing the "pend" root can help you figure out the meanings of other words as well. Below are eight such words to help you hone your language skills.

1. **append** (ə pend′) to add as a supplement or accessory.

    My supervisor asked me to append this material to the report we completed yesterday.

2. **appendage** (ə pen′dij) a subordinate part attached to something; a person in a subordinate or dependent position.

    The little boy had been hanging on his mother's leg for so long that she felt he was a permanent appendage.

3. **compendium** (kəm pen′dē əm) a brief treatment or account of a subject, especially an extensive subject.

    The medical editors put together a compendium of modern medicine.

4. **stipend** (stī′pend) fixed or regular pay; any periodic payment, especially a scholarship allowance. From Latin "stips," *a coin* + "pendere," *to weigh, pay out.*

    The graduate students found their stipends inadequate to cover the cost of living in a big city.

5. **pendulous** (pen′jə ləs, pend′yə-) hanging down loosely; swinging freely.

    She had pendulous jowls.

6. **pendant** (pen′ dənt) a hanging ornament.

    She wore a gold necklace with a ruby pendant.

7. **impending** (im pen′ding) about to happen; imminent.

    The impending storm filled them with dread.

8. **perpendicular** (pûr′pən dik′yə lər) vertical; upright.

    They set the posts perpendicular to the ground.

Quiz 27: Matching Synonyms

Match each of the numbered words with its closest synonym.
Write your answer in the space provided.

1. APPENDAGE	a. upright	_____
2. COMPENDIUM	b. salary	_____
3. IMPENDING	c. hanging	_____
4. PENDULOUS	d. adjunct	_____
5. PERPENDICULAR	e. ornament	_____
6. APPEND	f. summary	_____
7. PENDANT	g. attach	_____
8. STIPEND	h. imminently menacing	_____

Quiz 28: True/False

In the space provided, write T if the definition of the numbered
word is true or F if it is false.

		T or F
1. PENDULOUS	swinging freely	_____
2. PERPENDICULAR	curved	_____
3. PENDANT	hanging ornament	_____
4. STIPEND	fasten	_____
5. APPEND	add	_____
6. COMPENDIUM	excised section	_____
7. APPENDAGE	adjunct	_____
8. IMPENDING	imminent	_____

LESSON 15. "OH GOD!": *THE, THEO*

Atheism is the doctrine that denies the existence of a supreme
deity. Many people have been incorrectly labeled atheists because they rejected some popular belief in divinity. The Romans,
for example, felt the early Christians were atheists because they
did not worship the pagan gods; Buddhists and Jains have been
called atheistic because they deny a personal God. The word
"atheism" comes from the Greek prefix "a-," *without,* and the
root "the, theo," meaning *god.*

Many words derive from this root; the following section provides just a few useful examples.

1. **theology** (thē ol′ə jē) the field of study that deals with God
   or a deity.
   Modern theology is chiefly concerned with the relation
   between humanity and God.

2. **theism** (thē'iz' əm) the belief in the existence of a God or deity as the creator and ruler of the universe.

    The religious seminary taught its students the philosophy of theism.

3. **monotheism** (mon'ə thē iz'əm) the doctrine or belief that there is only one God.

    Judaism and Christianity preach monotheism.

4. **theocracy** (thē ok'rə sē) a form of government in which God or a deity is recognized as the supreme ruler.

    Puritan New England was a theocracy, with ministers as governors and the Bible as the constitution.

5. **pantheism** (pan' thē iz'əm) the doctrine that God is the transcendent reality of which the material universe and human beings are only manifestations.

    The New England philosophy of Transcendentalism that flourished in the mid-nineteenth century included elements of pantheism.

6. **apotheosis** (ə poth'ē ō'sis, ap'ə thē'ə sis) the exaltation of a person to the rank of a god; ideal example; epitome.

    This poem is the apotheosis of the Romantic spirit.

7. **theogony** (thē og'ə nē) an account of the origin of the gods.

    Hesiod wrote a theogony of the Greek gods.

Quiz 29: Defining Words

Define each of the following words.

1. pantheism _____
2. theology _____
3. theogony _____
4. theism _____
5. apotheosis _____
6. theocracy _____
7. monotheism _____

Suggested Answers: 1. the doctrine that God is the transcendent reality of which the material universe and human beings are only manifestations 2. the field of study that treats of the deity, its attributes, and its relation to the universe 3. an account of the origin of the gods 4. the belief in one God as the creator and ruler of the universe 5. the exaltation of a person to the rank of a god; the glorification of a person, act, principle, etc., as an ideal 6. a form of government in which God or a deity is recognized as the supreme civil ruler 7. the doctrine or belief that there is only one God

Quiz 30: True/False

In the space provided, write T if the definition of the numbered word is true or F if it is false.

		T or F
1. APOTHEOSIS	epitome	_____
2. THEOGONY	account of the origin of the gods	_____
3. THEOCRACY	religious government	_____
4. THEISM	belief in rebirth	_____
5. MONOTHEISM	viral illness	_____
6. PANTHEISM	rejected beliefs	_____
7. THEOLOGY	study of divine things	_____

LESSON 16. "CALL OUT!": *VOC*

The voice box (more properly called the "larynx") is the muscular and cartilaginous structure in which the vocal cords are located. The vibration of the vocal cords by air passing out of the lungs causes the formation of sounds that are then amplified by the resonating nature of the oral and nasal cavities. The root "voc," meaning *call* or *voice,* is the basis of words like "vocal," as well as a host of other powerful words. Now study the following ten "vocal" words.

1. **avocation** (av′ə kā′shən) a minor or occasional occupation; hobby. From Latin "avocatio," *distraction,* derived from "avocare," *to call away.*
   His avocation is bird-watching.
2. **vocable** (vō′ kə bəl) a word, especially one considered without regard to meaning. From Latin "vocabulum," derived from "vocare," *to call,* from "voc-, vox," *voice.*
   Lewis Carroll coined many nonsense vocables, such as *jabberwocky* and *bandersnatch.*
3. **vociferous** (vō sif′ər əs) crying out noisily; clamorous; characterized by noise or vehemence.
   She was vociferous in her support of reform legislation.
4. **advocate** (ad′və kāt′) to plead in favor of; support.
   The citizens' committee advocated a return to the previous plan.
5. **convoke** (kən vōk′) to summon to meet. From Latin "convocare" ("con-," *with, together* + "vocare," *to call*).
   They will convoke the members for a noon meeting.

6. **evoke** (i vōk′) to call up, as memories or feelings. From Latin "evocare."

   The music evoked the mood of spring.

7. **revoke** (ri vōk′) to take back or withdraw; cancel. From Latin "revocare," *to call again, recall.*

   The king revoked his earlier decree.

8. **invoke** (in vōk′) to call forth or pray for; appeal to or petition; declare to be in effect. From Latin "invocare."

   The defendant invoked the Fifth Amendment so as not to incriminate himself.

9. **equivocal** (i kwiv′ə kəl) of uncertain significance; not determined; dubious. From Latin "aequivocus" ("aequus," *equal* + "voc-, vox," *voice*).

   Despite his demands for a clear-cut decision, she would give only an equivocal response.

10. **irrevocable** (i rev′ə kə bəl) incapable of being revoked or recalled; unable to be repealed or annulled.

    Once Caesar crossed the Rubicon, his decision to begin the civil war against Pompey was irrevocable.

Quiz 31: Matching Synonyms

Match each of the numbered words with its closest synonym. Write your answer in the space provided.

1. CONVOKE	a. word	_____
2. ADVOCATE	b. hobby	_____
3. REVOKE	c. uncertain	_____
4. EQUIVOCAL	d. permanent	_____
5. INVOKE	e. summon	_____
6. VOCABLE	f. pray for	_____
7. EVOKE	g. support	_____
8. VOCIFEROUS	h. loud	_____
9. IRREVOCABLE	i. cancel	_____
10. AVOCATION	j. call up; produce	_____

Quiz 32: True/False

In the space provided, write T if the definition of the numbered word is true or F if it is false.

T or F

1. REVOKE	restore	_____
2. AVOCATION	profession	_____
3. VOCIFEROUS	quiet	_____

4. ADVOCATE   oppose   _____
5. EVOKE   stifle   _____
6. EQUIVOCAL   unambiguous   _____
7. INVOKE   suppress   _____
8. IRREVOCABLE   changeable   _____
9. CONVOKE   summon   _____
10. VOCABLE   word   _____

ANSWERS TO QUIZZES IN CHAPTER 9

Answers to Quiz 1

1. d 2. f 3. i 4. h 5. b 6. e 7. a 8. g 9. c

Answers to Quiz 3

1. a 2. c 3. b 4. d 5. a 6. b 7. b 8. c 9. d 10. d

Answers to Quiz 4

1. T 2. T 3. T 4. F 5. T 6. T 7. F 8. F 9. F 10. F

Answers to Quiz 5

1. c 2. d 3. a 4. a 5. b 6. d

Answers to Quiz 6

1. T 2. F 3. F 4. F 5. T 6. T

Answers to Quiz 7

1. d 2. e 3. g 4. b 5. c 6. a 7. f

Answers to Quiz 8

1. d 2. b 3. c 4. a 5. c 6. b 7. c

Answers to Quiz 9

1. T 2. T 3. F 4. T 5. F 6. F 7. F

Answers to Quiz 10

1. c 2. g 3. f 4. a 5. e 6. b 7. d

Answers to Quiz 11

1. d 2. f 3. i 4. c 5. h 6. b 7. g 8. a 9. e

Answers to Quiz 12

1. F 2. F 3. F 4. T 5. T 6. F 7. T 8. F 9. T

Answers to Quiz 13

1. a 2. b 3. c 4. d 5. c 6. b 7. a 8. a

Answers to Quiz 14

1. F 2. F 3. F 4. T 5. T 6. T 7. T 8. F

Answers to Quiz 15

1. T 2. T 3. F 4. T 5. F 6. F 7. F 8. T

Answers to Quiz 16

1. f 2. h 3. a 4. g 5. b 6. c 7. e 8. d

Answers to Quiz 17

1. F 2. T 3. F 4. T 5. T 6. F

Answers to Quiz 18

1. c 2. b 3. c 4. a 5. c 6. b

Answers to Quiz 19

1. b 2. d 3. a 4. b 5. c 6. d 7. a 8. c

Answers to Quiz 20

1. e 2. g 3. c 4. h 5. a 6. d 7. f 8. b

Answers to Quiz 21

1. b 2. c 3. d 4. a 5. a 6. c 7. b 8. d

Answers to Quiz 22

1. T 2. T 3. T 4. T 5. T 6. F 7. F 8. F

Answers to Quiz 23

1. c 2. d 3. b 4. a 5. b 6. d

Answers to Quiz 24

1. c 2. f 3. d 4. a 5. e 6. b

Answers to Quiz 25

1. a 2. b 3. c 4. d 5. c 6. b 7. d 8. d 9. a 10. b

Answers to Quiz 26

1. T 2. T 3. T 4. T 5. T 6. F 7. F 8. F 9. F 10. F

Answers to Quiz 27

1. d 2. f 3. h 4. c 5. a 6. g 7. e 8. b

Answers to Quiz 28

1. T 2. F 3. T 4. F 5. T 6. F 7. T 8. T

Answers to Quiz 30

1. T 2. T 3. F 4. F 5. F 6. F 7. T

Answers to Quiz 31

1. e 2. g 3. i 4. c 5. f 6. a 7. j 8. h 9. d 10. b

Answers to Quiz 32

1. F 2. F 3. F 4. F 5. F 6. F 7. F 8. F 9. T 10. T

10. GLOSSARY OF IMPORTANT ROOTS TO KNOW

In the previous section, you learned that *roots* are forms like *-term-*, *-theo-*, and *-vac-*, that occur frequently in words taken from other languages, chiefly Latin and Greek. The root *-term-* appeared in such English words borrowed from Latin as *determine*, *exterminate*, *interminable*, *term*, and *terminal*. Learning common roots helps you remember roots and their spellings and figure out their meanings. The following alphabetical list contains the most common roots found in English words.

-acr-, *root.* from Latin, meaning "sharp." This meaning is found in such words as: *acerbic, acrid, acrimonious, exacerbate.*

-acro- *root.* from Greek, meaning "high." This meaning is found in such words as: *acrobat, acronym, acrophobia.*

-act-, *root.* from Latin, meaning "to do; move." It is related to the root -AG-. This meaning is found in such words as: *act, action, exact, transact.*

-ag-, *root.* from Latin and Greek, meaning "to move, go, do." This meaning is found in such words as: *agent, agenda, agile, agitate.*

-agon-, *root.* from Greek, meaning "struggle, fight." This meaning is found in such words as: *agony, antagonist, protagonist.*

-agr-, *root.* from Latin, meaning "farming; field." This meaning is found in such words as: *agriculture, agronomy.*

-alesc-, *root.* from Latin, meaning "grow, develop." This meaning is found in such words as: *adolescence, adolescent, coalesce.*

-alg-, *root.* from Greek, meaning "pain." This meaning is found in such words as: *analgesic, neuralgia, nostalgia.*

-ali-, *root.* from Latin, meaning "other, different." This meaning is found in such words as: *alias, alibi, alien, alienate.*

-alte-, *root.* from Latin, meaning "other, different." This meaning is found in such words as: *alter, alternate, alternative, alternator, altruism, altruist.*

-alti-, *root.* from Latin, meaning "high; height." This meaning is found in such words as: *altimeter, altitude, alto, exalt.*

-am-[1] *root.* from Latin, meaning "love, like." This meaning is found in such words as: *amiable, amorous, amour, paramour.*

-am-² *root.* from Latin, meaning "take out; come out." This meaning is found in such words as: *example, sample.*

-ambl-, *root.* from Latin, meaning "walk." This meaning is found in such words as: *amble, ambulance, ambulate, perambulator, circumambulate.*

-ampl-, *root.* from Latin, meaning "enough; enlarge." This meaning is found in such words as: *ample, amplify, amplitude.*

-andro-, *root.* from Greek, meaning "male; man." This meaning is found in such words as: *androgynous, android, polyandry.*

-anima-, *root.* from Latin, meaning "spirit, soul." This meaning is found in such words as: *animate, animosity, animus, equanimity, inanimate.*

-ann-, *root.* from Latin, meaning "year." This meaning is found in such words as: *annals, anniversary, annual, annuity, biannual, semiannual, superannuated.*

-anthro-, *root.* from Greek, meaning "man; human." This meaning is found in such words as: *anthropocentric, anthropoid, anthropology, anthropomorphism, misanthrope.* See -ANDRO-.

-apt-, *root.* from Latin, meaning "fit, proper." This meaning is found in such words as: *adapt, apt, aptitude, inept.*

-arch-, *root.* **1.** from Greek, meaning "chief; leader, ruler." This meaning is found in such words as: *archbishop, archdiocese, archpriest, monarch, matriarch, patriarch, anarchy, hierarchy, monarchy.* **2.** also used to form nouns that refer to persons who are the most important, most notable, or the most extreme examples of (the following noun): *archenemy (= the most important enemy); archconservative (= the most extreme example of a conservative).* **3.** also appears with the meaning "first, earliest, original, oldest in time." This meaning is found in such words as: *archaeology, archaism, archaic, archetype.*

-arm-, *root.* from Latin, meaning "weapon." This meaning is found in such words as: *armada, armament, arms, disarmament.*

-astro- (or **-aster-**), *root.* from Greek, meaning "star; heavenly body; outer space." These meanings are found in such words as: *aster, asterisk, asteroid, astrology, astronomy, astronaut, disaster.*

-athl-, *root.* from Greek, meaning "contest, prize." This meaning is found in such words as: *athlete, athletics, pentathlon.*

-aud-, *root.* from Latin, meaning "hear." This meaning is found in such words as: *audible, audience, audio, audit, audition, auditorium.*

-bat-, *root.* from Latin, meaning "beat, fight." This meaning is found in such words as: *battalion, batten, batter, battle, combat.*

-bell-, *root.* from Latin, meaning "war." This meaning is found in such words as: *antebellum, bellicose, belligerence, belligerent.*

-bene-, *root.* from Latin, meaning "well." This meaning is found in such words as: *benediction, benefactor, beneficial, benefit, benevolent, beneficent.*

-biblio-, *root.* from Greek, meaning "book." This meaning is found in such words as: *bible, bibliography, bibliophile.*

-botan-, *root.* from Greek, meaning "plant, herb." This meaning is found in such words as: *botanical, botany.*

-brev-, *root.* from Latin, meaning "short." This meaning is found in such words as: *abbreviate, abridge, brevity, brief.*

-cad- (or **-cas-**), *root.* from Latin, meaning "fall." This meaning is found in such words as: *cadence, cadenza, decadent.* See -CIDE-².

-cap-, *root.* from Latin, meaning "take, hold." This meaning is found in such words as: *capacious, captures, caption.*

-caut-, *root.* from Latin, meaning "care; careful." This meaning is found in such words as: *caution, cautious, caveat, precaution.*

-cede-, *root.* from Latin, meaning "go away from; withdraw; yield." This meaning is found in such words as: *accede, antecedent, cede, concede, precede, precedent, recede, secede.* See -CEED-, -CESS-.

-ceed-, *root.* from Latin, meaning "go; move; yield." It is related to -CEDE-. This meaning is found in such words as: *proceed, succeed.*

-ceive-, *root.* from Latin, meaning "get, receive." This meaning is found in such words as: *conceive, deceive, misconceive, perceive, receive, transceiver.*

-celer-, *root.* from Latin, meaning "swift, quick." This meaning is found in such words as: *accelerate, celerity, decelerate.*

-cent-, *root.* from Latin, meaning "one hundred." This meaning is found in such words as: *cent, centavo, centigrade, centimeter, centennial, centipede, century, percent.*

-cep-, *root.* from Latin, meaning "get, receive, take." This meaning is found in such words as: *accept, anticipate, perception, reception.* See -CEIVE-.

-cern-, *root.* from Latin, meaning "separate; decide." These meanings are found in such words as: *concern, discern.*

-cert-, *root.* from Latin, meaning "certain; sure; true." This meaning is found in such words as: *ascertain, certain, certificate, certify, concert, disconcerted.*

-cess-, *root.* from Latin, meaning "move, yield." It is related to -CEDE-. This meaning is found in such words as: *access, accessible, accessory, cession, process, procession, recess, recession, success, succession.*

-chor-, *root.* from Greek, meaning "sing; dance." This meaning is found in such words as: *choir, choral, chord, chorus, choreograph, chorister.*

-chrom-, *root.* from Greek, meaning "color." This meaning is found in such words as: *chromatic, chromosome, lipochrome, monochrome, polychromatic.*

-chron-, *root.* from Greek, meaning "time." This meaning is found in such words as: *anachronism, chronic, chronicle, chronology, synchronize.*

-cide-¹, *root.* from Latin, meaning "kill; cut down." This meaning is found in such words as: *biocide, genocide, germicide, herbicide, homicide, insecticide, matricide, patricide, suicide.*

-cide-², *root.* from Latin, meaning "fall; happen." It is related to -CAD-. This meaning is found in such words as: *accident, incident.*

-cise-, *root.* from Latin, meaning "cut (down)." It is related to -CIDE-². This meaning is found in such words as: *circumcise, decisive, incision, incisor, incisive, precise, scissors.*

-claim-, *root.* from Latin, meaning "call out; talk; shout." This meaning is found in such words as: *acclaim, claim, clamor, exclaim, proclaim.*

-clos-, *root.* from Latin, meaning "close." This meaning is found in such words as: *cloister, close, closet, disclose, enclose.*

-clud- (or **-clus-**), *root.* from Latin, meaning "to close, shut." This meaning is found in such words as: *include, seclude, inclusion, seclusion.*

-cord-, *root.* from Latin, meaning "heart." This meaning is found in such words as: *accord, concord, concordance, cordial, discord.*

-corp-, *root.* from Latin, meaning "body." This meaning is found in such words as: *corpora, corporal, corporation, corps, corpse, corpus, corpuscle, incorporate.*

-cosm-, *root.* from Greek, meaning "world, universe; order, arrangement." This meaning is found in such words as: *cosmetic, cosmic, cosmopolitan, cosmos, microcosm.*

-cour-, *root.* ultimately from Latin where it has the meaning "run; happen." It is related to -CUR-. This meaning is found in such words as: *concourse, courier, course, discourse, recourse.*

-cred-, *root.* from Latin, meaning "believe." This meaning is found in such words as: *credence, credential, credible, credit, credo, credulous, creed, incredible.*

-cres-, *root.* from Latin, meaning "grow." This meaning is found in such words as: *crescendo, crescent, decrease, increase.*

-culp-, *root.* from Latin, meaning "blame." This meaning is found in such words as: *culpable, culprit, exculpate.*

-cum-, *root.* from Latin, meaning "with." It is used between two words to mean "with; combined with; along with": *a garage-cum-workshop (= a garage that is combined with a workshop).*

-cur-, *root.* from Latin, meanings "run; happen." These meanings are found in such words as: *concur, concurrent, currency, current, curriculum, cursive, cursor, cursory, occur, occurrence, recur, recurrence.* See -COUR-.

-cura-, *root.* from Latin, meaning "help; care." This meaning is found in such words as: *accurate, curable, curate, curator, curative, cure, manicure, pedicure, secure, sinecure.*

-cycle-, *root.* from Greek, meaning "cycle; circle; wheel." This meaning is found in such words as: *bicycle, cycle, cyclo, cyclone, cyclotron, recycle, tricycle.*

-dece- *root.* from Latin, meaning "correct, proper." This meaning is found in such words as: *decent, indecent.*

-dent-, *root.* from Latin, meaning "tooth." This meaning is found in such words as: *dental, dentifrice, dentist, dentistry, denture.*

-derm-, *root.* from Greek, meaning "skin." This meaning is found in such words as: *dermatitis, dermatology, dermis, epidermis, hypodermic, pachyderm, taxidermy.*

-dict-, *root.* from Latin, meaning "say, speak." This meaning is found in such words as: *benediction, contradict, Dictaphone, dictate, dictator, diction, dictionary, dictum, edict, predict.*

-doc-, *root.* from Latin, meaning "to teach." This meaning is found in such words as: *docile, doctor, doctrine, document.*

-dox-, *root.* from Greek, meaning "opinion, idea, belief." This meaning is found in such words as: *doxology, orthodox.*

-drom-, *root.* from Greek, meaning "run; a course for running." This meaning is found in such words as: *aerodrome, dromedary, hippodrome, palindrome, syndrome, velodrome.*

-du-, *root.* from Latin, meaning "two." This meaning is found in such words as: *dual, duel, duet, duo, duplex, duplicity.*

-duc-, *root.* from Latin, meaning "to lead." This meaning is found in such words as: *abduct, abduction, adduce, aqueduct, conducive, conduct, deduce, deduct, ducal, duct, duke, educate, induce, induction, introduce, oviduct, produce, production, reduce, reduction, seduce, seduction, viaduct.*

-dur-, *root.* from Latin, meaning "hard; strong; lasting." These meanings are found in such words as: *durable, duration, duress, during, endure.*

-dyn-, *root.* from Greek, meaning "power." This meaning is found in such words as: *dynamic, dynamism, dynamite, dynamo, dynasty.*

-equa- (or **-equi-**), *root.* from Latin, meaning "equal; the same." This meaning is found in such words as: *equable, equal, equanimity, equilibrium, equity, equivocal, inequality, inequity, unequal.*

-fac-, *root.* from Latin, meaning "do; make." This meaning is found in such words as: *benefactor, de facto, facsimile, fact, faction, faculty, manufacture.* See -FEC-, -FIC-.

-face-, *root.* from Latin, meaning "form; face; make." It is related to -FAC-. This meaning is found in such words as: *deface, efface, facade, face, facet, facial, surface.*

-fec-, *root.* from Latin, meaning "do; make." It is related to the root -FAC-. This meaning is found in such words as: *affect, defecate, defect, effect, infect.*

-fed-, *root.* from Latin, meaning "group; league; trust." This meaning is found in such words as: *confederate, federal, federalize, federation.*

-fend-, *root.* from Latin, meaning "strike." This meaning is found in such words as: *defend, defense, defensive, fend, forfend, indefensible, offend, offense, offensive.*

-fer-, *root.* from Latin, meaning "carry." This meaning is found in such words as: *confer, defer, differ, efferent, ferrous, ferry, infer, pestiferous, prefer, transfer.*

-fess-, *root.* from Latin, meaning "declare; acknowledge." This meaning is found in such words as: *confess, confession, confessional, profess, profession, professional, professor.*

-fic-, *root.* from Latin, meaning "make, do." It is related to -FAC- and -FEC-. This meaning is found in such words as: *beneficial, certificate, efficacy, fiction, honorific, horrific, pacific, prolific, simplification.*

-fid-, *root.* from Latin, meaning "faith; trust." This meaning is found in such words as: *confide, confidence, fidelity, fiduciary.*

-fin- *root.* from Latin, meaning "end; complete; limit." This meaning is found in such words as: *confine, define, definite, definition, final, finale, finance, fine, finish, finite.*

-fix-, *root.* from Latin, meaning "fastened; put; placed." This meaning is found in such words as: *affix, fixation, infix, prefix, suffix.*

-flat-, *root.* from Latin, meaning "blow; wind." This meaning is found in such words as: *conflate, deflate, flatulence, inflate.*

-flect-, *root.* from Latin, meaning "bend." It is related to -FLEX-. This meaning is found in such words as: *deflect, inflect, genuflect, reflect.*

-flex-, *root.* from Latin, meaning "bend." It is related to -FLECT-. This meaning is found in such words as: *circumflex, flex, flexible, reflex, reflexive.*

-flor-, *root.* from Latin, meaning "flower." This meaning is found in such words as: *efflorescence, flora, floral, florescence, florid, florist, flour, flourish, flower.*

-flu-, *root.* from Latin, meaning "flow." This meaning is found in such words as: *affluence, affluent, confluence, effluence, effluent, flu, flue, fluctuate, fluent, fluid, flume, fluoride, flux, influence, influenza.*

-foli-, *root.* from Latin, meaning "leaf." This meaning is found in such words as: *defoliate, foil, foliage, folio, portfolio.*

-form-, *root.* from Latin, meaning "form, shape." This meaning is found in such words as: *conform, deform, formalize, format, formula, malformed, multiform, nonconformist, perform, platform, reform, transform, uniform.*

-fort-, *root.* from Latin, meaning "strong; strength." This meaning is found in such words as: *comfort, discomfort, effort, fort, forte, fortify, fortitude, fortress, uncomfortable.*

-fortun-, *root.* from Latin, meaning "by chance; luck." This meaning is found in such words as: *fortuitous, fortunate, fortune, misfortune, unfortunate.*

-frac-, *root.* Latin, meaning "break; broken." This meaning is found in such words as: *fractious, fracture, fragile, fragment, frail, infraction, refraction.*

-frat-, *root.* from Latin, meaning "brother." This meaning is found in such words as: *fraternal, fraternity, fratricide.*

-fug-, *root.* from Latin, meaning "flee; move; run." This meaning is found in such words as: *centrifugal, centrifuge, fugitive, fugue, refuge, subterfuge.*

-funct-, *root.* from Latin, meaning "perform, execute; purpose, use." This meaning is found in such words as: *defunct, disfunction, function, functional, malfunction, perfunctory.*

-fus-, *root.* from Latin, meaning "pour, cast; join; blend." This meaning is found in such words as: *confuse, defuse, diffuse, effusive, fuse, fusion, infuse, profuse, suffuse, transfusion.*

-gam-, *root.* from Greek, meaning "marriage." This meaning is found in such words as: *bigamy, bigamist, gamete, misogamist, polygamy.*

-gen-, *root.* from Greek and Latin, meaning "race; birth; born; produced." These meanings are found in such words as: *antigen, carcinogen, congenital, degenerate, engender, erogenous, eugenics, gender, gene, generate, genus, homogenize.*

-geo-, *root.* from Greek, meaning "the earth; ground." This meaning is found in such words as: *apogee, geography, geology, geopolitics, perigee.*

-gest-, *root.* from Latin, meaning "carry; bear." This meaning is found in such words as: *congestion, digest, gestation, gesticulate, gesture, ingest, suggest.*

-glot-, *root.* from Greek, meaning "tongue." This meaning is found in such words as: *diglossia, epiglottis, gloss, glossary, glossolalia, glottis, isogloss, polyglot.*

-gnos-, *root.* from Greek and Latin, meaning "knowledge." This meaning is found in such words as: *agnostic, cognition, cognizant, diagnosis, diagnostic, incognito, precognition, prognosis, recognize.*

-grad-, *root.* from Latin, meaning "step; degree; rank." This meaning is found in such words as: *biodegradable, centigrade, degrade, grad, gradation, gradient, gradual, graduate, retrograde, undergraduate, upgrade.* See -GRESS-.

-graph-, *root.* from Greek, meaning "written down, printed, drawn." This meaning is found in such words as: *autograph, bibliography, biography, calligraphy, cartography, choreography, cinematography, cryptography, demographic, digraph, epigraph, ethnography, geography, graph, graphic, graphite, hagiography, holography, homograph, ideograph, lexicography, lithography, mimeograph, monograph, oceanography, orthography, paragraph, phonograph, photograph, pictograph, polygraph, pornography, seismograph, telegraph, typography.* See -GRAM.

-grat-, *root.* from Latin, meaning "pleasing; thankful; favorable." This meaning is found in such words as: *congratulate, grateful, gratify, gratis, gratitude, gratuitous, gratuity, ingrate, ingratiate, ingratitude.*

-greg-, *root.* from Latin, meaning "group; flock." This meaning is found in such words as: *aggregate, congregate, desegregate, egregious, gregarious, segregate.*

-gress- *root.* from Latin, meaning "step; move." It is related to -GRAD-. This meaning is found in such words as: *aggression, congress, digress, egress, ingress, progress, regress, transgress.*

-gyn-, *root.* from Greek, meaning "wife; woman." This meaning is found in such words as: *androgyny, gynecology, misogyny.*

-hab-, *root.* from Latin, meaning "live, reside." This meaning is found in such words as: *cohabit, habitant, habitable, habitat, habitation, inhabit.*

-habil-, *root.* from Latin, meaning "handy; apt; able." These meanings are found in such words as: *ability, able, habilitate, rehabilitate.*

-hale-, *root.* from Latin, meaning "breathe." This meaning is found in such words as: *exhale, halitosis, inhale.*

-hap-, *root.* from Old Norse, meaning "luck; chance." This meaning is found in such words as: *haphazard, hapless, happen, mishap, perhaps.*

-helio-, *root.* from Greek, meaning "sun." This meaning is found in such words as: *aphelion, heliocentric, helium, perihelion.*

-here-, *root.* from Latin, meaning "cling, stick tight." It is related to -HES-. This meaning is found in such words as: *adhere, adherent, cohere, coherence, coherent.* See -HES-.

-hes-, *root.* Latin, meaning "cling, stick to." It is related to -HERE-. This meaning is found in such words as: *adhesive, cohesive, hesitate.*

-hetero-, *root.* from Greek, meaning "the other of two; different." This meaning is found in such words as: *heterogeneous, heterosexual.*

-hexa-, *root.* from Greek, meaning "six." This meaning is found in such words as: *hexagon, hexameter.*

-homo-, *root.* from Greek, meaning "same, identical." This meaning is found in such words as: *homogeneous, homogenize, homonym.*

-horr-, *root.* from Latin, meaning "shake, tremble." This meaning is found in such words as: *abhor, abhorrent, horrendous, horrible, horrify, horror.*

-hum-, *root.* from Latin, meaning "ground." This meaning is found in such words as: *exhume, humble, humiliate, humility, humus, posthumous.*

-hydr-, *root.* from Greek, meaning "water." This meaning is found in such words as: *anhydrous, carbohydrate, dehydration, hydrant, hydrate, hydraulic, hydrocarbon, hydroelectric, hydrofoil, hydrogen, hydrophobia, hydroplane, hydroponics, hydrotherapy.*

-jec-, *root.* from Latin, meaning "throw; be near; place." This meaning is found in such words as: *eject, adjacent, adjective, ejaculate, abject, dejection, conjecture, object, reject, inject, project, interject, trajectory, subject.*

-jour-, *root.* from French and ultimately from Latin, meaning "daily; of or relating to one day." This meaning is found in such words as: *adjourn, journal, journey, sojourn.*

-jud-, *root.* from Latin, meaning "judge." It is related to -JUR- and -JUS-. This meaning is found in such words as: *adjudge, adjudicate, injudicious, judge, judicial, misjudge, nonjudgmental, prejudgment, prejudice.*

-junc-, *root.* from Latin, meaning "join; connect." This meaning is found in such words as: *adjoin, adjunct, conjunction, disjointed, disjunctive, enjoin, injunction, join(t), rejoinder, subjunctive.*

-jur-, *root.* from Latin, meaning "swear." It is related to the root -JUS-, meaning "law; rule." This meaning is found in such words as: *abjure, conjure, injure, juridical, jurisdiction, jury, perjure.*

-jus-, *root.* from Latin, meaning "law; rule; fair; just." It is related to the root -JUR-. This meaning is found in such words as: *adjust, just, justice, maladjusted, readjust, unjust.*

-lab-, *root.* from Latin, meaning "work." This meaning is found in such words as: *belabor, collaborate, elaborate, labor, laborious.*

-laps-, *root.* from Latin, meaning "slip; slide; fall; make an error." This meaning is found in such words as: *collapse, elapse, lapse, prolapse, relapse.*

-lat-¹, *root.* from Latin, meaning "carried." This meaning is found in such words as: *ablative, collate, correlate, dilatory, elated, oblate, prelate, prolate, relate, relative.*

-lat-², *root.* from Latin, meaning "line; side." This meaning is found in such words as: *bilateral, collateral, dilate, equilateral, lateral, latitude, unilateral, vasodilator.*

-lax-, *root.* from Latin, meaning "loose, slack." This meaning is found in such words as: *lax, laxative, relax.*

-lec-, *root.* from Latin (and sometimes Greek), meaning "gather; choose" and also "read." This meaning is found in such words as: *collect, eclectic,* *eligible, elite, ineligible, election, lectern, lector, lecture, recollect, select*. See -LEG-.

-leg-, *root.* from Latin, meaning "law" and "to gather," also "to read." It is related to -LEC-. These meanings are found in such words as: *delegate, eclectic, illegal, illegible, intellect, intelligent, legacy, legal, legate, legend, legible, legion, legitimate, legislate, paralegal, privilege, relegate, sacrilege.*

-lev-, *root.* from Latin, meaning "lift; be light." This meaning is found in such words as: *alleviate, cantilever, elevate, elevator, levee, lever, leverage, levitate, levity, levy, relevant, relieve.*

-liber-, *root.* from Latin, meaning "free." This meaning is found in such words as: *deliver, liberal, liberate, libertine, liberty, livery.*

-libr-, *root.* from Latin, meaning "book." This meaning is found in such words as: *libel, library, libretto.*

-libra-, *root.* from Latin, where it has the meaning "balance; weigh." This meaning is found in such words as: *deliberate, equilibrium, librate.*

-lig-, *root.* from Latin, meaning "to tie; bind." This meaning is found in such words as: *ligament, ligature, obligate, oblige, religion.*

-lim-, *root.* from Latin, meaning "line; boundary; edge; threshold." This meaning is found in such words as: *eliminate, illimitable, limbic, limbo, liminal, limit, preliminary, sublime, subliminal*. See -LIN-.

-lin-, *root.* from Latin, meaning "string; line." This meaning is found in such words as: *crinoline, colinear, curvilinear, delineate, line, lineage, lineal, lineament, linear, linen, lingerie, matrilinear, patrilineal, rectilinear.* The meaning is also found in many compound words with *line* as the last part, such as *baseline, guideline, hairline, pipeline, sideline, underline*. See -LIM-.

-ling-, *root.* from Latin, meaning "tongue." This meaning is found in such words as: *bilingual, interlingual, language, lingo, linguine, linguistic, monolingual.*

-lit-, *root.* from Latin, meaning "letter; read; word." This meaning is found in such words as: *alliteration, illiterate, letter, literacy, literal, literary, obliterate, transliteration.*

-lith-, *root.* from Greek, meaning "stone." This meaning is found in such words as: *lithium, lithography, megalith, microlith, monolith, neolithic, paleolithic.*

-loc-, *root.* from Latin, meaning "location; place." This meaning is found in such words as: *allocate, collocation, dislocate, echolocation, local, locale, locate, locative, locomotive, locus, relocate.*

-log-, *root.* from Greek, meaning "speak; word; speech." This meaning is found in such words as: *analog, apology, chronology, decalogue, dialogue, doxology, epilogue, eulogy, ideology, homologous, illogical, logarithm, logic, logo, monologue, neologism, philology, syllogism, tautology, terminology.* See -LOGY.

-loq- (or **-loc-**), *root.* from Latin, meaning "speak; say." This meaning is found in such words as: *circumlocution, elocution, eloquent, grandiloquent, interlocutor, locution, loquacious, magniloquent, soliloquy, ventriloquist.*

-lu- (or **-lav-**), *root.* from Latin, meaning "wash." this meaning is found in such words as: *dilute, lavatory, ablution.*

-luc-, *root.* from Latin, meaning "light." This meaning is found in such words as: *elucidate, lucid, Lucite, lucubrate, pellucid, relucent, translucent.*

-lud- (or **-lus-**), *root.* from Latin, meaning "to play." This meaning is found in such words as: *allude, allusion, collusion, delude, elusive, illusion, illusory, interlude, ludicrous, prelude.*

-lys-, *root.* from Greek and Latin, meaning "to break down, loosen, dissolve." This meaning is found in such words as: *analysis, catalyst, dialysis, electrolysis, electrolyte, hydrolysis, paralysis, paralytic, palsy, urinalysis.*

-man-[1], *root.* from Latin, meaning "hand." This meaning is found in such words as: *amanuensis, legerdemain, maintain, manacle, manage, manual, maneuver, manufacture, manure, manuscript.*

-man-[2], *root.* -man- comes from Latin, meaning "stay; to last or remain." This meaning is found in such words as: *immanent, impermanent, permanent, remain.*

-mand-, *root.* from Latin, meaning "order." This meaning is found in such words as: *command, countermand, demand, mandate, mandatory, remand.*

-mater-, *root.* from Latin, meaning "mother." This meaning is found in such words as: *maternal, maternity, matriarch, matricide, matrimony, matrix, matron.*

-mech-, *root.* from Greek (but for some words comes through Latin), meaning "machine," and therefore "instrument or tool." This meaning is found in such words as: *machination, machine, machinery, mechanic, mechanical, mechanize.*

-medi-, *root.* from Latin, meaning "middle." This meaning is found in such words as: *immediate, intermediate, media, medial, median, mediate, mediator, medieval, mediocre, medium, multimedia.*

-mem-, *root.* from Latin, meaning "mind; memory." This meaning is found in such words as: *commemorate, immemorial, memento, memo, memorandum, memoir, memorabilia, memorial, memory, remember, remembrance.*

-men-, *root.* from Latin, meaning "mind." This meaning is found in such words as: *commentary, mental, mentality, mention, reminiscent.*

-merc-, *root.* from Latin, meaning "trade." This meaning is found in such words as: *commerce, commercial, infomercial, mercantile, mercenary, merchant.*

-merg-, *root.* from Latin, meaning "plunge; dip; mix." This meaning is found in such words as: *emerge, emergency, immerse, immmersion, merge, merger, submerge.*

-meter-, *root.* from Greek, where it has the meaning "measure." This meaning is found in such words as: *anemometer, barometer, centimeter, chronometer, diameter, geometry, kilometer, meter, metric, metronome, nanometer, odometer, parameter, pedometer, perimeter, symmetry.*

-migr-, *root.* from Latin, meaning "move to a new place; migrate." This meaning is found in such words as: *emigrant, emigrate, immigrate, migrant, migrate, transmigration.*

-min-, *root.* from Latin, meaning "least; smallest." This meaning is found in such words as: *diminish, diminution, diminutive, miniature, minimal, minimum, minor, minority, minuend, minus, minute.*

-mir-, *root.* from Latin, meaning "look at." This meaning is found in such words as: *admirable, admire, admiration, miracle, miraculous, mirage, mirror.*

-mis-, *root.* from Latin, meaning "send." It is related to -MIT-. This meaning is found in such words as: *admission, commissar, commissary, commission, compromise, demise, dismiss, emissary, impermissible, intermission, missal, missile, mission, missionary, missive, omission, permission, permissive, promise, promissory, remiss, submission, surmise, transmission.*

-misc-, *root.* from Latin, meaning "mix." This meaning is found in such words as: *miscegenation, miscellaneous, miscellany, miscible, promiscuous.*

-miser-, *root.* from Latin, meaning "wretched." This meaning is found in such words as: *commiserate, miser, miserable, miserly, misery.*

-mit-, *root.* from Latin, meaning "send." It is related to -MIS-. This meaning is found in such words as: *admit, commit, committee, emit, intermittent, noncommittal, omit, permit, remit, remittance, submit, transmit.*

-mne-, *root.* from Greek, meaning "mind; remembering." This meaning is found in such words as: *amnesia, amnesty, mnemonic.*

-mob-, *root.* from Latin, meaning "move." It is related to -MOT- and -MOV-. This meaning is found in such words as: *automobile, mobile, mobility, mobilize.*

-mod-, *root.* from Latin, meaning "manner; kind; measured amount." This meaning is found in such words as: *accommodate, commodious, immoderate, immodest, modal, mode, model, modern, modicum, module, mood, outmoded, remodel.*

-mon-, *root.* from Latin, meaning "warn." This meaning is found in such words as: *admonish, admonitory, admonition, monitor, monitory, monition, monster, monstrous, monument, premonition, summon.*

-monstr-, *root.* from Latin, meaning "show; display." This meaning is found in such words as: *demonstrate, monstrance, muster, remonstrate.*

-mor-, *root.* from Latin, meaning "custom; proper." This meaning is found in such words as: *amoral, demoralize, immoral, moral, morale, morality, mores.*

-morph-, *root.* from Greek, meaning "form; shape." This meaning is found in such words as: *allomorph, amorphous, anthropomorphism, metamorphic, metamorphosis, morph, morpheme, morphine.*

-mort-, *root.* from Latin, meaning "death." This meaning is found in such words as: *amortize, immortal, immortality, immortalize, morgue, mortal, mortality, mortgage.*

-mot-, *root.* from Latin, meaning "move." It is related to -MOV-. This meaning is found in such words as: *automotive, commotion, demote, emote, emotion, immotile, locomotive, motif, motion, motive, motivate, motor, promote, remote.*

-mov-, *root.* from Latin, meaning "move." It is related to -MOT-. This meaning is found in such words as: *movable, move, movement, removal, remove, unmoving.*

-mut-, *root.* from Latin, meaning "change." This meaning is found in such words as: *commute, commutation, immutable, mutate, mutation, mutual, pari-mutuel, permutation, permute, transmute.*

-nat- (or **-nasc-**), *root.* from Latin, meaning "born; birth." This meaning is found in such words as: *cognate, denatured, innate, naive, nascent, natal, nativity, nation, national, native, nature, naturalize, supernatural.*

-naut-, *root.* from Greek, meaning "sailor." It has become generalized to mean "traveler." These meanings are found in such words as: *aeronautic, astronaut, cosmonaut, nautical, nautilus.*

-nav-, *root.* from Latin, meaning "boat, ship." It is related to -NAUT-. This meaning is found in such words as: *circumnavigate, naval, nave, navicular, navigable, navigate, navy.*

-nec- (or **-nex-**), *root.* from Latin, meaning "tie; weave; bind together." This meaning is found in such words as: *annex, connect, disconnect, interconnect, nexus, unconnected.*

-neg-, *root.* from Latin, meaning "deny; nothing." This meaning is found in such words as: *abnegate, negate, negation, negative, neglect, negligee, negligence, negligible, renegade, renege.*

-noc- (or **-nox-**), *root.* from Latin, meaning "harm; kill." This meaning is found in such words as: *innocent, innocuous, nocuous, noxious, obnoxious.*

-noct-, *root.* from Latin, meaning "night." This meaning is found in such words as: *equinoctial, noctambulism, nocturnal, nocturne.*

-nom-¹, *root.* from Greek, meaning "custom; law; manage; control." This meaning is found in such words as: *agronomy, anomalous, anomaly, anomie, astronomy, autonomic, autonomous, autonomy, economy, gastronome, gastronomy, taxonomy.*

-nom-², *root.* from Latin and from Greek, meaning "name." This meaning is found in such words as: *binomial, cognomen, denomination, ignominous, ignominy, monomial, nomen, nomenclature, misnomer, nominal, nominate, nominative, noun, onomastic, onomatopoeia, polynomial, pronominal.*

-norm-, *root.* from Latin, meaning "a carpenter's square; a rule or pattern." This meaning is found in such words as: *abnormal, enormous, enormity, norm, normal, normalcy, normalize, paranormal, subnormal.*

-nota-, *root.* from Latin, meaning "note." This meaning is found in such words as: *annotate, connotation, denote, notable, notary, notarize, notation, note, notorious, notoriety.*

-nounce-, *root.* from Latin, meaning "call; say." It is related to -NUNC-. This meaning is found in such words as: *announce, denounce, mispronounce, pronounce, renounce.*

-nov-, *root.* from Latin, meaning "new." This meaning is found in such words as: *innovate, innovation, nova, novel, novella, novelette, novelist, novelty, novice, novitiate, renovate, renovation.*

-null-, *root.* from Latin, meaning "none; not one." This meaning is found in such words as: *annul, null, nullify.*

-num-, *root.* from Latin, meaning "number." This meaning is found in such words as: *enumerate, innumerable, number, numeral, numerator, numerous, outnumber, supernumerary.*

-nunc-, *root.* from Latin, meaning "call; say." It is related to -NOUNCE-. This meaning is found in such words as: *annunciation, denunciation, enunciate, mispronunciation, nuncio, renunciation.*

-ocul-, *root.* from Latin, meaning "eye." This meaning is found in such words as: *binocular, monocle, ocular, oculist.*

-oper-, *root.* from Latin, meaning "work." This meaning is found in such words as: *cooperate, inoperative, opera, operate, opus.*

-opt-, *root.* from Latin, meaning "choose; choice." This meaning is found in such words as: *adopt, co-opt, opt, option, optional.*

-opti-, *root.* from Greek, meaning "light; sight." This meaning is found in such words as: *autopsy, biopsy, myopia, myopic, ophthalmology, optic, optical, optician, optometrist, optometry, synoptic.*

-ord-, *root.* from Latin, meaning "order; fit." This meaning is found in such words as: *coordinate, extraordinary, inordinate, insubordinate, ordain, order, ordinance, ordinal, ordinary, ordination, subordinate.*

-orga-, *root.* from Greek, meanings "tool; body organ; musical instrument." These meanings are found in such words as: *disorganize, homorganic, inorganic, microorganism, organ, organize, reorganize.*

-ori-, *root.* from Latin, meaning "rise; begin; appear." This meaning is found in such words as: *aboriginal, aborigine, abort, abortion, disorient, orient, orientation, origin, original.*

-pac-, *root.* from Latin, meaning "peace." This meaning is found in such words as: *pacific, pacify, pact.*

-pact-, *root.* from Latin, meaning "fasten." This meaning is found in such words as: *compact, impact, impacted, subcompact.*

-pand-, *root.* from Latin, meaning "spread; get larger." This meaning is found in such words as: *expand, expansion, expanse, expansive, spandrel.*

-par-, *root.* from Latin, meaning "equal; a piece." This meaning is found in such words as: *apart, apartheid, bipartisan, comparable, compare, compartment, counterpart, depart, department, departure, disparage, impart, incomparable, pair, par, parenthesis, part, partial, participle, particle, particular, partisan, partition, party, repartee.*

-pare-[1], *root.* from Latin, meaning "prepare." This meaning is found in such words as: *apparatus, disparate, pare, prepare, preparation, rampart, repair, separate.*

-pare-[2], *root.* from Latin, meaning "to bring forth; breed." This meaning is found in such words as: *multiparous,. parent, postpartum, parturition, viviparous.*

-pass-[1], *root.* from Latin, meaning "step; pace." This meaning is found in such words as: *bypass, compass, encompass, impasse, pass, passable, passage, passageway, passport, surpass, trespass, underpass.*

-pass-[2], *root.* from Latin, meaning "suffer; experience." It is related to -PAT-. This meaning is found in such words as: *compassion, compassionate, dispassionate, impassioned, impassive, passion, passive.*

-pat-, *root.* from Latin, meaning "suffer; experience." It is related to -PASS-[2]. This meaning is found in such words as: *compatible, impatience, impatient, incompatible, patience, patient, simpatico.*

-path-, *root.* from Greek, meaning "suffering; disease; feeling." This meaning is found in such words as: *antipathy, apathetic, apathy, empathy, homeopathy, osteopath, pathetic, pathology, pathos, psychopath, sympathetic, sympathize, sympathy, telepathy.*

-patr-, *root.* from Latin, meaning "father." This meaning is found in such words as: *compatriot, expatriate, paterfamilias, paternal, paternity, patriarch, patrician, patricide, patriot, patron, patroon, patronymic.*

-ped-¹, *root.* from Latin, meaning "foot." This meaning is found in such words as: *biped, centipede, expedient, expedite, expedition, impede, impediment, millipede, moped, pedal, pedicure, pedestal, pedestrian, pedometer, quadruped.*

-ped-², *root.* from Greek, meaning "child." This meaning is found in such words as: *encyclopedia, orthopedic, pedagogue, pedagogy, pederasty, pediatrics, pediatrician, pedophile.*

-pel-, *root.* from Latin, meaning "drive; push." It is related to the root -PULS-. This meaning is found in such words as: *compel, dispel, expel, impel, propel, propeller, repel, repellant.*

-pen- *root.* from Latin and Greek, meaning "penalty; wrong," and hence "repent." These meanings are found in such words as: *impenitent, penal, penalize, penitence, penology, repent, repentance, subpoena.*

-pend-, *root.* from Latin, meaning "hang; be suspended or weighed." This meaning is found in such words as: *append, appendage, appendix, compendium, depend, expend, impending, independent, pending, pendant, pendulum, pendulous, spend, stipend, suspend.*

-pet-, *root.* from Latin, meaning "seek; strive for." This meaning is found in such words as: *appetite, centripetal, compete, competition, competence, competent, impetigo, impetuous, impetus, perpetual, petition, petulant, repeat, repetition.*

-phil-, *root.* from Greek, meaning "love; loving." This meaning is found in such words as: *hemophilia, necrophilia, philander, philanthropic, philanthropy, philharmonic, philodendron, philology, philosophy.*

-phon-, *root.* from Greek, meaning "sound; voice." This meaning is found in such words as: *cacophony, euphony, homophone, microphone, megaphone, phoneme, phonetic, phonics, phonograph, phonology, polyphony, saxophone, stereophonic, symphony, telephone, xylophone.*

-phys-, *root.* from Greek, meaning "origin; form; nature; natural order." This meaning is found in such words as: *geophysics, metaphysics, physic, physician, physics, physiognomy, physiology, physique.*

-plac-, *root.* from Latin, meaning "to please." This meaning is found in such words as: *complacent, implacable, placate, placebo, placid.*

-plaud-, *root.* from Latin, meaning "clap; noise." It is related to the root -PLOD-. This meaning is found in such words as: *applaud, plaudit, plausible.*

-plen-, *root.* from Latin, meaning "full." It is related to the root -PLET-. This meaning is found in such words as: *plenary, plenipotentiary, plenitude, plenteous, plenty, plenum, replenish.*

-plet-, *root.* from Latin and Greek, meaning "full." This meaning is found in such words as: *complete, deplete, plethora, replete.* See -PLEN-.

-plex-, *root.* from Latin, meaning "fold." It is related to the root -PLIC-. This meaning is found in such words as: *complex, duplex, multiplex, perplex, Plexiglas, plexus.*

-plic-, *root.* from Latin, meaning "fold, bend." This meaning is found in such words as: *accomplice, application, complicate, complicity, duplicate, duplicity, explicable, explicate, explicit, implicate, implicit, inexplicable, multiplication, replica, replicate, supplicant.* See -PLEX-

-plod-, *root.* from Latin, meaning "noise." This meaning is found in such words as: *explode, implode.* See -PLAUD-.

-ploy-, *root.* from French and ultimately from Latin, meaning "bend; fold; use; involve." It is related to -PLIC-. This meaning is found in such words as: *deploy, employ, employee, employer, employment, ploy.*

-pod-, *root.* from Greek, meaning "foot." This meaning is found in such words as: *antipode, arthropod, chiropodist, podiatrist, podiatry, podium, pseudopod, tripod.*

-point-, *root.* from French and ultimately from Latin, meaning "point, prick, pierce." It is related to the root -PUNCT-. This meaning is found in such words as: *appoint, disappoint, midpoint, pinpoint, point, pointless, viewpoint.*

-poli-, *root.* from Latin, meaning "polish, smooth." This meaning is found in such words as: *impolite, polish, polite.*

-polis-, *root.* from Greek, meaning "city." This meaning is found in such words as: *cosmopolitan, geopolitical, impolitic, megalopolis, metropolis, metropolitan, necropolis, police, policy, politicize, political, politico, politics, polity.*

-pon-, *root.* from Latin, meaning "put, place." It is related to the root -POSIT-. This meaning is found in such words as: *component, deponent, exponent, opponent, postpone, proponent.*

-pop-, *root.* from Latin, meaning "people." This meaning is found in such words as: *populace, popular, popularity, popularize, populate, populous.*

-port-, *root.* from Latin, meaning "carry; bring." This meaning is found in such words as: *comport, comportment, deport, export, import, importance, important, opportune, opportunity, portable, portage, portfolio, porter, portmanteau, purport, rapport, report, support, transport, transportation.*

-posit-, *root.* from Latin, meaning "to put, place." It is related to the root -PON-. This meaning is found in such words as *deposit, position, postpone.*

-pot-, *root.* from Latin, meaning "power; ability." This meaning is found in such words as: *impotence, impotent, omnipotent, plenipotentiary, potent, potential, potency.*

-pound-, *root.* from French and ultimately from Latin, meaning "put; place." It is related to the root -PON-. This meaning is found in such words as: *compound, expound, impound, propound.*

-preci-, *root.* from Latin, meaning "value; worth; price." This meaning is found in such words as: *appreciate, depreciate, precious, price, semiprecious.*

-prehend-, *root.* from Latin, meaning "seize; grasp hold of; hold on to." This meaning is found in such words as: *apprehend, comprehend, misapprehend, prehensile.* See -PRIS-.

-press-, *root.* from Latin, meaning "squeeze; press (down)." This meaning is found in such words as: *acupressure, compress, compression, decompress, decompression, depress, depression, express, impress, impressive, irrepressible, oppress, press, pressure, repress, suppress.*

-prim-, *root.* from Latin, meaning "first." This meaning is found in such words as: *primacy, primary, primal, primeval, primate, prime, primitive, primo, primogeniture, primordial, prince, principal, principle, unprincipled.*

-pris-, *root.* from French and ultimately from Latin, meaning "grasp; take hold; seize." It is related to the root -PREHEND-. This meaning is found in such words as: *apprise, comprise, enterprise, prison, prize, reprisal, reprise, surprise.*

-priv-, *root.* from Latin, meaning "separated; apart; restricted." This meaning is found in such words as: *deprivation, deprive, privacy, private, privation, privatize, privilege, privy, underprivileged.*

-prob-, *root.* from Latin, meaning "prove." This meaning is found in such words as: *approbation, improbable, opprobrious, opprobrium, probable, probability, probate, probation, probe, probity, reprobate.* See -PROV-.

-propr-, *root.* from Latin, meaning "one's own." This meaning is found in such words as: *appropriate, expropriate, improper, impropriety, misappropriate, proper, property, proprietary, proprietor, propriety.*

-prov-, *root.* from French and ultimately from Latin, meaning "prove." It is related to the root -PROB-. This meaning is found in such words as: *approve, approval, disapprove, disprove, improve, proof, prove, proven.*

-prox-, *root.* from Latin, meaning "close; near." This meaning is found in such words as: *approximate, approximation, proximity.*

-pter-, *root.* from Greek, meaning "wing; feather." This meaning is found in such words as: *archaeopteryx, dipterous, helicopter, monopterous, pterodactyl.*

-pugn-, *root.* from Latin, meaning "fight; fist." This meaning is found in such words as: *impugn, pugilism, pugnacious, repugnant.*

-puls-, *root.* from Latin, meaning "push; drive." This meaning is found in such words as: *compulsion, expulsion, impulse, impulsive, propulsion, pulsar, pulsation, pulse, repulse, repulsive.* See -PEL-.

-punct-, *root.* from Latin, meaning "point; prick; pierce." This meaning is found in such words as: *acupuncture, compunction, expunge, punctilious, punctual, punctuality, punctuation, puncture, pungent.* See -POINT-.

-pur-, *root.* from Latin, meaning "pure." This meaning is found in such words as: *expurgate, impure, impurity, pure, purée, purgative, purgatory, purge, purify, puritan, purity.*

-pute-, *root.* from Latin, meaning "to clean, prune; consider; think." This meaning is found in such words as: *amputate, compute, computation, deputy, dispute, disreputable, impute, indisputable, putative, reputable, reputation.*

-quad-, *root.* from Latin, meaning "four, fourth." This meaning is found in such words as: *quad, quadrangle, quadrant, quadriplegic, quadruped, quadruplet.*

-quer-, *root.* from Latin, meaning "seek; look for; ask." This meaning is found in such words as: *conquer, query.* See -QUIR-, -QUES-, -QUIS-.

-ques-, *root.* from Latin, meaning "seek; look for; ask." This meaning is found in such words as: *conquest, inquest, quest, question, request.*

-quie-, *root.* from Latin, meaning "quiet, still." This meaning is found in such words as: *acquiesce, acquiescent, disquieting, quiescent, quiet, quietude.*

-quir-, *root.* from Latin, meaning "seek; look for." This meaning is found in such words as: *acquire, enquiry, inquire, inquiry, require, requirement.* See -QUIS-, -QUER-.

-quis-, *root.* from Latin, meaning "seek; look for." This meaning is found in such words as: *acquisition, exquisite, inquisitive, inquisition, perquisite, prerequisite, requisite.* See -QUIR-.

-quit-, *root.* from Latin, meaning "release; discharge; let go." This meaning is found in such words as: *acquit, quit, quite, requite, unrequited.*

-quot-, *root.* from Latin, meaning "how many; divided." This meaning is found in such words as: *quota, quotation, quote, quotidian, quotient.*

-rape-, *root.* from Latin, meaning "carry off by force." This meaning is found in such words as: *enrapture, rape, rapid, rapine, rapt, rapture.*

-rase-, *root.* from Latin, meaning "rub; scrape." This meaning is found in such words as: *abrasion, erase, raze, razor.*

-ratio-, *root.* from Latin, meaning "logic; reason; judgment." This meaning is found in such words as: *irrational, overrated, rate, ratify, ratio, ration, rational.*

-real-, *root.* from Latin, meaning "in fact; in reality." This meaning is found in such words as: *real, reality, realistic, realize, really, surreal.*

-rect-, *root.* from Latin, meaning "guide; rule; right; straight." This meaning is found in such words as: *correct, direct, erect, indirect, insurrection, misdirect, resurrection, rectangle, rectify, rectitude, rector, rectum.*

-reg-, *root.* from Latin, meaning "rule; direct; control." This meaning is found in such words as: *deregulate, interregnum, irregular, regal, regalia, regency, regular, regicide, regime, regimen, regiment, region, regional.*

-rend-, *root.* from Latin, meaning "give." This meaning is found in such words as: *render, rendition, surrender.*

-roga-, *root.* from Latin, meaning "ask; demand." This meaning is found in such words as: *abrogate, arrogant, derogatory, interrogate, prerogative, surrogate.*

-rota-, *root.* from Latin, meaning "round." This meaning is found in such words as: *orotund, rotary, rotate, rotation, rotogravure, rotor, rotund, rotunda.*

-rupt-, *root.* from Latin, meaning "break." This meaning is found in such words as: *abrupt, corrupt, disrupt, erupt, eruption, incorruptible, interrupt, rupture.*

-salv-, *root.* from Latin, meaning "save." This meaning is found in such words as: *salvation, salvage, salver, salvo.*

-san-, *root.* from Latin, meaning "health." This meaning is found in such words as: *insane, insanitary, sanatorium, sane, sanitary, sanitize.*

-sanct-, *root.* from Latin, meaning "holy." This meaning is found in such words as: *sacrosanct, sanctify, sanction, sanctity, sanctuary.*

-sat-, *root.* from Latin, meaning "full, enough, sufficient." This meaning is found in such words as: *dissatisfy, dissatisfaction, insatiable, sate, satiated, satire, satisfy, satisfaction, saturate, unsatisfied.*

-scend-, *root.* from Latin, meaning "climb." This meaning is found in such words as: *ascend, condescend, descend, transcend, transcendent.*

-schol-, *root.* from Latin, meaning "school." This meaning is found in such words as: *scholar, scholastic, school, unschooled.*

-sci-, *root.* from Latin, meaning "to know." This meaning is found in such words as: *conscience, conscious, omniscient, omniscience, prescient, prescience, science, scientific.*

-scope-, *root.* from Greek, meaning "see." This meaning is found in such words as: *fluoroscope, gyroscope, horoscope, microscope, microscopic, oscilloscope, periscope, radioscopy, spectroscope, stethoscope, telescope, telescopic.*

-scrib-, *root.* from Latin, meaning "write." This meaning is found in such words as: *ascribe, circumscribe, conscribe, describe, indescribable, inscribe, prescribe, proscribe, scribble, scribe, subscribe, transcribe.*

-script-, *root.* from Latin, meaning "writing." This meaning is found in such words as: *description, inscription, scripture.*

-sect-, *root.* from Latin, meaning "cut." This meaning is found in such words as: *bisect, dissect, intersect, resection, section, sector, vivisection.*

-semble-, *root.* from Latin, meaning "seem; appear(ance)." This meaning is found in such words as: *assemble, assembly, dissemble, ensemble, resemblance, resemble, semblance.*

-sene-, *root.* from Latin, meaning "old." This meaning is found in such words as: *senate, senescence, senescent, senile, senior.*

-sens-, *root.* from Latin, meaning "sense; feel." This meaning is found in such words as: *consensus, dissension, extrasensory, insensible, insensitive, nonsense, sensation, sensational, sense, senseless, sensitive, sensor, sensory, sensual, sensuous.* See -SENT-.

-sent-, *root.* from Latin, meaning "feel." It is related to the root -SENS-. This meaning is found in such words as: *assent, consent, dissent, presentiment, resent, resentful, resentment, scent, sentence, sentient, sentiment.*

-seq-, *root.* from Latin, meaning "follow." This meaning is found in such words as: *consequence, consequent, consequential, inconsequential, obsequious, sequel, sequence, sequential, subsequent.*

-serv-[1], *root.* from Latin, meaning "slave." This meaning is found in such words as: *deserve, disservice, servant, serve, service, servile, servitude, subservient.*

-serv-[2], *root.* from Latin, meaning "save." This meaning is found in such words as: *conserve, conservation, observe, observation, preserve, preservation, reserve, reservation, reservoir, unreserved.*

-sess-, *root.* from Latin, meaning "sit; stay." It is related to the root -SID-. This meaning is found in such words as: *assess, assessor, dispossess, intersession, obsession, possession, repossession, session.*

-sid-, *root.* from Latin, meaning "sit; stay; live in a place." This meaning is found in such words as: *assiduous, dissident, insidious, preside, president,* *presidium, presidio, reside, residual, residue, siege, subside, subsidiary, subsidy, subsidize.* See -SESS-.

-sign-, *root.* from Latin, meaning "sign; have meaning." This meaning is found in such words as: *assign, assignation, consign, cosign, design, designate, ensign, insignia, insignificant, resign, signal, signature, signet, significant, signify.*

-simil-, *root.* from Latin, meaning "alike, similar." This meaning is found in such words as: *assimilate, assimilation, dissimilar, dissimulate, facsimile, similar, simile, simulcast, simulate, simultaneous, verisimilitude.*

-sist-, *root.* from Latin, meaning "remain; stand; stay." This meaning is found in such words as: *assist, consist, desist, inconsistent, insist, irresistible, persist, resist, subsist, subsistence.*

-soc-, *root.* from Latin, meaning "partner; comrade." This meaning is found in such words as: *associate, association, disassociate, disassociation, social, socialize, society, socio-, unsociable.*

-sola-, *root.* from Latin, meaning "soothe." This meaning is found in such words as: *console, consolation, disconsolate, inconsolable, solace.*

-sole-, *root.* from Latin, meaning "only; alone." This meaning is found in such words as: *desolate, desolation, sole, soliloquy, solipsism, solitaire, solitary, solitude, solo.*

-solv-, *root.* from Latin, meaning "loosen; release; dissolve." This meaning is found in such words as: *absolve, dissolve, insolvent, resolve, solve.*

-som-, *root.* from Greek, meaning "body." This meaning is found in such words as: *chromosome, psychosomatic, ribosome, somatic.*

-son-, *root.* from Latin, meaning "sound." This meaning is found in such words as: *consonant, dissonant, dissonance, resonant, resonance, resonate, resound, sonar, sonata, sonic, sonnet, sonogram, sound, supersonic, ultrasonic, unison.*

-soph-, *root.* from Greek, meaning "wise." This meaning is found in such words as: *philosopher, philosophy, sophism, sophistry, sophisticated, sophomore, theosophical, theosophy, unsophisticated.*

-sort-, *root.* from Latin, meaning "kind; type; part." This meaning is found in such words as: *assorted, consort, consortium, resort, sort.*

-spec-, *root.* from Latin, meaning "look at; examine." This meaning is found in such words as: *aspect, expect, inspect, inspector, inspection, introspection, irrespective, perspective, prospect, prospective, prospectus, respect, respectable, retrospect, special, specialty, specialize, specie, species, specific, specify, specimen, specious, spectacle, spectacular, spectrum, speculate, suspect.*

-sper-, *root.* from Latin, meaning "hope; hope for; expect." This meaning is found in such words as: *desperado, desperate, prosper, prosperity, prosperous.*

-spir-, *root.* from Latin, meaning "breathe; have a longing for." This meaning is found in such words as: *aspire, conspire, expire, inspire, perspire, respiration, respiratory, respire, spiracle, spirit, transpire.*

-spond-, *root.* from Latin, meaning "pledge; promise." This meaning is found in such words as: *correspond, correspondent, correspondence, despondent, respond, transponder.*

-stab-, *root.* from Latin, meaning "stand." This meaning is found in such words as: *establish, instability, stabilize, stable, unstable.*

-stan-, *root.* from Latin, meaning "stand; remain." This meaning is found in such words as: *constant, circumstance, distance, distant, happenstance, inconstant, inconstancy, insubstantial, stance, stanch, stanchion, stand, stanza, stanch, substance, substantial, substantive, transubstantiation.*

-stat-, *root.* from Latin (and in some cases from Greek), meaning "stand; remain." This meaning is found in such words as: *hemostat, instate, interstate, misstate, overstate, photostat, prostate, reinstate, rheostat, state, static, station, statistics, stative, statue, status, statute, statutory, thermostat, understate.*

-stin-, *root.* from Latin, meaning "separate; mark by pricking." This meaning is found in such words as: *distinct, distinguish, indistinct, indistinguishable, instinct.*

-stit-, *root.* from Latin, meaning "remain; stand." This meaning is found in such words as: *constitute, constitution, destitute, institute, prostitute, prostitution, reconstitute, restitution, substitute, superstition, unconstitutional.*

-strain-, *root.* from French and ultimately from Latin, meaning "stretch; tighten; bind." It is related to the root -STRICT-. This meaning is found in such words as: *constrain, restrain, strain, strait, straiten, unrestrained.*

-strat-, *root.* from Latin, meaning "cover; throw over" and "level." These meanings are found in such words as: *prostrate, strata, stratify, stratosphere, stratum, substrate.*

-strict-, *root.* from Latin, meaning "draw tight; bind; tighten." This meaning is found in such words as: *constrict, district, redistrict, restrict, strict, stricture, vasoconstrictor.*

-stroph-, *root.* from Greek, meaning "turn; twist." This meaning is found in such words as: *apostrophe, catastrophe, strophe.*

-stru-, *root.* from Latin, meaning "build, as by making layers; spread." This meaning is found in such words as: *construct, construction, construe, destruct, destruction, indestructible, infrastructure, instruct, instruction, instrument, instrumentation, misconstrue, obstruct, reconstruct, structure.*

-stud-, *root.* from Latin, meaning "be busy with; devote oneself to." This meaning is found in such words as: *student, studio, study, understudy.*

-suade-, *root.* from Latin, meaning "recommend; urge as being agreeable or sweet." This meaning is found in such words as: *dissuade, persuade.*

-sum-, *root.* from Latin, meaning "take up; pick up." This meaning is found in such words as: *assume, assumption, consume, consumption, presume, presumption, presumptuous, resume, resumé, resumption, subsume, sumptuous.*

-tact- (or **-tang-**), *root.* from Latin, meaning "touch." This meaning is found in such words as: *contact, intact, tact, tactile, tangent, tangible.*

-tail-, *root.* from French and ultimately from Latin, meaning "cut." This meaning is found in such words as: *curtail, detail, entail, retail, tailor.*

-tain-, *root.* from French and ultimately from Latin, meaning "hold." It is related to the root -TEN-. This meaning is found in such words as: *abstain,* *attain, contain, detain, entertain, maintain, obtain, pertain, rein, retain, retinue, sustain.*

-tech-, *root.* from Greek, meaning "skill; ability." This meaning is found in such words as: *polytechnic, pyrotechnic, tech, technical, technician, technique, technology.*

-temp-, *root.* from Latin, meaning "time." This meaning is found in such words as: *contemporary, contretemps, extemporaneous, tempo, temporary, temporize.*

-ten-, *root.* from Latin, meaning "hold." This meaning is found in such words as: *abstinence, content, continent, countenance, incontinent, impertinent, incontinence, lieutenant, pertinent, retentive, sustenance, tenable, tenacious, tenant, untenable.* See -TAIN-.

-tend-, *root.* from Latin, meaning "stretch; stretch out; extend; proceed." This meaning is found in such words as: *attend, contend, distend, extend, intend, portend, pretend, superintend, tend, tender, tendency, tendon.*

-term-, *root.* from Latin, meaning "end; boundary; limit." This meaning is found in such words as: *determine, exterminate, indeterminate, interminable, predetermine, term, terminal, terminate, terminology, terminus.*

-terr-, *root.* from Latin, meaning "earth; land." This meaning is found in such words as: *extraterrestrial, extraterritorial, subterranean, terrace, terrain, terrarium, terrestrial, terrier, territory.*

-test-, *root.* from Latin, meaning "witness." This meaning is found in such words as: *attest, contest, detest, incontestable, intestate, pretest, protest, protestation, Protestant, test, testament, testate, testify, testimonial, testimony.*

-theo-, *root.* from Greek, meaning "god." This meaning is found in such words as: *atheism, atheist, monotheism, pantheon, polytheism, theocracy, theology, theosophy.*

-therm-, *root.* from Greek, meaning "heat." This meaning is found in such words as: *hypothermia, thermal, thermodynamics, thermometer, thermostat.*

-thes-, *root.* from Greek, meaning "put together; set down." This meaning is found in such words as: *antithesis, epenthesis, hypothesis, parenthesis, photosynthesis, prosthesis, synthesis, synthetic, thesis.*

-tom-, *root.* from Greek, meaning "cut." This meaning is found in such words as: *anatomy, appendectomy, atom, diatom, dichotomy, hysterectomy, lobotomy, mastectomy, tome, tomography, tonsilectomy, vasectomy.*

-ton-, *root.* from Greek, meaning "sound." This meaning is found in such words as: *atonal, baritone, detonate, intonation, intone, monotone, monotonous, overtone, semitone, tonal, tone, tonic, undertone.*

-tort-, *root.* from Latin, meaning "twist." This meaning is found in such words as: *contort, distort, extort, retort, tort, torte, tortilla, tortuous, torture.*

-tox-, *root.* from Latin, meaning "poison." This meaning is found in such words as: *antitoxin, detoxify, intoxicated, intoxication, toxic, toxin.*

-trac-, *root.* from Latin, meaning "pull." This meaning is found in such words as: *abstract, attract, attraction, contract, contraction, detract, dis-*

tract, extract, extractor, intractable, protracted, protractor, retract, subcontract, subtract, tract, tractable, traction, tractor.

-troph-, *root.* from Greek, meaning "food, nourishment." This meaning is found in such words as: *atrophy, isotrophy, phototrophic, trophic.*

-trude-, *root.* from Latin, meaning "thrust, push." This meaning is found in such words as: *extrude, intrude, obtrude, protrude.*

-turb-, *root.* from Latin, meaning "stir up." This meaning is found in such words as: *disturb, disturbance, imperturbable, masturbate, perturb, perturbation, turbid, turbine, turbo, turbulent.*

-type-, *root.* from Greek, meaning "impression." This meaning is found in such words as: *archetype, atypical, prototype, stereotype, type, typical, typify, typography.*

-ult-, *root.* from Latin, meaning "beyond; farther." This meaning is found in such words as: *antepenultimate, penultimate, ulterior, ultimatum, ultimate, ultra-.*

-uni-, *root.* from Latin, meaning "one." This meaning is found in such words as: *reunion, reunite, unicameral, unicorn, unicycle, uniform, unify, unilateral, union, unique, unisex, unit, unitary, unite, university.*

-urb-, *root.* from Latin, meaning "city." This meaning is found in such words as: *conurbation, suburb, suburban, suburbanite, suburbia, urb, urban, urbane.*

-vac-, *root.* from Latin, meaning "empty." This meaning is found in such words as: *evacuate, vacancy, vacant, vacate, vacation, vacuous, vacuum.*

-vade-, *root.* from Latin, meaning "go." This meaning is found in such words as: *evade, invade, pervade.*

-val-, *root.* from Latin, meaning "value; worth; health; be strong." This meaning is found in such words as: *devalue, equivalent, evaluate, prevalent, undervalue, value, valiant, valid, validate, valor.*

-var-, *root.* from Latin, meaning "change." This meaning is found in such words as: *invariable, variable, variance, variant, variation, varied, variegate, variety, variform, various, vary.*

-vec-, *root.* from Latin, meaning "drive; convey." This meaning is found in such words as: *convection, invective, vector.*

-ven-, *root.* from Latin, meaning "come." This meaning is found in such words as: *advent, adventure, avenue, circumvent, contravene, convene, convention, convenience, convent, covenant, event, eventual, inconvenience, inconvenient, intervene, invent, invention, inventory, misadventure, prevent, provenance, revenue, souvenir, unconventional, uneventful, venture, venturesome, venue.*

-venge-, *root.* from Latin, meaning "protect, avenge, punish." This meaning is found in such words as: *avenge, revenge, vengeance.*

-ver-, *root.* from Latin, meaning "true; truth." This meaning is found in such words as: *veracious, veracity, verily, verify, verisimilitude, veritably, verity.*

-verb-, *root.* from Latin, meaning "word." This meaning is found in such words as: *adverb, adverbial, proverb, proverbial, verb, verbal, verbalize, verbatim, verbiage, verbose.*

-verg-, *root.* from Latin, meaning "turn; bend." This meaning is found in such words as: *converge, diverge, verge.* See -VERT-.

-vert- (or **-vers-**), *root.* from Latin, meaning "turn; change." This meaning is found in such words as: *adversary, adverse, advertise, advertisement, aversion, avert, controversial, controversy, conversation, conversant, converse, conversion, convert, diverse, diversion, divert, extrovert, extroversion, inadvertent, incontrovertible, introvert, invert, inversion, irreversible, obverse, perverse, perversion, pervert, reversal, reverse, revert, subversive, subversion, subvert, transverse, traverse, universal, universe, versatile, verse, versed, version, versus, vertebra, vertebrate, vertex, vertical, vertiginous, vertigo.*

-via-, *root.* from Latin, meaning "way; route; a going." This meaning is found in such words as: *deviant, devious, obviate, trivial, via, viaduct.*

-vict-, *root.* from Latin, meaning "conquer." It is related to the root -VINC-. This meaning is found in such words as: *convict, evict, victor, victorious, victory.*

-vide-, *root.* from Latin, meaning "see." It is related to the root -VIS-. This meaning is found in such words as: *evidence, evident, provide, providence, providential, video, videodisc, videocassette, videotape.*

-vinc-, *root.* from Latin, meaning "conquer; defeat." This meaning is found in such words as: *convince, evince, invincible, vincible.* See -VICT-.

-vis-, *root.* from Latin, meaning "see." This meaning is found in such words as: *advice, advisable, advise, envisage, envision, inadvisable, invisible, provision, proviso, revise, revision, supervise, supervision, supervisor, television, visa, visage, vis-à-vis, visible, vision, visit, visor, vista, visual.* See -VIDE-.

-vit-, *root.* from Latin, meaning "life; living." It is related to the root -VIV-. This meaning is found in such words as: *aqua vitae, curriculum vitae, revitalize, vita, vital, vitalize, vitamin.*

-viv-, *root.* from Latin, meaning "life; alive; lively." This meaning is found in such words as: *convivial, revival, revive, survival, survive, survivor, viva, vivacious, vivid, viviparous, vivisection.*

-voc- *root.* from Latin, meaning "call." This meaning is found in such words as: *advocate, avocation, convocation, convoke, equivocal, evocative, evoke, invocation, invoke, irrevocable, provocation, provocative, provoke, revocation, revoke, unequivocal, unprovoked, vocabulary, vocal, vocation, vociferous.*

-vol-, *root.* from Latin, meaning "wish; will." This meaning is found in such words as: *benevolent, involuntary, malevolent, volition, voluntary, volunteer.*

-volv- (or **-volut-**), *root.* from Latin, meaning "turn, roll." This meaning is found in words such as: *evolve, revolve, evolution, revolution.*

-vor-, *root.* from Latin, meaning "eat." This meaning is found in such words as: *carnivore, carnivorous, devour, herbivore, omnivore, omnivorous, voracious.*

-vot-, *root.* from Latin, meaning "vow." This meaning is found in such words as: *devote, devotee, devout, vote.*

-voy-, *root.* from French, ultimately from Latin VIA, meaning "way; send." This meaning is found in such words as: *envoy, invoice, voyage.*

11. LEARNING WORDS FROM THEIR HISTORIES

LESSON 1.

Words, like people, have a past, and as with people, some words have more interesting stories than others. Knowing a word's history can help you remember it and incorporate it into your daily speech. The following ten words have especially intriguing backgrounds. Read through the histories, then complete the quizzes that follow.

1. **bootlegger** (boot′leg′ər) Originally, a "bootlegger" was a person who smuggled outlawed alcoholic liquor in the tops of his tall boots. Today the term is used to mean *someone who unlawfully makes, sells, or transports alcoholic beverages* without registration or payment of taxes.

2. **bugbear** (bug′bâr′) The word refers to *a source of fears, often groundless.* It comes from a Welsh legend about a goblin in the shape of a bear that ate up naughty children.

3. **fiasco** (fē as′kō) "Fiasco" is the Italian word for *flask* or *bottle.* How it came to mean *a complete and ignominious failure* is obscure. One theory suggests that Venetian glassblowers set aside fine glass with flaws to make into common bottles.

4. **jackanapes** (jak′ə nāps′) Today the word is used to describe *an impertinent, presumptuous young man; a whippersnapper.* Although its precise origin is uncertain, we know that the term was first used as an uncomplimentary nickname for William de la Pole, Duke of Suffolk, who was murdered in 1450. His badge was an ape's clog and chain. In a poem of the time, Suffolk was called "the Ape-

clogge," and later referred to as an ape called "Jack Napes."

5. **jeroboam** (jer′ə bō′əm) We now use the term "jeroboam" to refer to *a wine bottle having a capacity of about three liters.* Historically, Jeroboam was the first king of the Biblical kingdom of Israel, described in I Kings 11:28 as "a mighty man of valor," who, three verses later, "made Israel to sin." Some authorities trace the origin of today's usage to the king, reasoning that since an oversized bottle of wine can cause sin, it too is a jeroboam.

6. **nonplus** (non plus′, non′plus) The word "nonplus" means *to make utterly perplexed, to puzzle completely.* The original Latin phrase was "non plus ultra," meaning *no more beyond,* allegedly inscribed on the Pillars of Hercules, beyond which no ship could safely sail.

7. **quisling** (kwiz′ling) This term refers to *a traitor,* a person who betrays his or her own country by aiding an enemy and often serving later in a puppet government. It is directly derived from the name of Vidkun Quisling (1887–1945), a Norwegian army officer turned fascist who collaborated with the Nazis early in World War II.

8. **bowdlerize** (bōd′lə rīz′, boud′-) In 1818, Scottish physician Dr. Thomas Bowdler published a new edition of Shakespeare's works. The value of his edition, he stated, lay in the fact that he had edited it so that all "words and expressions are omitted which cannot with propriety be read aloud to the family." Good intentions aside, he found himself being held up to ridicule. From his name is derived the word "bowdlerize," meaning *to expurgate a literary text in a prudish manner.*

9. **boycott** (boi′kot) In an attempt to break the stranglehold of Ireland's absentee landlords, Charles Stewart Parnell advocated in 1880 that anyone who took over land from which a tenant had been evicted for nonpayment of rent should be punished "by isolating him from his kind as if he was a leper of old." The most famous application of Parnell's words occurred soon after on the estate of the Earl of Erne. Unable to pay their rents, the earl's tenants suggested a lower scale, but the manager of the estate, Captain Charles Cunningham Boycott, would not accept the reduction. In retaliation, the tenants applied the measures proposed by Parnell, not only refusing to gather crops and run

the estate, but also intercepting Boycott's mail and food, humiliating him in the street, and threatening his life. Their treatment of Boycott became so famous that within a few months the newspapers were using his name to identify any such nonviolent coercive practices. Today "boycott" means *to join together in abstaining from, or preventing dealings with, as a protest.*

10. **chauvinism** (shō′və niz′əm) One of Napoleon's most dedicated soldiers, Nicolas Chauvin was wounded seventeen times fighting for his emperor. After he retired from the army, he spoke so incessantly of the majestic glory of his leader and the greatness of France that he became a laughingstock. In 1831, his name was used for a character in a play who was an almost idolatrous worshiper of Napoleon. The word "chauvin" became associated with this type of extreme hero worship and exaggerated patriotism. Today we use the term "chauvinism" to refer to *zealous and belligerent nationalism.*

Quiz 1: Matching Synonyms

Match each of the numbered words with its closest synonym. Write your answer in the space provided.

1. BOOTLEGGER	a. fanatical patriotism	_____
2. BUGBEAR	b. total failure	_____
3. FIASCO	c. expurgate	_____
4. JACKANAPES	d. groundless fear	_____
5. JEROBOAM	e. oversized wine bottle	_____
6. NONPLUS	f. unlawful producer of alcohol	_____
7. QUISLING	g. rude fellow	_____
8. BOWDLERIZE	h. perplex	_____
9. BOYCOTT	i. traitor	_____
10. CHAUVINISM	j. strike	_____

Quiz 2: True/False

In the space provided, write T if the definition of the numbered word is true or F if it is false.

		T or F
1. BOWDLERIZE	expurgate	_____
2. BOYCOTT	male child (Scottish)	_____
3. BOOTLEGGER	petty thief	_____

4. FIASCO	celebration	_____
5. CHAUVINISM	fanatical patriotism	_____
6. JACKANAPES	jack-of-all-trades	_____
7. QUISLING	turncoat	_____
8. BUGBEAR	baseless fear	_____
9. JEROBOAM	ancient queen	_____
10. NONPLUS	certain	_____

LESSON 2.

The origins of most of the following words can be traced to Latin. Read through the histories, then complete the quizzes.

1. **aberration** (ab'ə rā'shən) This word comes from the Latin verb "aberrare," *to wander away from.* A person with a psychological "aberration" exhibits behavior that strays from the accepted path; hence the word means *deviation from what is common, normal, or right.*

2. **abominate** (ə bom'ə nāt') "Abominate" is from the Latin "abominor," meaning *I pray that the event predicted by the omen may be averted.* The Romans murmured the word to keep away the evil spirits whenever anyone said something unlucky. Today we use it to mean *to regard with intense aversion or loathing; abhor.*

3. **abracadabra** (ab'rə kə dab'rə) This intriguing-sounding word was first used as a charm in the second century. The Romans believed that the word had the ability to cure toothaches and other illnesses. Patients seeking relief wrote the letters in the form of a triangle on a piece of parchment and wore it around their necks on a length of thread. Today "abracadabra" is used as a pretend conjuring word. It also means *meaningless talk; nonsense.*

4. **wiseacre** (wīz'ā'kər) Although the word "acre" in "wiseacre" makes it appear that the term refers to a unit of measurement, "wiseacre" is actually used contemptuously to mean *a wise guy* or *a smart aleck.* The term comes from the Dutch "wijssegger," which means *soothsayer.* Since soothsayers were considered learned, it was logical to call them "wise," which is what "wijs" means. The word "acre" is a mispronunciation of the Dutch "segger," *sayer.* There is a famous story in which the word was used in its present sense. In response to the bragging of a wealthy

landowner, the English playwright Ben Jonson is said to have replied, "What care we for your dirt and clods? Where you have an acre of land, I have ten acres of wit." The chastened landowner is reported to have muttered: "He's Mr. Wiseacre."

5. **ebullient** (i bul′yənt, i bŏŏl′-) This word derives from the Latin "ebullire," *to boil over.* A person who is "ebullient" is *overflowing with fervor, enthusiasm, or excitement.*

6. **enclave** (en′klāv, än′-) The word "enclave" refers to *a country or territory entirely or mostly surrounded by another country.* More generally, it means *a group enclosed or isolated within a larger one.* The word comes ultimately from Latin "inclavare," *to lock in.*

7. **expedite** (ek′spi dīt′) The word "expedite" means *to speed up the progress of something.* It comes from the Latin "expedire," *to set the feet free.*

8. **expunge** (ik spunj′) To indicate that a soldier had retired from service, the ancient Romans wrote a series of dots or points beneath his name on the service lists. The Latin "expungere" thus meant both *to prick through* and *to mark off on a list.* Similarly, the English word "expunge" means *to strike or blot out; to erase.*

9. **inchoate** (in kō′it, -āt) "Inchoate" comes from the Latin "inchoare," *to begin.* Thus, an "inchoate" plan is *not yet fully developed,* or *rudimentary.*

10. **prevaricate** (pri var′i kāt′) Today "prevaricate" means *to speak falsely or misleadingly with deliberate intent; to lie.* It has its origin in a physical act. The Latin verb "praevaricare" means *to spread apart.* The plowman who "prevaricated," then, made crooked ridges, deviating from straight furrows in the field.

Quiz 3: True/False

In the space provided, write T if the definition of the numbered word is true or F if it is false.

		T or F
1. ENCLAVE	rendezvous	_____
2. ABOMINATE	detest	_____
3. WISEACRE	large ranch	_____
4. EXPUNGE	erase	_____
5. PREVARICATE	preplan	_____
6. INCHOATE	illogical	_____

7. ABERRATION	fidelity	_____
8. EXPEDITE	slow down	_____
9. ABRACADABRA	hocus-pocus	_____
10. EBULLIENT	enthusiastic	_____

Quiz 4: Matching Synonyms

Match each of the following numbered words with its closest synonym. Write your answer in the space provided.

1. WISEACRE	a. dispatch	_____
2. ENCLAVE	b. divergence	_____
3. INCHOATE	c. smarty-pants	_____
4. ABOMINATE	d. obliterate	_____
5. ABERRATION	e. misstate	_____
6. ABRACADABRA	f. enclosure	_____
7. EXPUNGE	g. detest	_____
8. EXPEDITE	h. mumbo-jumbo	_____
9. EBULLIENT	i. incipient	_____
10. PREVARICATE	j. high-spirited	_____

LESSON 3.

Powerful words may have their beginnings in historical events, myths and legends, and special terminology. Here are ten more powerful words with interesting or unusual histories. Read through the etymologies (word origins), then complete the quizzes that follow.

1. **impeccable** (im pek′ə bəl) The word comes from the Latin "impeccabilis," *without sin.* The religious meaning has been only slightly extended over the years. Today an "impeccable" reputation is *faultless, flawless, irreproachable.*

2. **ambrosia** (am brō′zhə) Originally, "ambrosia" was the food of the Olympian gods (as "nectar" was their drink). The word comes from the Greek "a-," *not,* and "brostos," *mortal;* hence, eating ambrosia conferred immortality. Today the word means *an especially delicious food,* with the implication that the concoction is savory enough to be fit for the gods. One popular dessert by this name contains shredded coconut, sliced fruits, and cream.

3. **gerrymander** (jer′i man′dər, ger′-) In 1812, Massachusetts governor Elbridge Gerry conspired with his party to

change the boundaries of voting districts to enhance their own political clout. Noticing that one such district resembled a salamander, a newspaper editor coined the term "gerrymander" to describe *the practice of dividing a state, county, etc., into election districts so as to give one political party a majority while concentrating the voting strength of the other party into as few districts as possible.*

4. **mesmerize** (mez′mə rīz′, mes′-) The Austrian doctor Friedrich Anton Mesmer first publicly demonstrated the technique of hypnotism in 1775. Today the term "mesmerize" is still used as a synonym for "hypnotize," but it has broadened to also mean *spellbind* or *fascinate.*

5. **quintessence** (kwin tes′əns) The word comes from the medieval Latin term "quinta essentia," *the fifth essence.* This fifth primary element was thought to be ether, supposedly the constituent matter of the heavenly bodies, the other four elements being air, fire, earth, and water. The medieval alchemists tried to isolate ether through distillation. These experiments gave us the contemporary meaning of the word: *the pure and concentrated essence of a substance.*

6. **desultory** (des′əl tôr′ē) Some Roman soldiers went into battle with two horses, so that when one steed wearied, the soldier could vault onto the second horse striding along parallel to the first without losing any time. The same skill was employed by circus performers, especially charioteers, who could leap between two chariots riding abreast. Such a skilled horseman was called a "desultor," *a leaper.* Perhaps because these equestrians stayed only briefly on their mounts, the word "desultory" acquired its present meaning, *lacking in consistency, constancy, or visible order.*

7. **aegis** (ē′jis) When Zeus emerged victorious from his rebellion against the Titans, he attributed his success in part to his shield, which bore at its center the head of one of the Gorgons. The shield was reputedly made of goatskin, and hence its name, "aigis," was said to derive from the Greek "aig-," the stem of "aix," *goat.* Our present use of the word to mean *protection* or *sponsorship* evolved from the notion of eighteenth-century English writers who assumed that the "egis" of Zeus or Athena—or their Roman counterparts Jove and Minerva—protected all those who came under its influence. Today the preferred spelling of the word is "aegis."

8. **adieu** (ə dōō′, ə dyōō′) The French expression "à Dieu" literally means *to God.* It is an abbreviation of the sentence "Je vous recommande à Dieu," *I commend you to God,* used between friends at parting. Both in French and in English the word means *good-bye* or *farewell.*

9. **aloof** (ə lōōf′) The word was originally a sailor's term, "a loof," *to the luff or windward direction,* perhaps from the Dutch "te loef," *to windward.* Etymologists believe that our use of the word to mean *at a distance, especially in feeling or interest,* comes from the idea of keeping a ship's head to the wind, and thus clear of the lee shore toward which it might drift.

10. **bluestocking** (blōō′stok′ing) A "bluestocking" is *a woman with considerable scholarly, literary, or intellectual ability or interest.* The word originated in connection with intellectual gatherings held in London about 1750 in the homes of women bored by the more frivolous pastimes of their age. Lavish evening dress was not required at these affairs; in fact, to put at ease visitors who could not afford expensive clothing, the women themselves dressed simply. One of the male guests went so far as to wear his everyday blue worsted stockings rather than the black silk ones usually worn at evening social gatherings. In response to their interests and dress, the English naval officer Admiral Edward Boscawen (1711–1761) is said to have sarcastically called these gatherings "the Blue Stocking Society."

Quiz 5: Definitions
Select the best definition for each numbered word. Circle your answer.

1. mesmerize
   a. attack   b. burst forth   c. fascinate
2. desultory
   a. aggressive   b. fitful   c. nasty
3. aloof
   a. remote   b. sailing   c. windy
4. aegis
   a. intense interest   b. goat   c. sponsorship
5. gerrymander
   a. medieval gargoyle   b. combine for historical sense
   c. redistrict for political advantage

6. impeccable
   a. guileless   b. perfect   c. impeachable
7. adieu
   a. good-bye   b. hello   c. about-face
8. ambrosia
   a. suppository   b. flower   c. delicious food
9. quintessence
   a. pith   b. fruit   c. oil
10. bluestocking
   a. ill-dressed woman   b. intellectual woman   c. poor man

Quiz 6: Matching Synonyms

Select the best synonym for each numbered word. Write your answer in the space provided.

1. ADIEU	a. delicious food	_____
2. ALOOF	b. inconsistent; random	_____
3. GERRYMANDER	c. distant; remote	_____
4. AMBROSIA	d. farewell	_____
5. IMPECCABLE	e. sponsorship	_____
6. BLUESTOCKING	f. enthrall	_____
7. DESULTORY	g. without fault	_____
8. AEGIS	h. concentrated essence	_____
9. MESMERIZE	i. divide a political district	_____
10. QUINTESSENCE	j. a well-read woman	_____

Lesson 4.

The following words are all based on Greek myths and legends. Read through their histories, then complete the quizzes.

1. **amazon** (am′ə zon′) The word comes ultimately from the Greek, but the origin of the Greek word is uncertain. "Amazon" refers to *a tall, powerful, aggressive woman.* The Amazons of legend were female warriors, allied with the Trojans against the Greeks.
2. **anemone** (ə nem′ə nē′) This spring flower is named for Anemone, daughter of the wind. It comes from Greek "anemos," *the wind.*
3. **cornucopia** (kôr′nə kō′pē ə, -nyə-) According to Greek mythology, to save the infant Zeus from being swallowed by his father, Cronus, his mother, Rhea, hid her son in a

cave and tricked Cronus into swallowing a stone wrapped in a cloth. The infant was then entrusted to the care of the nymph Amaltheia, who fed him on goat's milk. One day she filled a goat's horn with fresh fruit and herbs. The horn was thereafter magically refilled, no matter how much the child ate. To the Greeks, this boundless source was the horn of Amaltheia; to the Romans, it was the "cornu copiae," from "cornu," *horn,* and "copia," *plenty.* We know a "cornucopia" as *a horn containing food or drink in endless supply* or *horn of plenty.* It is often used as a symbol of abundance.

4. **diadem** (dī′ə dem′) In his quest to create a vast, unified empire with Babylon as its capital, the Macedonian hero Alexander the Great adopted a number of Persian and Oriental customs. He began to wear a blue-edged white headband with two ends trailing to the shoulders, a Persian symbol of royalty. The Greeks called this headpiece a "diadema," literally *a binding over.* The headpiece was adopted by other monarchs down through the ages and further embellished with gold and gems, eventually evolving into a rich crown. Today a "diadem" is *a crown* or *a headband worn as a symbol of royalty.*

5. **epicure** (ep′i kyo͞or′) Epicurus was a Greek philosopher who lived from 342 to 270 B.C. He believed that pleasure, attained mainly through pure and noble thoughts, constituted the highest happiness. After his death, his disciples spread his views. Their critics argued that Epicurus's theory was little more than an excuse for debauchery. From this argument we derive the present-day meaning of "epicure," *a person with luxurious tastes or habits, especially in eating or drinking.*

6. **esoteric** (es′ə ter′ik) From the Greek "esoterikos," *inner,* the word was used to describe the secret doctrines taught by the philosopher Pythagoras to a select few of his disciples. Hence "esoteric" means *understood by or meant only for those who have special knowledge or interest; recondite.*

7. **labyrinth** (lab′ə rinth) According to the Greek myth, King Minos of Crete ordered Daedalus to build a prison for the Minotaur, a half-bull, half-human monster. Daedalus succeeded by creating a series of twisting passageways that kept the monster imprisoned. Today a "labyrinth" is *a devious arrangement of linear patterns forming a design; a maze.*

8. **lethargy** (leth′ər jē) The Greeks believed in an afterlife. In their mythology, the dead crossed the river Lethe, which flowed through Hades, the underground realm. Anyone who drank its water forgot the past. The Greek word "lethargia" derives from "lethe," *forgetfulness.* Hence our English word "lethargy," *drowsiness* or *sluggishness.*

9. **mentor** (men′tôr, -tər) In the *Odyssey* of Homer, Mentor is Odysseus's friend and tutor to his son Telemachus. Today the word "mentor" means *trusted teacher or guide.*

10. **nemesis** (nem′ə sis) Nemesis was the Greek goddess of vengeance, whose task it was to punish the proud and the insolent. Today a "nemesis" is *an agent or act of retribution or punishment,* or *something that a person cannot conquer or achieve.*

Quiz 7: True/False

In the space provided, write T if the definition of the numbered word is true or F if it is false.

		T or F
1. DIADEM	crown	_____
2. LABYRINTH	lazy	_____
3. MENTOR	mendacious	_____
4. AMAZON	female warrior	_____
5. ANEMONE	mollusk	_____
6. ESOTERIC	arcane	_____
7. LETHARGY	lassitude	_____ .
8. NEMESIS	downfall	_____
9. CORNUCOPIA	foot ailment	_ -
10. EPICURE	hidden	_____

Quiz 8: Defining Words

Define each of the following words.

1. diadem _____
2. esoteric _____
3. mentor _____
4. nemesis _____
5. amazon _____
6. epicure _____
7. anemone _____
8. cornucopia _____

9. labyrinth _____
10. lethargy _____

Suggested Answers: 1. crown 2. meant only for the select few with special knowledge or interest 3. trusted teacher or guide 4. act of retribution, or that which a person cannot conquer or achieve 5. female warrior 6. a person with luxurious tastes or habits, especially in eating or drinking 7. flower 8. boundless source 9. maze 10. sluggishness; weariness

Lesson 5.

Now study the curious origins of these ten words and work through the two quizzes that follow.

1. **ostracize** (os′trə sīz′) The word "ostracize" comes originally from the Greek "ostrakon," *tile, potsherd, shell.* It refers to the ancient Greek practice of banishing a man by writing his name on a shell or a bit of earthen tile. Anyone considered dangerous to the state was sent into exile for ten years. The judges cast their votes by writing on the shells or pottery shards and dropping them into an urn. The word "ostracize" still retains the same sense, *to exclude, by general consent, from society.*

2. **sycophant** (sik′ə fənt, -fant′) The word "sycophant" now means *a self-seeking, servile flatterer.* Originally, it was used to refer to an informer or slanderer. Curiously, it comes from Greek "sykon," *fig,* and "-phantes," *one who shows;* thus, *a fig-shower.* One explanation for this odd coinage is that in ancient Greece a sycophant was an informer against merchants engaged in the unlawful exportation of figs.

3. **cynosure** (sī′nə shŏŏr′, sin′ə-) According to the myth, Zeus chose to honor the nymph who cared for him in his infancy by placing her in the sky as a constellation. One of her stars was so brilliant and stationary that all the other stars seemed to revolve around it. To the practical-minded ancient mariners, however, the bottom three stars of the constellation looked like a dog's tail. They named the entire constellation "Cynosura," *dog's tail.* From its name we get our word "cynosure," *something that attracts attention by its brilliance or interest.* By the way, we now call the constellation "Ursa Minor," *Little Bear,* and the bright star "Polaris," *Pole Star* or *North Star.*

4. **belfry** (bel′frē) Oddly enough, this word has nothing to do with bells, except by association. Originally, a "belfry" was a movable tower rolled up close to the walls of a besieged city by soldiers in wartime. Later, a belfry was a tower to protect watchmen, or a watchtower in which alarm bells were hung, through which usage it finally became *a bell tower.* The word came into English from Old French, which in turn may have taken it from a Germanic military term.

5. **debauch** (di bôch′) Today we define the word "debauch" as *to corrupt by sensuality, intemperance, etc.* It comes from the French word "débaucher," meaning *to entice away from work or duty.*

6. **eldorado** (el′də rä′dō, -rā′-) The word comes from Spanish legends of an incredibly wealthy city in South America, so rich that its streets were paved with gold. Many adventurers set off to find this elusive city; in 1595 Sir Walter Raleigh ventured into Guiana in a vain attempt to locate it. Among the Spaniards, the king of this fabulous land came to be called "El Dorado," *the Golden One.* Today "eldorado" is used generally to mean *any fabulously wealthy place.*

7. **esquire** (es′kwī³r) In medieval times, young men who wished to become knights first had to serve other knights. Their primary duty was to act as shield bearer. Because of this duty, the young man was called an "esquire," from the French "esquier," *shield bearer,* ultimately going back to the Latin "scutum," *shield.* Later the title "esquire" came to be attached to the sons of a nobleman; eventually it referred to any man considered a gentleman. Today it is often appended to a lawyer's name; in Britain, it is applied to a member of the gentry ranking next below a knight.

8. **filibuster** (fil′ə bus′tər) In the seventeenth century, English seamen who attacked Spanish ships and brought back wealth from New Spain were called "buccaneers." In Holland, they were known as "vrijbuiters," *free robbers.* In French, the word became first "fribustier" and then "flibustier." In Spain, the term was "filibustero." Then, when the nineteenth-century American soldier of fortune William Walker tried to capture Sonora, Mexico, the Mexicans promptly dubbed him a "filibuster." Today the term refers to *the use of irregular or disruptive tactics, such as exceptionally long speeches, by a member of a legislative as-*

sembly. The current use of the word may have arisen through a comparison of a legislator's determination to block a bill with the tactics used by William Walker to evade the law.

9. **furlong** (fûr′lông, -long) In the twelfth century, an acre of land was defined as the area a yoke of oxen could plow in one day. As such, the size varied from place to place but always greatly exceeded what we accept today as an acre. In some places, an acre was defined by the area a team of eight oxen could plow in a day—about an eighth of a Roman mile, also called a "stadium." The length of the plow's furrows were thus each about a stadium in length; this became a convenient measure of distance—a "fur-lang" in Old English, from "furh," *furrow,* and "lang," *long.* This measure was then standardized to an area forty rods in length by four rods in width; however, the rod was not a standard measure either. Later, when the length of a yard was standardized, "furlong" came to be used simply as a term for *a unit of distance an eighth of a mile or 220 yards in length.*

10. **galvanism** (gal′və niz′əm) In the mid-eighteenth century, Luigi Galvani, a professor of anatomy at the University of Bologna, concluded that the nerves are a source of electricity. Although Volta later proved his theory incorrect, Galvani's pioneering work inspired other scientists to produce electricity by chemical means. Today the term "galvanism," *electricity,* honors Galvani.

Quiz 9: Definitions

Each of the following phrases contains an italicized word. See how many you can define correctly. Write your answer in the space provided.

_____ 1. bats in the *belfry*
    a. cave b. brain c. bell tower d. tropical tree

_____ 2. *ostracized* from society
    a. banished b. beaten c. walked d. welcomed

_____ 3. a hopeless *sycophant*
    a. dreamer b. alcoholic c. romantic d. toady

_____ 4. travel a *furlong*
    a. acre b. year c. week d. less than a mile

_____ 5. seek *eldorado*
    a. physical comfort b. delicious food c. wealthy place d. death

_____ 6. add the title *esquire*
   a. gentleman   b. married man   c. duke
   d. professional
_____ 7. *debauched* by the experience
   a. impoverished   b. corrupted
   c. strengthened   d. enriched
_____ 8. a lengthy *filibuster*
   a. entertainment   b. obstructive tactics
   c. childhood   d. voyage
_____ 9. powerful *galvanism*
   a. electric current   b. discoveries   c. gases
   d. weapons
_____ 10. the *cynosure* of all eyes
   a. defect   b. attraction   c. sky-blue color
   d. cynicism

Quiz 10: True/False

In the space provided, write T if the definition of the numbered word is true or F if it is false.

			T or F
1.	BELFRY	steeple	_____
2.	DEBAUCH	corrupt	_____
3.	ESQUIRE	attorney's title	_____
4.	OSTRACIZE	exclude	_____
5.	FILIBUSTER	obstruction	_____
6.	FURLONG	eighth of a mile	_____
7.	CYNOSURE	sarcasm	_____
8.	ELDORADO	Spain	_____
9.	GALVANISM	atomic power	_____
10.	SYCOPHANT	flatterer	_____

LESSON 6.

Our language is enriched by many exotic words with curious histories. Here are ten new ones to add to your growing vocabulary. Read through the etymologies and complete the two quizzes that follow.

1. **juggernaut** (jug′ər nôt′, -not′) Our modern word "juggernaut" comes from the Hindi name for a huge image of the god Vishnu, "Jagannath," at Puri, a city in Orissa, India.

Each summer, the statue is moved to a new location a little less than a mile away from the old one. Early tourists to India brought back strange stories of worshipers throwing themselves under the wheels of the wagon carrying the idol. Since any shedding of blood in the presence of the god is sacrilege, what these travelers probably witnessed was a weary pilgrim being accidentally crushed to death. Thus, thanks to exaggeration and ignorance, "juggernaut" came to mean *blind and relentless self-sacrifice.* In addition, the word means *any large, overpowering, or destructive force.*

2. **iconoclast** (ī kon′ə klast′) An "iconoclast" is *a person who attacks cherished beliefs or traditional institutions.* It is from the Greek "eikon," *image,* and "klastes," *breaker.* Although the contemporary usage is figurative, the word was originally used in a literal sense to describe the great controversy within the Christian church in the eighth century over religious images. One camp held that all visual representations should be destroyed because they encouraged idol worship; the other, that such artworks simply inspired the viewers to feel more religious. By the mid-eighth century, untold numbers of relics and images had been destroyed. The issue was not settled for nearly a century, when the images were restored to the church in Constantinople.

3. **laconic** (lə kon′ik) In Sparta, the capital of the ancient Greek region of Laconia, the children were trained in endurance, cunning, modesty, and self-restraint. From the terse style of speech and writing of the Laconians we derive the English word "laconic." Today the word retains this meaning, *expressing much in few words.*

4. **gamut** (gam′ət) Guido of Arezzo, one of the greatest musicians of medieval times, is credited with being first to use the lines of the staff and the spaces between them. He used the Greek letter "gamma" for the lowest tone in the scale. This note was called "gamma ut." Contracted to "gamut," it then designated the entire scale. The word quickly took on a figurative as well as a literal sense. Today "gamut" is defined as *the entire scale or range.*

5. **guillotine** (gil′ə tēn′, gē′ə-) After the outbreak of the French Revolution, Dr. Joseph Ignace Guillotin became a member of the National Assembly. During an early debate, he proposed that future executions in France be conducted by a humane beheading machine that he had seen in

operation in another country. His suggestion was received favorably; in 1791, after Dr. Guillotin had retired from public service, the machine that bears his name was designed by Antoine Louis and built by a German named Schmidt. The guillotine was first used in 1792 to behead a thief. At that time, the device was called a "Louisette" after its designer; but the public began calling it after Dr. Guillotin, the man who had first advocated its use.

6. **horde** (hôrd) Upon the death of Genghis Khan, his grandson Batu Khan led the Mongol invasion of Europe, cutting a merciless swath from Moscow to Hungary. At each post, Batu erected a sumptuous tent made of silk and leather. His followers called it the "sira ordu," *the silken camp.* In Czech and Polish the Turkic "ordu" was changed to "horda." The name came to be applied not only to Batu's tent but also to his entire Mongol army. Because of the terror they inspired across the land, "horde" eventually referred to any Tartar tribe. Today, it means *any large crowd; swarm.*

7. **lyceum** (lī sē′əm) The Lyceum was the shrine dedicated to Apollo by the Athenians. The name came from the Greek "Lykeion," meaning *Wolf Slayer,* a nickname of Apollo. The shrine was a favorite haunt of the Athenian philosophers, especially Aristotle, who taught his disciples while walking along its paths. Thus, the word "lyceum" came to mean *an institute for popular education, providing discussions, lectures, concerts, and so forth.*

8. **macabre** (mə kä′brə, -kä′bər) In modern usage, "macabre" means *gruesome and horrible, pertaining to death.* Its history is uncertain. However, most etymologists believe that the word's use in the French phrase "Danse Macabre," *dance of Macabre,* a translation of Medieval Latin "chorea Macchabeorum," connects the word with the Maccabees, the leaders of the Jewish rebellion against Syria about 165 B.C., whose death as martyrs is vividly described in the Book of Maccabees (a part of the Apocrypha).

9. **gargantuan** (gär gan′ ch‍oo ən) The sixteenth-century French writer François Rabelais created a giant he named "Gargantua" after a legendary giant of the Middle Ages. To fuel his enormous bulk—Gargantua rode on a horse as large as six elephants—he had to consume prodigious

amounts of food and drink. Today we use the word "gargantuan" to mean *gigantic, enormous.*
10. **libertine** (lib′ər tēn′) In ancient Rome, "libertinus" referred to a freed slave. Since those freed from slavery were
unlikely to be strict observers of the laws that had enslaved
them in the first place, "libertine" came to designate *a person who is morally or sexually unrestrained.*

Quiz 11: Matching Synonyms

Match each of the numbered words with its closest synonym.
Write your answer in the space provided.

1. LYCEUM	a. skeptic	_____
2. LIBERTINE	b. academy	_____
3. ICONOCLAST	c. overpowering force	_____
4. HORDE	d. terse	_____
5. GARGANTUAN	e. gruesome	_____
6. LACONIC	f. dissolute person	_____
7. GUILLOTINE	g. beheading machine	_____
8. JUGGERNAUT	h. entire range	_____
9. GAMUT	i. huge	_____
10. MACABRE	j. crowd	_____

Quiz 12: Defining Words

Define each of the following words.

1. iconoclast _____
2. libertine _____
3. gamut _____
4. macabre _____
5. guillotine _____
6. laconic _____
7. gargantuan _____
8. lyceum _____
9. horde _____
10. juggernaut _____

Suggested Answers: 1. a person who attacks cherished beliefs or traditional
institutions 2. a rake 3. the entire scale or range 4. horrible, gruesome 5. a
machine used to behead criminals 6. terse 7. enormous, colossal 8. institute
for popular education 9. large group 10. an overpowering force

LESSON 7.

The English language has adopted a prodigious number of words from unexpected sources. Read through the histories of the ten unusual words that follow and then complete the quizzes.

1. **imp** (imp) In Old English, an imp was originally a young plant or seedling. Eventually, the term came to be used figuratively to indicate a descendant of a royal house, usually a male. Probably because of the behavior of such children, the word became synonymous with a young demon. Since the sixteenth century, the original meaning of "imp" as *scion* has been completely dropped, and the word is now used exclusively to mean *a little devil or demon, an evil spirit,* or *an urchin.*

2. **kaleidoscope** (kə lī′də skōp′) Invented in 1816 by Scottish physicist Sir David Brewster, the "kaleidoscope" is a scientific toy constructed of a series of mirrors within a tube. When the tube is turned by hand, symmetrical, ever-changing patterns can be viewed through the eyepiece. Brewster named his toy from the Greek "kalos," *beautiful;* "eidos," *form;* and "skopos," *watcher.*

3. **knave** (nāv) In Old English, the word "knave" (then spelled "cnafa") referred to a male child, a boy. It was later applied to a boy or man employed as a servant. Many of these boys had to be wily to survive their hard lot; thus the word gradually evolved to mean *a rogue* or *rascal.*

4. **Machiavellian** (mak′ē ə vel′ē ən) The Florentine political philosopher Nicolò Machiavelli (1469–1527) was a fervent supporter of a united Italy. Unfortunately, his methods for achieving his goals placed political expediency over morality. His masterpiece, *The Prince* (1513), advocated deception and hypocrisy on the grounds that the end justifies the means. Therefore, the adjective "Machiavellian" means *unscrupulous, cunning,* and *deceptive in the pursuit of power.*

5. **indolence** (in′dl əns) Originally, "indolence" meant *indifference.* The word was used in that sense until the sixteenth century. Probably because indifference is frequently accompanied by an unwillingness to bestir oneself, the term has now come to mean *lazy* or *slothful.*

6. **incubus/succubus** (in′kyə bəs, ing′-; suk′yə bəs) In the Middle Ages, women were thought to give birth to witches after being visited in their sleep by an "incubus," or *evil*

male spirit. The female version of this spirit, said to be the cause of nightmares, was a "succubus." Because the evil spirit pressed upon the sleeper's body and soul, the term "incubus" also means *something that oppresses like a nightmare.*

7. **hoyden** (hoid′n) A "hoyden" is *a boisterous, ill-bred girl; a tomboy.* The word is usually linked to the Dutch "heyden," meaning *a rustic person* or *rude peasant,* originally *a heathen* or *pagan,* and is related to the English word "heathen." At first in English the word meant *a rude, boorish man,* but beginning in the 1600s it was applied to girls in the sense of *a tomboy.* How the change came about is uncertain.

8. **guinea** (gin′ē) The guinea was a gold coin first minted in 1663 for the use of speculators trading with Africa. The coins were called "guineas" because the trade took place along the coast of Guinea. The British guinea came to be worth 21 shillings. After the establishment of the gold standard in the early nineteenth century, no more guineas were struck. In Great Britain, a pound and one shilling is still often called a "guinea."

9. **macadam** (mə kad′əm) While experimenting with methods of improving road construction, John McAdam, a Scotsman, concluded that the prevailing practice of placing a base of large stones under a layer of small stones was unnecessary. As surveyor-general for the roads of Bristol, England, in the early nineteenth century, McAdam built roads using only six to ten inches of small crushed stones, thereby eliminating the cost of constructing the base. Not only were the results impressive, the savings were so remarkable that his idea soon spread to other countries. McAdam's experiments led to our use of the term "macadam" for *a road surface* or *pavement.*

10. **mackintosh** (mak′in tosh′) In 1823, Scottish chemist Charles Macintosh discovered that the newfangled substance called "rubber" could be dissolved with naphtha. This solution could be painted on cloth to produce a waterproof covering. Clothing made from Macintosh's invention came to be called "mackintoshes," or *raincoats.*

Quiz 13: True/False

In the space provided, write T if the definition of the numbered word is true or F if it is false.

T or F

1. INCUBUS	evil spirit	_____
2. HOYDEN	howl	_____
3. GUINEA	rush basket	_____
4. MACADAM	raincoat	_____
5. MACKINTOSH	road surface	_____
6. IMP	male servant	_____
7. MACHIAVELLIAN	principled	_____
8. KALEIDOSCOPE	optical toy	_____
9. INDOLENCE	laziness	_____
10. KNAVE	dishonest fellow	_____

Quiz 14: Matching Synonyms

Select the best definition for each numbered word. Write your answer in the space provided.

1. MACADAM	a. raincoat	_____
2. HOYDEN	b. little mischiefmaker	_____
3. GUINEA	c. laziness	_____
4. MACKINTOSH	d. optical toy	_____
5. MACHIAVELLIAN	e. pavement	_____
6. IMP	f. rogue	_____
7. KALEIDOSCOPE	g. evil spirit	_____
8. KNAVE	h. gold coin	_____
9. INDOLENCE	i. sly and crafty	_____
10. INCUBUS	j. tomboy	_____

LESSON 8.

Now read about these ten words and complete the quizzes that follow.

1. **maelstrom** (māl′strəm) The word's figurative meaning, *a restless, disordered state of affairs,* is derived from its literal one. Today's meaning comes from "Maelstrom," the name of a strong tidal current off the coast of Norway. The current creates a powerful whirlpool because of its configuration. According to legend, the current was once so strong that it could sink any vessel that ventured near it.

2. **insolent** (in′sə lənt) The word comes from the Latin "insolentem," which literally meant *not according to custom.* Since those who violate custom are likely to offend, "inso-

lent" evolved to imply that the person was also vain and conceited. From this meaning we derive our present usage, *contemptuously rude or impertinent in speech or behavior.*

3. **interloper** (in′tər lō′pər) The word "interloper" was used in the late sixteenth century to describe Spanish traders who carved out for themselves a piece of the successful trade the British had established with the Russians. The word was formed on the analogy of "landloper," meaning *one who trespasses on another's land,* from a Dutch word literally meaning *land runner.* Although the dispute over the Spanish intrusion was settled within a few years, the word remained in use to mean *one who intrudes into some region or field of trade without a proper license* or *thrusts himself or herself into the affairs of others.*

4. **halcyon** (hal′sē ən) According to classical mythology, the demigod Halcyone threw herself into the sea when she saw the drowned body of her beloved mortal husband. After her tragic death, the gods changed Halcyone and her husband into birds, which they called "halcyons," our present-day kingfishers. The Greeks believed the sea calmed as the birds built their nests and hatched their eggs upon its waves during the seven days before and after the winter solstice. This period came to be known as "halcyon days." The adjective is now used to mean *calm, peaceful, prosperous,* or *joyful.*

5. **hector** (hek′tər) Hector was a great Trojan hero, son of King Priam. As Homer recounts in the *Iliad,* Hector took advantage of his enemy Achilles's departure from the Greek camp to drive the Greeks back to their ships and slay Achilles's dearest friend, Patroclus. To the Romans, who regarded themselves as descendants of the Trojans, Hector was a symbol of courage. But in the seventeenth century, the name was applied to the gangs of bullies who terrorized the back streets of London. It is to their transgressions that we owe the present use of "hector," *to harass or persecute.*

6. **helpmeet** (help′mēt′) This synonym for *helpmate, companion, wife,* or *husband* is the result of a misunderstanding. The word comes from Genesis 2:18, "And the Lord God said, It is not good that the man should be alone; I will make him an help meet for him." In this passage, "meet" means *proper* or *appropriate,* but the two words came to be read as one, resulting in the word's current spelling.

7. **hermetic** (hûr met′ik) The Greeks linked the Egyptian god Thoth with Hermes, calling him "Hermes Trismegistus," Hermes Three-Times Greatest. He was accepted as the author of the books that made up the sum of Egyptian learning, called the "Hermetic Books." Since these forty-two works largely concerned the occult sciences, "hermetic" came to mean *secret,* and in a later usage, *made airtight by fusion or sealing.*

8. **intransigent** (in tran′si jənt) When Amadeus, the son of Victor Emmanuel II of Italy, was forced to abdicate the throne of Spain in 1873, those favoring a republic attempted to establish a political party. This group was called in Spanish "los intransigentes" (from "in-," *not* + "transigente," *compromising*) because they could not come to terms with the other political parties. The term passed into English as "intransigent." Today the word retains the same meaning: *uncompromising* or *inflexible.*

9. **jitney** (jit′nē) The origin of this term has long baffled etymologists. The word first appeared in American usage in the first decade of the twentieth century as a slang term for a nickel. The word then became associated with the public motor vehicles whose fare was five cents. Some authorities have theorized that the term is a corruption of "jeton," the French word for *token.* Today a "jitney" is *a small passenger bus following a regular route at varying hours.*

10. **junket** (jung′kit) At first, the word referred to a basket of woven reeds used for carrying fish, and was ultimately derived from Latin "juncus," *reed.* Then the basket was used to prepare cheese, which in turn came to be called "junket." Since the basket also suggested the food it could carry, "junket" later evolved to mean *a great feast.* Today we use the term in closely related meanings: *a sweet custardlike food* or *flavored milk curdled with rennet* or *a pleasure excursion.*

Quiz 15: Matching Synonyms

Match each numbered word with its closest synonym. Write your answer in the space provided.

1. HALCYON   a. tightly sealed   _____
2. INTRANSIGENT   b. intruder   _____
3. JITNEY   c. impertinent   _____

4. MAELSTROM   d. peaceful   _____
5. JUNKET   e. inflexible   _____
6. HECTOR   f. small bus   _____
7. INSOLENT   g. companion   _____
8. HERMETIC   h. pleasure trip   _____
9. INTERLOPER   i. harass   _____
10. HELPMEET   j. disorder   _____

Quiz 16: True/False

In the space provided, write T if the definition of the numbered word is true or F if it is false.

		T or F
1. HALCYON	calm	_____
2. JITNEY	juggler	_____
3. MAELSTROM	masculine	_____
4. INTRANSIGENT	uncompromising	_____
5. INSOLENT	rude	_____
6. INTERLOPER	welcome guest	_____
7. JUNKET	refuse	_____
8. HECTOR	helper	_____
9. HERMETIC	airtight	_____
10. HELPMEET	newcomer	_____

LESSON 9.

The interesting origins of these ten words can help you remember their current meanings. Complete the quizzes after your reading.

1. **knickers** (nik′ərz) The descendants of the Dutch settlers in New York are sometimes known as "Knickerbockers." Thus, the term for the *loosely fitting short trousers gathered at the knee* that we call "knickers" derives from the name of the people who wore them, the Knickerbockers. The pants first came to public attention in the illustrations to Washington Irving's *A History of New York from the Beginning of the World to the End of the Dutch Dynasty,* published in 1809 under the pen name Diedrich Knickerbocker. Knickers were formerly extremely popular attire for boys and young men.

2. **magenta** (mə jen′tə) On June 4, 1859, the French and Sar-

dinian armies of Napoleon III won a decisive victory over the Austrian army in the northern fields of Italy near the small town of Magenta. At the time of the victory, scientists had just created a dye imparting a lovely reddish-purple color but had not yet named it. When the French chemists heard of the momentous triumph for their country, they named the dye "magenta" in honor of the victory. Today we call this *reddish-purple color* "magenta," but the dye itself is technically known as "fuchsin" (as in "fuchsia").

3. **garret** (gar′it) Originally, the French word "garite" referred to a watchtower from which a sentry could look out for approaching enemies. Among the things the Normans brought when they conquered England was the word "garite." In England the word came to mean a *loft* or *attic* and its spelling was altered to "garret."

4. **mandrake** (man′drāk) The original name for this narcotic herb was "mandragora," which is still its scientific name; the word comes from Greek "mandragoras," of unknown origin. In the Middle Ages, Englishmen erroneously assumed that "mandragora" came from "mandragon," a combination of "man," because of the appearance of its forked root, and "dragon," because of its noxious qualities. Since a dragon was then commonly called a "drake," the plant came to be called "mandrake."

5. **gazette** (gə zet′) In the beginning of the sixteenth century, Venetians circulated a small tin coin of little value they called a "gazzetta," a diminutive of the word "gaza," magpie. Soon after, the government began to print official bulletins with news of battles, elections, and so forth. Because the cost of the newspaper was one gazzetta, the leaflet itself eventually came to be called a "gazzetta." By the end of the century, the term was used in England as well. The present spelling is the result of French influence. Today a "gazette" refers to *a newspaper* or *official government journal.*

6. **martinet** (mär′tn et′, mär′tn et′) Seeking to improve his army, in 1660 Louis XIV hired Colonel Jean Martinet, a successful infantry leader, to devise a drill for France's soldiers. Martinet drilled his soldiers to such exacting standards that his name came to be applied to any officer intent on maintaining military discipline or precision. Thus, in English, a "martinet" is *a strict disciplinarian, especially a*

military one. Interestingly, in France, Martinet's name acquired no such negative connotation.

7. **gorgon** (gôr′gən) The name comes from the Greek myth of the three monstrous sisters who inhabited the region of Night. Together they were known as the "Gorgons"; their individual names were Stheno, Euryale, and Medusa. Little has been written about the first two. Medusa was the most hideous and dangerous; her appearance, with her head of writhing serpents, was so ghastly that anyone who looked directly at her was turned to stone. A secondary meaning of "gorgon" is *a mean or repulsive woman.*

8. **maudlin** (môd′lin) This word, meaning *tearfully or weakly emotional,* comes from the miracle plays of the Middle Ages. Although these plays depicted many of the Biblical miracles, the most popular theme was the life of Mary Magdalene. The English pronounced her name "maudlin," and since most of the scenes in which she appeared were tearful, this pronunciation of her name became associated with mawkish sentimentality.

9. **meander** (mē an′dər) In ancient times, the Menderes River in western Turkey was so remarkable for its twisting path that its Greek name, "Maiandros," came to mean *a winding.* In Latin this word was spelled "maeander," hence English "meander," used mainly as a verb and meaning *to proceed by a winding or indirect course.*

10. **gossamer** (gos′ə mər) In fourth-century Germany, November was a time of feasting and merrymaking. The time-honored meal was roast goose. So many geese were eaten that the month came to be called "Gänsemonat," *goose month.* The term traveled to England but in the course of migration, it became associated with the period of unseasonably warm autumn weather we now call "Indian summer." During the warm spell, large cobwebs are found draped in the grass or suspended in the air. These delicate, airy webs, which we call "gossamer," are generally believed to have taken their name from "goose summer," when their appearance was most noticeable. We now define "gossamer" as *something fine, filmy, or light;* it also means *thin and light.*

Quiz 17: Sentence Completion
Complete each sentence with the appropriate word from the following list.

gossamer   gorgon   maudlin
magenta   garret   meander
mandrake   knickers   gazette
martinet

1. It is pleasant to _____ slowly down picturesque country roads on crisp autumn afternoons.
2. The movie was so _____ that I was still crying when the closing credits began to roll.
3. The teacher was such a _____ that his students soon rebelled fiercely against his strict regulations.
4. In ancient days, the root of the _____ was surrounded by myths: it was believed that it could cast out demons from the sick, cause madness, or even make a person fall hopelessly in love.
5. Your entire load of white laundry will likely turn pink or even _____ if you include even a single new and previously unwashed red or purple sock.
6. Many budding artists have romantic fantasies about living in a wretched _____ and starving for the sake of their art.
7. Men rarely wear _____ any longer for playing golf, but the style was popular for many years.
8. The _____ cobwebs shredded at the slightest touch.
9. Since the daily _____ has excellent coverage of local sports, cultural events, and regional news, we tend to overlook its weak coverage of international events.
10. The gossip columnist was so mean and ugly that her victims referred to her as a _____ .

Quiz 18: Definitions

Select the correct definition for each numbered word. Write your answer in the space provided.

_____ 1. knickers
      a. short pants   b. soccer players   c. early settlers   d. punch line
_____ 2. meander
      a. moan   b. ramble   c. strike back   d. starve
_____ 3. gorgon
      a. misunderstood person   b. foregone conclusion   c. hideous monster   d. midget

_____ 4. magenta
   a. military victory   b. electricity
   c. machinations   d. reddish-purple color

_____ 5. mandrake
   a. myth   b. dragon   c. duck   d. narcotic plant

_____ 6. garret
   a. basement   b. attic   c. garage   d. unsuccessful
   artist

_____ 7. maudlin
   a. warlike   b. married   c. mawkish   d. intense

_____ 8. martinet
   a. strict disciplinarian   b. facile problem
   c. hawk   d. musical instrument

_____ 9. gazette
   a. journal   b. gazebo   c. silver coin   d. book of
   maps

_____ 10. gossamer
   a. variety of goose   b. grasp   c. flimsy
   material   d. idle talk

LESSON 10.

Knowing the backgrounds of the following ten words will give
you an edge in recalling their meanings and using them in conversation to make your speech and writing more powerful.
When you have studied each word, complete the two quizzes
that follow.

1. **meerschaum** (mēr′shəm, -shôm) Since it is white and soft
   and often found along seashores, ancient people believed
   this white claylike mineral was foam from the ocean turned
   into stone. As a result, in all languages it was called "sea
   foam." It was of little use until German artisans began to
   carve it into pipes, for as it absorbs the nicotine from the
   tobacco it acquires a deep honey color. Because the Germans were the first to find a use for it, the German name
   stuck: "meer," *sea;* "schaum," *foam.* In English "meerschaum" often means *a tobacco pipe with a bowl made of
   meerschaum* (the mineral).

2. **toady** (tō′dē) In the seventeenth century, people believed
   that toads were poisonous, and anyone who mistakenly ate
   a toad's leg instead of a frog's leg would die. Rather than

swearing off frogs' legs, people sought a cure for the fatal food poisoning. Charlatans would sometimes hire an accomplice who would pretend to eat a toad, at which point his employer would whip out his instant remedy and "save" his helper's life. For his duties, the helper came to be called a "toad-eater." Since anyone who would consume anything as disgusting as a toad must be completely under his master's thumb, "toad-eater" or "toady" became the term for *an obsequious sycophant; a fawning flatterer.*

3. **gregarious** (gri gâr′ē əs) The Latin term for a herd of animals is "grex." Because a group of people banded together in military formation resembles a herd of animals, the word "grex" was applied to people as well as animals. The way the people grouped together was called "gregarius," *like a herd.* The word has come down to us as "gregarious," meaning *friendly* or *fond of the company of others.*

4. **miscreant** (mis′krē ənt) The word's source, the Old French "mes-," *wrongly,* and "creant," *believing,* tells us that "miscreant" was originally used to describe a heretic. The word has evolved over the centuries, however, to refer to *a base, villainous, or depraved person.*

5. **sinecure** (sī′ni kyŏŏr′, sin′i-) "Sinecure," a word meaning *an office or position requiring little or no work, especially one yielding profitable returns,* originally began as a church term, from the Latin "beneficium sine cura," *a benefice without care.* It referred to the practice of rewarding a church rector by giving him a parish for which he had no actual responsibilities. The real work was carried on by a vicar, but his absent superior received the higher recompense. Although the church practice was abolished in the mid-nineteenth century, the term is often used today in a political context.

6. **ottoman** (ot′ə mən) In the late thirteenth century, the Muslim Turks, under the leadership of Othman (also known as Osman I) established Turkey as "the Ottoman Empire." The empire was noted for its exotic silk and velvet furnishings. Travelers to the realm took some of their luxurious couches and divans back to Europe, where they became popular in France under the Bourbon kings. The French dubbed a *low, backless cushioned seat or footstool* an "ottomane" after its country of origin. The English called it an "ottoman."

7. **namby-pamby** (nam′bē pam′bē) The term "namby-pamby," used to describe anything *weakly sentimental, pretentious, or affected,* comes from Henry Carey's parody of Ambrose Philips's sentimental children's poems. Carey titled his parody "Namby Pamby," taking the "namby" from the diminutive of "Ambrose" and using the first letter of his surname, "P," for the alliteration. Following a bitter quarrel with Philips, Alexander Pope seized upon Carey's parody in the second edition of his *Dunciad* in 1733. Through the popularity of Pope's poem, the term "namby-pamby" passed into general usage.

8. **mountebank** (moun′tə bangk′) During the Middle Ages, Italians conducted their banking in the streets, setting up business on convenient benches. In fact, the Italian word "banca" has given us our word "bank." People with less honest intentions realized that it would be relatively easy to cheat the people who assembled around these benches. To attract a crowd, these con men often worked with jugglers, clowns, rope dancers, or singers. Since they always worked around a bench, they were known as "montimbancos." Although the word was Anglicized to "mountebank," it still refers to *a huckster or charlatan* who sells quack medicines from a platform in a public place, appealing to his audience by using tricks, storytelling, and so forth.

9. **phaeton** (fā′i tn) In Greek mythology, Helios drove the chariot of the sun across the sky each day. Helios's son Phaëton implored his father to let him drive the glittering chariot. Against his better judgment, one day Helios acceded to his son's wishes and let him drive the chariot pulled by its four powerful horses. Phaëton began well enough, but by mid-morning he wearied and could no longer control the horses. The sun fluctuated between heaven and earth, causing great destruction. To stop the devastation, Zeus hurled a thunderbolt at Phaëton, who fell lifeless to the ground. In the sixteenth century, the English drew from this legend to describe a heedless driver as a "Phaeton." The word was later applied to *a light four-wheeled carriage* popular in the eighteenth century. Still later, it was applied to *a type of touring car.*

10. **mugwump** (mug′wump′) This word entered the English language in a most curious fashion. In the mid-1600s, the clergyman John Eliot, known as the Apostle to the Indians, translated the Bible into the Algonquian language.

When he came to the thirty-sixth chapter of Genesis, he had no word for "duke," so he used "mugquomp," an Algonquian term for *chief* or *great man*. Historians of the language theorize that the term might already have been in circulation at that time, but they know for certain that by 1884 it was in fairly general use. In the presidential election that year, a group of Republicans threw their support to Grover Cleveland rather than to the party's nominee, James G. Blaine. The newspapers scorned the renegade Republicans as "mugwumps," those who thought themselves too good to vote for Blaine. The scorned Republicans got the last word when they adopted the same term to describe themselves, saying they were independent men proud to call themselves "mugwumps," or *great men*. Today we use the term "mugwump" to desribe *a person who takes an independent position* or *one who is neutral on a controversial issue*.

Quiz 19: True/False

In the space provided, write T if the definition of the numbered word is true or F if it is false.

T or F

1. TOADY	sycophant	_____
2. MISCREANT	sociable person	_____
3. MUGWUMP	political ally	_____
4. NAMBY-PAMBY	cereal	_____
5. GREGARIOUS	affable	_____
6. PHAETON	ghost	_____
7. MOUNTEBANK	impostor	_____
8. MEERSCHAUM	mixup	_____
9. OTTOMAN	footstool	_____
10. SINECURE	sincere	_____

Quiz 20: Matching Synonyms

Match each of the following numbered words with its closest synonym. Write your answer in the space provided.

1. MOUNTEBANK	a. easy job	_____
2. GREGARIOUS	b. knave	_____
3. OTTOMAN	c. charlatan	_____
4. TOADY	d. carriage	_____
5. MISCREANT	e. sociable	_____

6. MUGWUMP	f. independent	_____
7. NAMBY-PAMBY	g. sycophant	_____
8. SINECURE	h. pipe	_____
9. PHAETON	i. low, backless seat	_____
10. MEERSCHAUM	j. sentimental	_____

ANSWERS TO QUIZZES IN CHAPTER 11

Answers to Quiz 1

1. f 2. d 3. b 4. g 5. e 6. h 7. i 8. c 9. j 10. a

Answers to Quiz 2

1. T 2. F 3. F 4. F 5. T 6. F 7. T 8. T 9. F 10. F

Answers to Quiz 3

1. F 2. T 3. F 4. T 5. F 6. F 7. F 8. F 9. T 10. T

Answers to Quiz 4

1. c 2. f 3. i 4. g 5. b 6. h 7. d 8. a 9. j 10. e

Answers to Quiz 5

1. c 2. b 3. a 4. c 5. c 6. b 7. a 8. c 9. a 10. b

Answers to Quiz 6

1. d 2. c 3. i 4. a 5. g 6. j 7. b 8. e 9. f 10. h

Answers to Quiz 7

1. T 2. F 3. F 4. T 5. F 6. T 7. T 8. T 9. F 10. F

Answers to Quiz 9

1. c 2. a 3. d 4. d 5. c 6. a 7. b 8. b 9. a 10. b

Answers to Quiz 10

1. T 2. T 3. T 4. T 5. T 6. T 7. F 8. F 9. F 10. T

Answers to Quiz 11

1. b 2. f 3. a 4. j 5. i 6. d 7. g 8. c 9. h 10. e

Answers to Quiz 13

1. T 2. F 3. F 4. F 5. F 6. F 7. F 8. T 9. T 10. T

Answers to Quiz 14

1. e 2. j 3. h 4. a 5. i 6. b 7. d 8. f 9. c 10. g

Answers to Quiz 15

1. d 2. e 3. f 4. j 5. h 6. i 7. c 8. a 9. b 10. g

Answers to Quiz 16

1. T 2. F 3. F 4. T 5. T 6. F 7. F 8. F 9. T 10. F

Answers to Quiz 17

1. meander 2. maudlin 3. martinet 4. mandrake 5. magenta 6. garret
7. knickers 8. gossamer 9. gazette 10. gorgon

Answers to Quiz 18

1. a 2. b 3. c 4. d 5. d 6. b 7. c 8. a 9. a 10. c

Answers to Quiz 19

1. T 2. F 3. F 4. F 5. T 6. F 7. T 8. F 9. T 10. F

Answers to Quiz 20

1. c 2. e 3. i 4. g 5. b 6. f 7. j 8. a 9. d 10. h

12. MORE WORD HISTORIES

LESSON 1.

Here are ten new words to enhance your word power. When you have finished reading the history of each word, complete the quizzes.

1. **oscillate** (os′ə lāt′) In ancient Rome, the grape growers hung little images with the face of Bacchus, the god of wine, on their vines. Since the Latin word for face is "os," a little face would be called an "oscillum." Because the images swung in the wind, some students of language concluded that the Latin verb "oscillare" came from a description of this motion. Most scholars have declined to make this connection, saying only that our present word "oscillate," *to swing to and fro,* is derived from Latin "oscillare," *to swing,* which in turn comes from "oscillum," *a swing.*

2. **nabob** (nā′bob) The Mogul emperors, who ruled India from the sixteenth until the middle of the nineteenth century, delegated authority to men who acted as governors of various parts of India. To the native Indians, such a ruler was known as a "nawwab," *deputy.* The word was changed by the Europeans into "nabob." The nabobs were supposed to tithe the money to the central government, but some of the nabobs withheld the money, and thereby became enormously wealthy. From their fortunes came the European custom of using the word "nabob" to refer to a person, especially a European, who had attained great wealth in India or another country of the East. The usage spread

to England, and today we use the term to describe *any very wealthy or powerful person.*

3. **pander** (pan′dər) "Pander," *to act as a go-between in amorous intrigues* or *to act as a pimp or procurer* or *to cater basely,* comes from the medieval story of Troilus and Cressida. In his retelling, Chaucer describes how the love-stricken Troilus calls upon his friend Pandarus, kin to Cressida, to aid him in his quest for her love. Much of Chaucer's tale is devoted to the different means used by Pandarus to help Troilus win his love. Shakespeare later recycled the same legend. As the story gained in popularity the name "Pandarus" was changed in English to "pandare" and then to "pander." The noun now has the negative connotation of *pimp* or *procurer for illicit sexual intercourse.*

4. **pedagogue** (ped′ə gog′, -gôg′) Wealthy Greek families kept a special slave to supervise their sons. The slave's responsibilities included accompanying the boys as they traveled to and from school and walked in the public streets. To describe a slave's chores, the Greeks coined the term "paidagogos," *a leader of boys.* Occasionally, when the slave was an educated man captured in warfare and sold into slavery, the slave also tutored his charges. From the Greek word we derived the English word "pedagogue," *teacher* or *educator.*

5. **quack** (kwak) Noticing how the raucous shouts of the charlatans selling useless concoctions sounded like the strident quacks of ducks, the sixteenth-century Dutch called these charlatans "quacksalvers"—literally, *ducks quacking over their salves.* The term quickly spread through Europe. The English shortened it to "quack," and used it to describe *any fraudulent or ignorant pretender to medical skills,* the meaning we retain today.

6. **nepotism** (nep′ə tiz′əm) This word for *patronage bestowed or favoritism shown on the basis of family relationships,* as in business or politics, can be traced to the popes of the fifteenth and sixteenth centuries. To increase their power, these men surrounded themselves with people they knew would be loyal—members of their own family. Among the most popular candidates were the popes' own illegitimate sons, called "nephews," from the Latin "nepos," *a descendant,* as a mark of respect. Eventually the term "nepo-

tism" came to mean favoritism to all family members, not just nephews.

7. **pompadour** (pom′pə dôr′, -dŏŏr′) Sheltered by a wealthy family and educated as though she were their own daughter, at twenty the exquisite Jeanne Antoinette Poisson Le Normant d'Étioles married her protector's nephew and began her reign over the world of Parisian fashion. Soon after, King Louis XV took her as his mistress, established her at the court of Versailles, and gave her the estate of Pompadour. The Marquise de Pompadour created a large and high-swept hairstyle memorialized by her name. Though it has been somewhat modified, the style is still known by her name.

8. **nostrum** (nos′trəm) The word "nostrum," *a patent or quack medicine,* became very current around the time of the Great Plague in the mid-seventeenth century. Doctors were helpless to combat the disease, so charlatans and quacks scurried to fill the gap, flooding the market with their own "secret"—and useless—concoctions. To make their medicines seem more effective, they labeled them with the Latin word "nostrum." The term came to be used as a general word for any quack medicine. Ironically, "nostrum" means *our own,* as in "nostrum remedium," *our own remedy;* thus it makes no claims at all for the remedy's effectiveness.

9. **narcissism** (när′sə siz′əm) The word "narcissism," *inordinate fascination with oneself,* comes from the Greek myth of Narcissus. According to one version of the legend, an exceptionally handsome young man fell in love with his own image reflected in a pool. Because he was unable to embrace his image, he died from unrequited love. According to another version, Narcissus fell in love with his identical twin sister. After her death, he sat and stared at his own reflection in the pool until he died from grief.

10. **nepenthe** (ni pen′thē) According to Greek legend, when Paris kidnapped Helen and took her to Troy, he wanted her to forget her previous life. In Homer's version of the tale, Paris gave Helen a drug thought to cause loss of memory. The drug was called "nepenthes." The word has come down to us with its meaning intact: *anything inducing a pleasurable sensation of forgetfulness.*

Quiz 1: True/False

In the space provided, write T if the definition of the numbered word is true or F if it is false.

		T or F
1. NEPENTHE	remembrance	_____
2. NEPOTISM	impartiality	_____
3. PANDER	procurer	_____
4. POMPADOUR	crewcut	_____
5. OSCILLATE	swing	_____
6. PEDAGOGUE	teacher	_____
7. NARCISSISM	self-love	_____
8. NABOB	pauper	_____
9. NOSTRUM	patent medicine	_____
10. QUACK	expert	_____

Quiz 2: Defining Words

Define each of the following words.

1. pompadour _____
2. nepenthe _____
3. oscillate _____
4. nostrum _____
5. quack _____
6. nabob _____
7. pander _____
8. nepotism _____
9. pedagogue _____
10. narcissism _____

Suggested Answers: 1. upswept hairstyle 2. something inducing forgetfulness 3. to swing back and forth 4. patent or useless remedy 5. medical charlatan 6. wealthy, powerful person 7. pimp or procurer 8. patronage given to family members 9. teacher 10. excessive self-love

LESSON 2.

Each of these ten words beginning with the letter "p" has a particularly captivating tale behind it. Read the stories, then complete the two quizzes at the end of the lesson.

1. **palaver** (pə lav′ər, -lä′vər) The word "palaver" derives ultimately from the Greek word "parabola," *comparison,* lit-

erally *a placing beside.* From this came English "parable," *a story that makes comparisons.* In Latin the word came to mean *speech, talk, word.* Later, Portuguese traders carried the term to Africa in the form "palavra" and used it to refer to the long talks with native chiefs required by local custom. English traders picked up the word in the eighteenth century, spelling it as we do today. The word retains its last meaning, *a long parley, especially one with people indigenous to a region* or *profuse, idle talk.*

2. **pannier** (pan′yər, -ē ər) The word "pannier" was first used in thirteenth-century France to mean *bread basket;* it is related to the French word "pain," *bread.* Soon it was also used to refer to a fish basket, and then a basket for toting any provisions. In later centuries, the term was applied to the baskets balanced on a donkey's back. Today we use the term to denote *a basket, especially a large one carried on a person's back.*

3. **pariah** (pə rī′ə) The term "pariah," *an outcast,* comes from the name of one of the lowest castes in India. Composed of agricultural laborers and household servants, it is not the lowest caste, but its members are still considered untouchable by the Brahmans. The British used the term "pariah" for anyone of low social standing. The term "pariah" now is used for *any outcast among his or her own people.*

4. **pecuniary** (pi kyōō′nē er′ē) The Romans measured a man's worth by the number of animals he kept on his farm. They adapted the Latin word for a farm animal, "pecu," to refer to individual wealth. But as people acquired new ways of measuring wealth, such as money and land, the Roman word evolved into "pecunia," which referred most specifically to money. From this came the adjective "pecuniary," *pertaining to or consisting of money.*

5. **phantasmagoria** (fan taz′mə gôr′ē ə) In the early years of the nineteenth century, an inventor named Philipstal created a wondrous device for producing optical illusions. By projecting colored slides onto a thin silk screen, Philipstal made his spectral images appear to move. Today, of course, we take such motion-picture illusions for granted, but in the age of the magic lantern, such visions were marvelous indeed. Philipstal named his invention "phantasmagoria," which we now apply to *a shifting series of phantasms or deceptive appearances, as in a dream.*

6. **poplin** (pop′lin) The origin of this word has nothing to do with its appearance or use. In the early fourteenth century, the papal seat was located in Avignon, France. Even after the papacy was moved to Rome, Avignon remained important for its production of a sturdy dress and upholstery fabric. The fabric came to be identified with the city in which it was made. Since Avignon remained a papal town until the late eighteenth century, the fabric came to be called "papelino," or *papal*. The English pronounced the word "poplin," giving us the present-day name for this *finely corded fabric of cotton, rayon, silk, or wool.*

7. **precipitate** (pri sip′i tāt′) The word "precipitate" is based on the Latin root "caput," meaning *head*. In fact, the word was first used to apply to those who had been executed or killed themselves by being hurled or jumping headlong from a "precipice" or high place. Later, the word came to mean *to rush headlong*. From this has come today's meaning, *to hasten the occurrence of; to bring about prematurely.*

8. **precocious** (pri kō′shəs) To the Romans, Latin "praecox," the source of English "precocious," was a culinary term meaning *precooked*. In time, however, its meaning was extended to *acting prematurely*. It is this later meaning of "precocious" that we use today, *unusually advanced in development, especially mental development.*

9. **pretext** (prē′tekst) "Pretext" comes from the Latin word "praetexta," meaning *an ornament,* such as the purple markings on a toga denoting rank. In addition to its literal sense, however, the word carried the connotation of something to cloak one's true identity. We have retained only the word's figurative meaning, *something that is put forward to conceal a true purpose or object; an ostensible reason.*

10. **procrustean** (prō krus′tē ən) According to one version of the Greek myth, Procrustes was a bandit who made his living waylaying unsuspecting travelers. He tied everyone who fell into his grasp to an iron bed. If they were longer than the bed, he cut short their legs to make their bodies fit; if they were shorter, he stretched their bodies until they fit tightly. Hence, "procrustean" means *tending to produce conformity through violent or arbitrary means.*

Quiz 3: True/False

In the space provided, write T if the definition of the numbered word is true or F if it is false.

		T or F
1. PROCRUSTEAN	marine life	_____
2. PECUNIARY	picayune	_____
3. PRECIPITATE	play	_____
4. PRETEXT	falsification	_____
5. PARIAH	outcast	_____
6. POPLIN	religious vestment	_____
7. PALAVER	serving tray	_____
8. PRECOCIOUS	advanced	_____
9. PANNIER	basket	_____
10. PHANTASMAGORIA	illusions	_____

Quiz 14: Matching Synonyms

Match each of the following numbered words with its closest synonym from the list of lettered words in the second column. Write your answer in the space provided.

1. POPLIN	a. excuse	_____
2. PALAVER	b. producing conformity by violent means	_____
3. PECUNIARY	c. fabric	_____
4. PHANTASMAGORIA	d. fantasy	_____
5. PRETEXT	e. expedite	_____
6. PRECOCIOUS	f. idle chatter	_____
7. PRECIPITATE	g. advanced	_____
8. PARIAH	h. outcast	_____
9. PROCRUSTEAN	i. basket	_____
10. PANNIER	j. monetary	_____

LESSON 3.

Read through the interesting stories behind these ten words. Then work through the two quizzes to see how many of the words you can use correctly.

1. **proletariat** (prō′li târ′ē ət) "Proletariat" derives from the Latin "proletarius," *a Roman freeman who lacked property and money.* The word came from "proles," *offspring, chil-*

dren. Although the freemen had the vote, many wealthy Romans despised them, saying they were useful only to have children. They called them "proletarii," *producers of children.* Karl Marx picked up the word in the mid-nineteenth century as a label for the lower-class working people of his age. "Proletariat" retains the same meaning today: *members of the working class, especially those who do not possess capital and must sell their labor to survive.*

2. **Arcadian** (är kā′dē ən) The residents of landlocked Arcadia, in ancient Greece, did not venture to other lands. As a result, they maintained traditional ways and lived what others imagined to be a simpler life. Ancient classical poets made "Arcadia" a symbol for a land of pastoral happiness. In the sixteenth century, English poet Sir Philip Sidney referred to a bucolic land he called "Arcadia." The word has retained this meaning, and today we consider residents of an "Arcadian" place to be *rustic, simple, and innocent.*

3. **rake** (rāk) "Rake," meaning *a dissolute person, especially a man,* was originally "rakehell." In the sixteenth century, this colorful term was used to describe a person so dissipated that he would "rake hell" to find his pleasures. "Rakehell" is now considered a somewhat archaic term to describe such roués; "rake" is the common word.

4. **pygmy** (pig′mē) The ancient Greeks were entranced by stories of a tribe of dwarfs in the upper Nile who were so small that they could be swallowed by cranes. To describe these tiny people, the Greeks used the word "pygmaios," which also referred to the distance on a person's arm from the elbow to the knuckles. The word became English "pygmy," *a tiny person or thing; a person or thing of small importance.*

5. **sardonic** (sär don′ik) The ancient Greeks described a plant on the island of Sardinia whose flesh, if eaten, caused the victim's face to become grotesquely convulsed, as if in scornful laughter. The Greek name for Sardinia was "Sardos"; therefore, "sardonios" came to refer to any mocking laughter. The English word eventually became "sardonic," *characterized by bitter irony or scornful derision.*

6. **tartar** (tär′tər) The fierce Genghis Khan and his successors led an army of bloodthirsty warriors, including the Ta-ta Mongols, in a series of conquests throughout Asia and into Europe. Their name, "Tartar" or "Tatar," became closely

associated with brutal massacres. Today the word "tartar" refers to *a savage, ill-tempered, or intractable person.*

7. **argosy** (är′gə sē) In the Middle Ages, cities on the Mediterranean coast maintained large fleets to ship goods around the known world. Ragusa was a Sicilian city well known for its large ships, called "ragusea." In English, the initial two letters became switched, creating "argusea." From there it was a short step to "argosy," *a large merchant ship, especially one with a rich cargo.* Because of Ragusa's wealth, the word "argosy" also came to mean *an opulent supply or collection.*

8. **Balkanize** (bôl′kə nīz′) After centuries of war, in 1912 the Balkan nations united to conquer the Turks and divide the spoils among themselves. The following year, however, the Balkan nations quarreled over how to divide their booty and began to fight among themselves. From this experience comes the verb "Balkanize," *to divide a country or territory into small, quarrelsome, ineffectual states.*

9. **cravat** (krə vat′) In the late seventeenth century, the French king Louis XIV formed a special division of Croats, a Slavic people, to serve in his army. The Croats wore colorful, much-admired neckties to distinguish themselves from the other regiments. Fashionable civilians took to wearing these neckties, calling them "cravats" after a variant spelling of "Croat." The term is still used to mean *necktie,* although it is somewhat out of fashion. It also refers to a scarf worn by men.

10. **hegira** (hi jī′rə, hej′ər ə) Around the year 600, the prophet Muhammad began to preach the new faith of Islam. To escape persecution, he was forced to flee his home in Mecca. Eventually, his followers increased, and by his death in 632, he controlled Arabia. Within a century, the empire of Islam had spread throughout western Asia and northern Africa. The turning point, Muhammad's flight from Mecca, came to be called the "Hegira," after the Arabic word for *flight* or *emigration.* The "Hegira" is the starting point on the Muslim calendar, and we now apply the word to *any flight or journey to a desirable or congenial place.*

Quiz 5: True/False

In the space provided, write T if the definition of the numbered word is true or F if it is false.

		T or F
1. RAKE	roué	_____
2. PROLETARIAT	wealthy persons	_____
3. HEGIRA	flight	_____
4. CRAVAT	craving	_____
5. TARTAR	disciple	_____
6. ARCADIAN	rustic	_____
7. SARDONIC	derisive	_____
8. PYGMY	monkey	_____
9. ARGOSY	rich supply	_____
10. BALKANIZE	vulcanize	_____

Quiz 6: Matching Synonyms

Select the best definition for each numbered word. Write your answer in the space provided.

1. RAKE	a. bucolic	_____
2. PYGMY	b. merchant ship	_____
3. CRAVAT	c. midget	_____
4. ARCADIAN	d. break up into antagonistic units	_____
5. ARGOSY	e. the working class	_____
6. HEGIRA	f. scornful; mocking	_____
7. BALKANIZE	g. necktie	_____
8. PROLETARIAT	h. bad-tempered person	_____
9. SARDONIC	i. journey or flight	_____
10. TARTAR	j. roué	_____

LESSON 4.

Now look at the backgrounds of these ten words. Then complete the two quizzes to help you add them to your vocabulary.

1. **ballyhoo** (bal'ē hōō') The word "ballyhoo" is of uncertain origin. Some, however, have connected it with the Irish town of Ballyhooy, known for the rowdy and often uncontrolled quarrels of its inhabitants. Today "ballyhoo" is an Americanism with a specific meaning: *a clamorous attempt to win customers or advance a cause; blatant advertising or publicity.*

2. **tawdry** (tô'drē) In the seventh century, an Englishwoman named Etheldreda fled her husband to establish an abbey.

When the Venerable Bede recounted her story in the early eighth century, he claimed that her death had been caused by a tumor in her throat, which she believed was a punishment for her early vanity of wearing jewelry about her neck. Her abbey eventually became the Cathedral of Ely; her name, Audrey. In her honor, the cathedral town held an annual fair where "trifling objects" were hawked. One theory as to the development of the word "tawdry" relates to the hawkers' cry, "Saint Audrey's lace!" This became "Sin t'Audrey lace" and then "tawdry lace." By association with these cheap trinkets, the word "tawdry" has come to mean *gaudy, showy,* or *cheap.*

3. **python** (pī'thon) According to Greek myth, the sacred oracle at Delphi was at one time threatened by a terrible serpent called "Python." It was finally killed by Apollo. About 150 years ago, *a large constrictor snake often measuring more than twenty feet long* was named after this mythical monster.

4. **recalcitrant** (ri kal'si trənt) The word was formed from the Latin prefix "re-," *back,* and "calcitrare," *to kick.* Thus, a recalcitrant person is one who kicks back, resisting authority or control.

5. **copperhead** (kop'ər hed') The term "copperhead" was coined by the New York *Tribune* in the early days of the Civil War to refer to *a Northerner who sympathized with the South.* The term came from the sneaky and poisonous copperhead snake, which strikes without warning.

6. **silhouette** (sil'ōō et') At the urging of his mistress, Madame de Pompadour, the French king Louis XV appointed Étienne de Silhouette as his finance minister. His mission was to enact strict economy measures to rescue the government from near-bankruptcy. At the same time, there was a revival of the practice of tracing profiles created by shadows. Since they replaced more costly paintings, these outlines came to be derided as "à la Silhouette"—another of his money-saving measures. Although Silhouette lasted in office less than a year, he achieved a sort of immortality when his name became permanently associated with *a two-dimensional representation of the outline of an object, as a person's profile, generally filled in with black.*

7. **remora** (rem'ər ə) Since this odd fish impeded the progress of Roman ships by attaching itself to the vessels with its sucking disks, the Romans named it a "remora," *that which holds back; hindrance.* Today we use the term only to

name the fish, though formerly it was also a synonym for *obstacle, hindrance.*

8. **caprice** (kə prēs′) "Caprice," *a sudden, unpredictable change of mind, a whim,* doesn't remind us of hedgehogs, yet these animals probably played a role in this word's past. "Caprice" comes ultimately from the Italian word "capriccio," which originally meant *fright, horror.* The word is thought to be a compound of "capo," *head,* and "riccio," *hedgehog,* because when people are very frightened, their hair stands on end, like a hedgehog's spines.

9. **treacle** (trē′kəl) Originally, "treacle" was an ointment used by the ancient Romans and Greeks against the bite of wild animals. But in the eighteenth and nineteenth centuries, competing quack medicine hawkers added sweetening to make their bitter potions more palatable. After a while, the sweetening agent itself, usually molasses, came to be called "treacle." We retain this meaning and have extended it to refer figuratively to *contrived or unrestrained sentimentality* as well.

10. **billingsgate** (bil′ingz gāt′) In the 1500s, "Belin's gate," a walled town within London, was primarily a fish market. The name was soon distorted to "billingsgate," and since many fishwives and seamen were known for their salty tongues, the word "billingsgate" came to mean *coarse or vulgar abusive language.*

Quiz 7: True/False

In the space provided, write T if the definition of the numbered word is true or F if it is false.

		T or F
1. RECALCITRANT	easygoing	_____
2. CAPRICE	capable	_____
3. REMORA	renovate	_____
4. COPPERHEAD	fierce warrior	_____
5. BALLYHOO	dance	_____
6. TAWDRY	gaudy	_____
7. BILLINGSGATE	profane language	_____
8. PYTHON	snake	_____
9. TREACLE	sugar	_____
10. SILHOUETTE	outline	_____

Quiz 8: Matching Synonyms

Match each of the following numbered words with its closest synonym. Write your answer in the space provided.

1. PYTHON	a. whim	____
2. BALLYHOO	b. cheap	____
3. TREACLE	c. verbal abuse	____
4. TAWDRY	d. snake	____
5. COPPERHEAD	e. outline	____
6. RECALCITRANT	f. clamor	____
7. SILHOUETTE	g. balky	____
8. CAPRICE	h. mawkish sentimentality	____
9. REMORA	i. fish	____
10. BILLINGSGATE	j. Southern sympathizer	____

LESSON 5.

The stories behind these ten words provide intriguing reading and can give your vocabulary true power. After you study the words, complete the two quizzes to see how many of the words you can use correctly.

1. **apartheid** (ə pärt′hāt, -hīt) "Apartheid," the term for *a policy of racial segregation and discrimination against non-whites,* entered English from Afrikaans, the language of South Africa's Dutch settlers, the Boers. They created the word from the Dutch word for "apart" and the suffix "-heid," related to our suffix "-hood." Thus, the word literally means *apartness* or *separateness.* It was first used in 1947, in a South African newspaper.

2. **quixotic** (kwik sot′ik) The word "quixotic," meaning *extravagantly chivalrous or romantic,* is based on the character of Don Quixote, the chivalrous knight in Cervantes' 1605 masterpiece *Don Quixote de la Mancha.* The impractical, visionary knight was ludicrously blind to the false nature of his dreams.

3. **bromide** (brō′mīd) "Bromides" are chemicals, several of which can be used as sedatives. In 1906, the American humorist Gelett Burgess first used the word to mean *a boring person,* one who is likely to serve the same purpose as a sedative. The term was then extended to mean *a platitude,*

the kind of remark one could expect from a tiresome person.

4. **profane** (prə fān', prō-) Only fully initiated men were allowed to participate in Greek and Roman religious rites; those not admitted were called "profane," from "pro," *outside,* and "fanum," *temple.* When the word came into English, it was applied to persons or things not part of Christianity. Probably in reference to the contempt of nonbelievers, "profane" now means *characterized by irreverence for God or sacred things.*

5. **rialto** (rē al'tō) In the late sixteenth century, the Venetians erected a bridge across the Grand Canal. Since the bridge spanned deep waters, it was called the "Rialto," *deep stream.* The bridge led to the creation of a busy shopping area in the center of the city. From this shopping center we derive our present meaning of "rialto," *an exchange or mart.*

6. **thespian** (thes'pē ən) A Greek poet named Thespis, who flourished circa 534 B.C., enlarged the traditional celebrations at the festival of Dionysus by writing verses to be chanted alternately by individuals and the chorus. This opportunity to be a solo performer was a first. From the poet's name we derive the word "thespian," *an actor or actress.*

7. **salver** (sal'vər) "Salver" came into English from Spanish "salva," a kind of tray. The Spanish word derived from Latin "salvare," *to save,* from the practice of having a servant taste one's food or drink to check for poison. Because poisoning was the method of choice for eliminating wealthy enemies in the Middle Ages, the practice of retaining a taster was commonplace among the affluent. The master's food was presented upon a separate tray, so the term "salva" came to apply to the tray as well as the tasting. Once the habit of poisoning people subsided, the English term "salver" came to mean *a tray, especially one used for serving food.*

8. **chagrin** (shə grin') The word "chagrin," meaning *a feeling of vexation due to disappointment,* does not derive from "shagreen," *a piece of hard, abrasive leather used to polish metal,* even though both words are spelled identically in French. French scholars connect "chagrin," *vexation, grief,* with an Old French verb, "chagreiner," *to turn mel-*

ancholy or gloomy, which evolved in part from a Germanic word related to English "grim."

9. **shibboleth** (shib′ə lith, -leth′) In the twelfth chapter of Judges, Jephthah and his men were victorious over the warriors of Ephraim. After the battle, Jephthah gave his guards the password "shibboleth" to distinguish friends from foes; he picked the word because the Ephraimites could not pronounce the "sh" sound. His choice was shrewd, and many of his enemies were captured and killed. Thus, "shibboleth" has come to mean *a peculiarity of pronunciation, usage, or behavior that distinguishes a particular class or set of persons.* It also can mean *slogan; catchword.*

10. **vie** (vī) The word "vie," *to strive in competition or rivalry with another, to contend for superiority,* was originally a shortened version of "envien," a sixteenth-century gaming term meaning *to raise the stake.* The contraction, "vie," came to mean *to contend, compete.*

Quiz 9: True/False

In the space provided, write T if the definition of the numbered word is true or F if it is false.

		T or F
1. CHAGRIN	chafe	_____
2. VIE	accede	_____
3. PROFANE	irreverent	_____
4. SALVER	tray	_____
5. QUIXOTIC	ill-tempered	_____
6. RIALTO	marketplace	_____
7. APARTHEID	foreigner	_____
8. SHIBBOLETH	platitude	_____
9. THESPIAN	actor	_____
10. BROMIDE	explosive	_____

Quiz 10: Definitions

Select the best definition for each numbered word. Circle your answer.

_____ 1. bromide
a. cliché   b. effervescence   c. angst

_____ 2. vie
a. treat   b. contend   c. despise

_____   3. quixotic
           a. alien b. romantic c. fictional
_____   4. salver
           a. salivate b. poison c. tray
_____   5. shibboleth
           a. peculiarity b. forbidden c. murdered
_____   6. profane
           a. pious b. irreverent c. exploding
_____   7. thespian
           a. actress b. speech impairment c. playwright
_____   8. apartheid
           a. discrimination b. unity c. hopelessness
_____   9. rialto
           a. shipyard b. reality c. exchange
_____   10. chagrin
           a. stiff b. vexation c. smirk

LESSON 6.

Knowing the histories of the following ten words can help you remember their meanings and use them in your speech and writing. Study the words, then work through the two quizzes that follow.

1. **Promethean** (prə mē′thē ən) According to Greek myth, as punishment for stealing fire from the gods and giving it to mortal humans, Prometheus was bound to the side of a mountain, where he was attacked daily by a fierce bird that feasted upon his liver. At night his wounds healed; the next day he was attacked anew. Because of his extraordinary boldness in stealing the divine fire, the word "Promethean" has come to mean *creative, boldly original.*

2. **sarcophagus** (sär kof′ə gəs) Although the majority of ancient Greeks favored burial or cremation, some obtained limestone coffins that could dissolve a body in little over a month. The coffin was called a "sarcophagus," from the Greek "sarx," *flesh,* and "phagos," *eating.* Today we use the term to refer to *a stone coffin, especially one bearing sculpture, an inscription, etc., often displayed as a monument.*

3. **quorum** (kwôr′əm) The word "quorum" was first used as part of a Latin phrase meaning *to select people for official*

court business. Ultimately, it came to mean *the number of members of a group or organization required to be present to transact business; legally, usually a majority.*

4. **antimacassar** (an′ti mə kas′ər) In the 1800s, macassar oil was imported from Indonesia to England as a popular remedy for baldness. Based on its reputation, men began to apply it liberally to their pates, but the oil stained the backs of sofas and chairs where they rested their oily heads. Therefore, homemakers began to place pieces of fabric over sofa and chair backs, since these scraps could be washed more easily than stained upholstery. These fabric pieces came to be called "antimacassars"—*against macassar oil.* They survive today in the *little doilies* fastidious homemakers drape over furniture.

5. **lackey** (lak′ē) After their invasion of Spain in 711, the Moors conquered nearly the entire country and established a glittering civilization. But it was not to last. By 1100, Christians had already wrested half of Spain from the Moors. Two hundred years later, the Moors retained only a small toehold; and a hundred years after that, they were driven out of Europe entirely. As the Moors suffered repeated defeats, their captured soldiers became servants to their Spanish conquerors. They were called "alacayo." The initial "a" was later dropped, and the word was rendered in English as "lackey," *a servile follower.*

6. **obelisk** (ob′ə lisk′) The word comes from the ancient Egyptian practice of erecting tall, thin pillars to pay homage to the sun god Ra. The Greeks called these shafts "obeliskoi." The word has come down to us as "obelisk," with its meaning intact, *a tapering four-sided shaft of stone with a pyramidal apex; a monument.*

7. **paladin** (pal′ə din) The original paladins were Charlemagne's twelve knights. According to legend, the famous paladin Roland was caught in an ambush and fought valiantly with his small band of followers to the last man. Because of his actions, "paladin" has come down to us as *any champion of noble causes.*

8. **hobnob** (hob′nob′) Those who "hobnob" with their buddies *associate on very friendly terms* or *drink together.* The word comes from the Anglo-Saxon "haebbe" and "naebbe," *to have* and *to have not.* In the 1700s, "hobnob" meant *to toast friends and host alternate rounds of drinks.* Each person thus had the pleasure of treating, creating a

sense of familiarity. Today this usage survives, even if those hobnobbing are teetotalers.

9. **helot** (hel′ət, hē′lət) Around the eighth century B.C., the Spartans conquered and enslaved the people of the southern half of the Peloponnesus. They called these slaves "helots," perhaps from the Greek word meaning *to enslave.* Today "helot" still means *serf or slave; bondsman.*

10. **kowtow** (kou′tou′) The Chinese people, who were largely isolated from the West until Portuguese traders established a post outside Canton, regarded their emperor as a representation of God on earth. Those approaching the emperor had to fall to the ground and strike their heads against the floor as a sign of humility. This was called a "kowtow," from the Chinese word that meant *knock-head.* As a verb, the English word follows the original meaning, *to touch the forehead to the ground while kneeling, as an act of worship;* but from this meaning we have derived a figurative use as well: *to act in an obsequious manner; show servile deference.*

Quiz 11: Defining Words

Define each of the following words.

1. obelisk _____
2. Promethean _____
3. helot _____
4. sarcophagus _____
5. kowtow _____
6. lackey _____
7. antimacassar _____
8. hobnob _____
9. quorum _____
10. paladin _____

Suggested Answers: 1. shaft 2. creative, boldly original 3. serf, slave 4. coffin 5. deference 6. a servile follower 7. doily 8. associate on friendly terms; drink together 9. majority 10. champion

Quiz 12: True/False

In the space provided, write T if the definition of the numbered word is true or F if it is false.

		T or F
1. LACKEY	servant	_____
2. QUORUM	majority	_____

3. OBELISK	shaft	_____
4. HOBNOB	twisted logic	_____
5. PROMETHEAN	creative	_____
6. SARCOPHAGUS	cremation	_____
7. HELOT	hell-on-wheels	_____
8. ANTIMACASSAR	against travel	_____
9. KOWTOW	bow low	_____
10. PALADIN	villain	_____

Lesson 7.

The quirky stories behind the following ten words can help you understand and remember them better. Read through the histories and complete the two quizzes to add to your mastery of language.

1. **quahog** (kwô′hôg, -hog) Despite the "hog" at the end of the word, a "quahog" has nothing to do with a pig. Rather, it is a clam; the word comes from the Algonquian (Narragansett) word "poquauhock."

2. **protean** (prō′tē ən) According to Greek legend, Proteus was a sea god who possessed the power to change his shape at will. He also had the ability to foretell the future, but those wishing to avail themselves of his power first had to steal upon him at noon when he checked his herds of sea calves, catch him, and bind him securely. Thus bound, Proteus would change shape furiously, but the petitioner who could keep him restrained until he returned to his original shape would receive the answer to his question—if he still remembered what he wanted to know. From Proteus, then, we get the word "protean," *readily assuming different forms or characters; variable.*

3. **noisome** (noi′səm) Although the words appear to have the same root, "noisome" bears no relation to "noise." "Noisome" means *offensive* or *disgusting,* as an odor, and comes from the Middle English word "noy," meaning *harm.* The root is related, however, to the word "annoy," *to molest or bother.*

4. **Ouija** (wē′jə) "Ouija" is a trademark for *a board game used to spell out messages in spiritualistic communication.* It consists of a small board, or planchette, resting on a larger board marked with words and letters. The name comes

from the French and German words for *yes,* "oui" and "ja."

5. **simony** (sī'mə nē, sim'ə-) Simon the sorcerer offered to pay the Apostle Peter to teach him the wondrous cures he had seen him perform, not understanding that his feats were miracles rather than magic tricks. From Simon's name comes the term "simony," *the sin of buying or selling ecclesiastical preferments.*

6. **rigmarole** (rig'mə rōl') In fourteenth-century England, a register of names was called a "rageman." Later it became a "ragman," then "ragman roll." As it changed, the term evolved to refer to a series of unconnected statements. By the 1700s, the word had become "rigmarole," with its present meaning, *an elaborate or complicated procedure.*

7. **bolshevik** (bōl'shə vik) At a rally of Communist leaders in 1903, Lenin garnered a majority of the votes. He cleverly dubbed his supporters "Bolsheviks," meaning *the majority.* His move was effective propaganda. Even though his supporters actually comprised only a minority, the name stuck and came to be associated with *a member of the Russian Communist party.* The word is also used in a derogatory sense to denote *an extreme political radical, a revolutionary.*

8. **misericord** (miz'ər i kôrd', mi zer'i kôrd') Both the *small projection on the underside of a hinged seat of a church stall that gives support, when the seat is lifted, to a person standing in the stall* and *a medieval dagger* have the same name, "misericord." In a curious sense, this is because they both provide mercy, the seat giving a parishioner a resting place during a long service, the dagger delivering the coup de grâce to a wounded foe. "Misericord" comes from the Latin "misericordia," meaning *compassion.*

9. **surplice** (sûr'plis) To keep themselves warm in damp, chilly stone churches, clergymen in the Middle Ages wore fur robes. But since fur was not considered proper attire for religious men, the priests covered their furs with loose-fitting white overgarments. The word "surplice" to describe these broad-sleeved white vestments came from their function: the Latin "super," *over,* and "pellicia," *fur garment.*

10. **sylph** (silf) A German alchemist of the 1700s coined the term "Sylphis" to describe the spirits of the air. He envisioned them as looking like humans but able to move more

swiftly and gracefully. Over the years, the word evolved to mean *a slender, graceful girl or woman*.

Quiz 13: True/False

In the space provided, write T if the definition of the numbered word is true or F if it is false.

			T or F
1.	MISERICORD	wretchedness	_____
2.	OUIJA	board game	_____
3.	SIMONY	slickness	_____
4.	BOLSHEVIK	sheik	_____
5.	PROTEAN	changeable	_____
6.	NOISOME	clamorous	_____
7.	SYLPH	svelte female	_____
8.	QUAHOG	bivalve	_____
9.	RIGMAROLE	simplification	_____
10.	SURPLICE	clerical vestment	_____

Quiz 14: Matching Synonyms

Match each of the numbered words with its closest synonym from the list of lettered words in the second column. Write your answer in the space provided.

1.	SYLPH	a. vestment	_____
2.	QUAHOG	b. medieval dagger	_____
3.	SURPLICE	c. ecclesiastical favors	_____
4.	BOLSHEVIK	d. slender girl	_____
5.	OUIJA	e. Communist	_____
6.	MISERICORD	f. involved process	_____
7.	NOISOME	g. variable	_____
8.	PROTEAN	h. clam	_____
9.	RIGMAROLE	i. foul	_____
10.	SIMONY	j. board game	_____

LESSON 8.

Now read the histories of these ten unique words. Fix them in your memory by completing the two quizzes that follow. The words can make your speech and writing more colorful, interesting, and effective.

1. **muumuu** (mōō′mōō′) This *loose dress, often brightly colored or patterned,* was first introduced into Hawaii by mis-

sionaries anxious to clothe their nude Hawaiian female converts. To accomplish their aims, the missionaries gave the Hawaiian women dresses cut in the European fashion, which the Hawaiians adapted to suit their needs and climate. The dress acquired the Hawaiian name "muumuu," which means *cut off,* because it lacked a yoke and therefore looked "cut off" at the neck.

2. **sybarite** (sib′ə rīt′) The ancient Greek colony of Sybaris in southern Italy was known for its luxurious life style. The residents were so famous for their opulent ways that the word "sybarite" came to be used for *any person devoted to luxury and pleasure.*

3. **rostrum** (ros′trəm) Today a "rostrum" is *any platform, stage, or the like for public speaking.* The word comes from the victory in 338 B.C. of the Romans over the pirates of Antium (Anzio), off the Italian coast. The victorious consul took back to Rome the prows of the six ships he had captured. These were attached to the lecterns used by Roman speakers. They came to be called "rostra," or *beaks.* We use the singular, "rostrum."

4. **lemur** (lē′mər) *An animal with a small foxlike face, woolly fur, and cute monkeylike body,* the "lemur" seems to some people to be an adorable creature. The scientist who first named this small nocturnal mammal, the eighteenth-century Swedish botanist Linnaeus, obviously had a less pleasant reaction to the animal, since the Latin word "lemur" denotes *malevolent, frightening spirits of the dead.*

5. **spoonerism** (spoo′nə riz′əm) The English clergyman W. A. Spooner (1844–1930) was notorious for his habit of transposing the initial letters or other sounds of words, as in "a blushing crow" for "a crushing blow." Since the good reverend was not unique in his affliction, we use the word "spoonerism" to describe these *unintentional transpositions of sounds.*

6. **vermicelli** (vûr′mi chel′ē) Anyone faced with a small child determined not to eat his or her spaghetti because "it looks like worms" had better avoid explaining the origin of "vermicelli." In Italian, "vermicelli" is the plural of "vermicello," a diminutive of "verme," which does indeed mean *worm.* When dealing with recalcitrant children, it's probably better to refer to these *long, slender threads of spaghetti* simply as "pasta."

7. **pundit** (pun′dit) Today we use the word "pundit" to mean

an expert or authority; but in the nineteenth century, the word was usually applied to a learned person in India. It comes from the Hindi word "pandit," meaning *learned man,* a Brahman with profound knowledge of Sanskrit, Hindu law, and so forth.

8. **yahoo** (yä′hōō) This word for a *coarse, uncouth person* was coined by Jonathan Swift in his 1726 novel *Gulliver's Travels.* In Swift's satire, the Yahoos were a race of humanoid brutes ruled by the Houyhnhnms, civilized horses.

9. **stoic** (stō′ik) The Stoics were philosophers of ancient Greece who believed in self-restraint. Their name comes from Greek *stoa,* "porch," where they habitually walked. Hence the word "stoic," which describes a person who is *impassive, calm, and austere.*

10. **wormwood** (wûrm′wŏŏd′) "Wormwood" is the active narcotic ingredient of absinthe, a bitter green liqueur now banned in most Western countries. Originally, however, the herb was used as a folk remedy for worms in the body. Because of the herb's bitter qualities, we also use it figuratively to mean *something bitter, grievous, or extremely unpleasant.*

Quiz 15: True/False

In the space provided, write T if the definition of the numbered word is true or F if it is false.

		T or F
1. SPOONERISM	Midwesterner	_____
2. YAHOO	oaf	_____
3. WORMWOOD	bitterness	_____
4. MUUMUU	murmur	_____
5. PUNDIT	bad kick	_____
6. LEMUR	monkeylike nocturnal mammal	_____
7. SYBARITE	slender	_____
8. STOIC	austere	_____
9. VERMICELLI	aggravation	_____
10. ROSTRUM	register	_____

Quiz 16: Matching Synonyms

Select the best definition for each numbered word. Write your answer in the space provided.

1. ROSTRUM   a. loose dress   _____
2. YAHOO   b. something bitter   _____
3. MUUMUU   c. small nocturnal
                       mammal   _____
4. SPOONERISM   d. long, thin threadlike
                       pasta   _____
5. WORMWOOD   e. impassive   _____
6. SYBARITE   f. stage or platform   _____
7. LEMUR   g. authority   _____
8. PUNDIT   h. lover of luxury   _____
9. VERMICELLI   i. transposition of
                       sounds in words   _____
10. STOIC   j. boor   _____

LESSON 9.

Here are ten more words with intriguing pasts. Read through the histories, then complete the quizzes that follow. Spend a few minutes using each of the words in a sentence to help you make them part of your everyday speech and writing.

1. **termagant** (tûr′mə gənt) The word "termagant," meaning *a violent, turbulent, or brawling woman,* comes from a mythical deity that many Europeans of the Middle Ages believed was worshiped by the Muslims. It often appeared in morality plays as a violent, overbearing personage in long robes. In modern usage, "termagant" is applied only to women.

2. **blarney** (blär′nē) According to Irish legend, anyone who kisses a magical stone set twenty feet beneath the ground of a castle near the village of Blarney, in Ireland, will henceforth possess the gift of eloquence. One story claims the Blarney stone got its powers from the eloquence of the seventeenth-century Irish patriot Cormac McCarthy, whose soft speech won favorable terms from Elizabeth I after an Irish uprising. From this stone-kissing custom, "blarney" has come to mean *flattering or wheedling talk; cajolery.*

3. **schooner** (skōō′nər) According to legend, Captain Andrew Robinson built the first "schooner," *a sailing vessel with a foremast and a mainmast.* As it cut smoothly into the water on its maiden voyage, someone presumably was heard to exclaim, "Oh, how she scoons!" Picking up on the

praise, Robinson decided to call his previously unnamed ship a "scooner." The "h" was added later. Scholars, however, doubt the veracity of this story and regard the word's source as uncertain.

4. **eunuch** (yōō'nək) A "eunuch" is *a castrated man,* especially formerly, one employed by Oriental rulers as a harem attendant. The word is based on the Greek "eunouchos," from "eune," *bed,* and "echein," *to keep,* since a eunuch is perfectly suited for guarding a woman's bed. The word is used figuratively to refer to *a weak, powerless person.*

5. **reefer** (rē'fər) The word "reefer" has several different meanings; but in the nineteenth century, the word was used to refer to sailors. The term came from a description of their duties, the taking in of the reefs. Heavy woolen coats hindered the seamen in the execution of their duties, so they wore close-fitting coats instead. These coats took their name from the sailors who wore them, and today we often refer to *any short coat or jacket of thick cloth* as a "reefer."

6. **shrew** (shrōō) In Old English, the word "shrew" described *a small, fierce rodent.* The word was later applied to *a person with a violent temper and tenacious personality* similar to the rodent's. Although "shrew" has retained this meaning, it is usually applied only to a woman.

7. **kudos** (kōō'dōz, kyōō'-) Although "kudos" has come down to us from the Greek intact in both form and meaning—*praise, glory*—in the process it has come to be regarded as a plural word, although it is singular. As a result, another new word has been formed, "kudo." Although purists still prefer "kudos is" to "kudos are," only time will tell if the transformation to kudo/kudos becomes permanent.

8. **bohemian** (bō hē'mē ən) In the early fifteenth century, a band of vagabond peasants took up residence in Paris. Knowing that they had come from somewhere in central Europe, the French dubbed the gypsies "Bohemians," in the belief that they were natives of Bohemia. Working from the stereotyped view of gypsies as free spirits, the French then applied the term "bohemian" to *a person, typically one with artistic or intellectual aspirations, who lives an unconventional life.*

9. **rhubarb** (rōō'bärb) In conventional usage, the word refers to *a long-stalked plant,* used in tart conserves and pie fill-

ings; it is also a slang term for *quarrel* or *squabble*. The ancient Greeks gave the plant its name. Since it grew in an area outside of Greece, they called it "rha barbaron." "Rha" was the name of the plant and "barbaron" meant *foreign*.

10. **lacuna** (lə kyoo′nə) "Lacuna," *a gap or missing part; hiatus,* comes from the identical Latin word, "lacuna," meaning *a hollow.* It first entered English to refer to a missing part in a manuscript. It is also the root of "lagoon."

Quiz 17: True/False

In the space provided, write T if the definition of the numbered word is true or F if it is false.

			T or F
1.	KUDOS	compliment	_____
2.	BLARNEY	cajolery	_____
3.	SHREW	cleverness	_____
4.	REEFER	woolen coat	_____
5.	LACUNA	hiatus	_____
6.	TERMAGANT	intermediate	_____
7.	BOHEMIAN	businesslike	_____
8.	SCHOONER	sailing vessel	_____
9.	RHUBARB	sweet	_____
10.	EUNUCH	castrated man	_____

Quiz 18: Definitions

Select the best definition for each numbered word. Write your answer in the space provided.

_____   1. kudos
a. enclave   b. martial arts   c. acclaim
d. humiliation

_____   2. eunuch
a. hero   b. warrior   c. castle   d. castrated man

_____   3. bohemian
a. free spirit   b. butcher   c. foreigner   d. master chef

_____   4. shrew
a. virago   b. sly   c. bibliophile   d. hearty

_____   5. lacuna
a. hot tub   b. gap   c. lake   d. cool water

_____ 6. termagant
   a. lease b. eternal c. possessive d. brawling woman
_____ 7. schooner
   a. release b. submarine c. possessive
   d. sailboat
_____ 8. rhubarb
   a. root b. ridicule c. squabble d. arrow
_____ 9. blarney
   a. mountain climbing b. sweet talk
   c. sightseeing d. luncheon meats
_____ 10. reefer
   a. coat b. renegade c. exotic fish d. regret

Lesson 10.

Recalling the history of these ten words can help you remember their meanings and make them part of your stock of words. Go through the following word histories and complete the quizzes that follow. Then review the histories to help you remember the words.

1. **solecism** (sol′ə siz′əm, sō′lə-) To the ancient Greeks, the people of the colony of Soloi spoke inexcusably poor Greek. The Greeks were perhaps most offended by the Solois' errors in grammar and usage. They called such barbarous speech "soloikismos," *the language of Soloi.* Through Latin, the word became "solecism," *a substandard or ungrammatical usage; a breech of good manners or etiquette.*

2. **requiem** (rek′wē əm) A "requiem" is a mass celebrated for the repose of the souls of the dead. It comes from the opening line of the Roman Catholic mass for the dead, "Requiem aeternam dona eis, Domine," meaning *Give them eternal rest, Lord.*

3. **tariff** (tar′if) "Tariff," *an official schedule of duties or customs imposed by a government on imports and exports,* comes from the Arabic term for *inventory,* "ta'rif." Perhaps because this story is so unexciting, a false etymology claims that the word instead comes from the name of a Moorish town near the straits of Gibraltar formerly used as a base for daring pirate raids. Colorful, but not true.

4. **blitzkrieg** (blits′krēg′) The German word "Blitzkrieg," literally *a lightning war,* describes the overwhelming Nazi attacks on Poland in 1940. In two weeks, Germany pounded Poland into submission; in six weeks, it crushed the French army. Although ultimately the Germans met defeat, their method of attack has found a place in our language, and "blitzkrieg" has come to denote *an overwhelming, all-out attack.*

5. **entrepreneur** (än′trə prə nûr′, -nŏŏr′, -nyŏŏr′) "Entrepreneur" came from the French word derived from the verb "entreprendre," *to undertake.* It was initially used in English to denote a musician's manager, the person responsible for such things as organizing concerts; in the nineteenth century, the word assumed its present meaning: *a person who organizes, manages, and assumes responsibility for a business or other enterprise.*

6. **spinnaker** (spin′ə kər) According to one story, in the mid-nineteenth century, a yachtsman devised a new racing sail. The name of the yacht was the "Sphinx," but the sailors had difficulty pronouncing the word. Their mispronunciation gave us the word "spinnaker," *a large, triangular sail carried by yachts as a headsail when running before the wind.*

7. **reynard** (rā′närd, -nərd, ren′ərd) This *poetic name given to the fox* comes from the medieval beast epic, stories first circulated orally throughout western Europe, then written down. Aside from countless hours of entertainment, these satirical tales have also provided us with words for other animals: "bruin" for *bear* and "chanticleer" for *rooster.*

8. **kibitzer** (kib′it sər) A "kibitzer" is *a spectator, especially at a card game, who gives unwanted advice to a player; a meddler.* This word came from Yiddish, which derived it from the German verb "kiebitzen," *to be a busybody; give unwanted advice to card players.* The verb, in turn, came from "Kiebitz," the German word for a lapwing, an inquisitive little bird given to shrill cries.

9. **lampoon** (lam pŏŏn′) "Lampoon," *a sharp, often virulent satire,* comes from the French word "lampon," which is thought to come from "lampons," *let's drink,* a common ending to seventeenth-century French satirical drinking songs. We also use the word as a verb meaning *to mock or ridicule.*

10. **scapegoat** (skăp'gōt') The term "scapegoat," *a person made to bear the blame for others or to suffer in their place,* comes from the sixteenth chapter of Leviticus, which describes how the high priest Aaron was directed to select two goats. One goat was to be a burnt offering to the Lord; the other, an "escape goat" for atonement, was presented alive to the Lord and sent away into the wilderness to carry away the sins of the people. The word "scape" was a shortening of "escape."

Quiz 19: True/False

In the space provided, write T if the definition of the numbered word is true or F if it is false.

		T or F
1. KIBITZER	busybody	____
2. REYNARD	goat	____
3. BLITZKRIEG	negotiations	____
4. SOLECISM	bad grammar	____
5. TARIFF	customs duties	____
6. SPINNAKER	craftsperson	____
7. REQUIEM	revival	____
8. LAMPOON	enlighten	____
9. SCAPEGOAT	substitute victim	____
10. ENTREPRENEUR	organizer and manager	____

Quiz 20: Matching Synonyms

Match each of the following numbered words with its closest synonym. Write your answer in the space provided.

1. TARIFF	a. sail	____
2. LAMPOON	b. mock	____
3. KIBITZER	c. funeral mass	____
4. SCAPEGOAT	d. fox	____
5. REYNARD	e. customs duties	____
6. REQUIEM	f. business manager	____
7. SOLECISM	g. busybody	____
8. BLITZKRIEG	h. grammatical error	____
9. SPINNAKER	i. victim	____
10. ENTREPRENEUR	j. all-out attack	____

ANSWERS TO QUIZZES IN CHAPTER 12

Answers to Quiz 1

1. F 2. F 3. T 4. F 5. T 6. T 7. T 8. F 9. T 10. F

Answers to Quiz 3

1. F 2. F 3. F 4. T 5. T 6. F 7. F 8. T 9. T 10. T

Answers to Quiz 4

1. c 2. f 3. j 4. d 5. a 6. g 7. e 8. h 9. b 10. i

Answers to Quiz 5

1. T 2. F 3. T 4. F 5. F 6. T 7. T 8. F 9. T 10. F

Answers to Quiz 6

1. j 2. c 3. g 4. a 5. b 6. i 7. d 8. e 9. f 10. h

Answers to Quiz 7

1. F 2. F 3. F 4. F 5. F 6. T 7. T 8. T 9. F 10. T

Answers to Quiz 8

1. d 2. f 3. h 4. b 5. j 6. g 7. e 8. a 9. i 10. c

Answers to Quiz 9

1. F 2. F 3. T 4. T 5. F 6. T 7. F 8. F 9. T 10. F

Answers to Quiz 10

1. a 2. b 3. b 4. c 5. a 6. b 7. a 8. a 9. c 10. b

Answers to Quiz 12

1. T 2. T 3. T 4. F 5. T 6. F 7. F 8. F 9. T 10. F

Answers to Quiz 13

1. F 2. T 3. F 4. F 5. T 6. F 7. T 8. T 9. F 10. T

Answers to Quiz 14

1. d 2. h 3. a 4. e 5. j 6. b 7. i 8. g 9. f 10. c

Answers to Quiz 15

1. F 2. T 3. T 4. F 5. F 6. T 7. F 8. T 9. F 10. F

Answers to Quiz 16

1. f 2. j 3. a 4. i 5. b 6. h 7. c 8. g 9. d 10. e

Answers to Quiz 17

1. T 2. T 3. F 4. T 5. T 6. F 7. F 8. T 9. F 10. T

Answers to Quiz 18

1. c 2. d 3. a 4. a 5. b 6. d 7. d 8. c 9. b 10. a

Answers to Quiz 19

1. T 2. F 3. F 4. T 5. T 6. F 7. F 8. F 9. T 10. T

Answers to Quiz 20

1. e 2. b 3. g 4. i 5. d 6. c 7. h 8. j 9. a 10. f

13. IMPORTED WORDS

A long with sushi, crêpes, and pizza—and their original names —English has borrowed numerous words from foreign cultures. Here is a selection of "imported" words for you to add to your vocabulary.

LESSON 1. FRENCH BORROWINGS

We've borrowed so many words from French that someone once half-seriously claimed that English is little more than French badly pronounced. Some of these words have kept their original spelling, while others have become so Anglicized you may not recognize them as originally French.

1. **envoy** (en′voi, än′-) a diplomatic agent; an accredited messenger or representative.
2. **résumé** (rez′o͞o mā′, rez′o͞o mā′) a summing up; a brief account of personal, educational, and professional qualifications and experience, as of an applicant for a job.
3. **coup d'état** (ko͞o′dä tä′) a sudden and decisive action in politics, especially one effecting a change of government, illegally or by force.
4. **cause célèbre** (kôz′sə leb′, -leb′rə) any controversy that attracts great public attention.
5. **avant-garde** (ə vänt′gärd′, ə vant′-, av′än-, ä′vän-) the advance group in any field, especially in the visual, literary, or musical arts, whose works are unorthodox and experimental.
6. **laissez-faire** (les′ā fâr′) the theory that government should intervene as little as possible in economic affairs.

7. **rendezvous** (rän′də vōō′, -dä-) an agreement between two or more people to meet at a certain time and place.

8. **cul-de-sac** (kul′də sak′) a street, lane, etc., closed at one end; blind alley.

9. **esprit de corps** (e sprē′ də kôr′) a sense of union and of common interests and responsibilities, as developed among a group of persons associated together.

10. **idée fixe** (ē′dā fēks′) a fixed idea; obsession.

11. **joie de vivre** (zhwä′də vēv′, vē′vrə) a delight in being alive.

12. **milieu** (mil yōō′, mēl-) an environment; medium.

13. **potpourri** (pō′pōō rē′) a mixture of dried petals of roses or other flowers with spices, kept in a jar for their fragrance.

14. **rapport** (ra pôr′, rə-) a harmonious or sympathetic relationship or connection.

15. **bon vivant** (bon′vē vänt′, bôn′vē vän′) a person who lives luxuriously and enjoys good food and drink.

Quiz 1: Matching Synonyms

Match each of the following numbered words with its closest synonym. Write your answer in the space provided.

1. RENDEZVOUS	a. togetherness	_____
2. RAPPORT	b. experimental artists	_____
3. CUL-DE-SAC	c. hands-off policy	_____
4. BON VIVANT	d. love of life	_____
5. IDÉE FIXE	e. meeting	_____
6. JOIE DE VIVRE	f. environment	_____
7. POTPOURRI	g. diplomatic agent	_____
8. MILIEU	h. harmony	_____
9. AVANT-GARDE	i. controversy	_____
10. COUP D'ÉTAT	j. government overthrow	_____
11. RÉSUMÉ	k. dead end	_____
12. ESPRIT DE CORPS	l. list of qualifications	_____
13. ENVOY	m. connoisseur	_____
14. CAUSE CÉLÈBRE	n. fragrant dried flowers	_____
15. LAISSEZ-FAIRE	o. obsession	_____

Quiz 2: True/False

In the space provided, write T if the definition of the numbered word is true or F if it is false.

		T or F
1. LAISSEZ-FAIRE	a policy of leaving alone	_____
2. ESPRIT DE CORPS	harmony and union	_____
3. MILIEU	setting	_____
4. RENDEZVOUS	meeting	_____
5. IDÉE FIXE	obsession	_____
6. POTPOURRI	cooking utensils	_____
7. ENVOY	letter	_____
8. RAPPORT	announcement	_____
9. JOIE DE VIVRE	good vintage	_____
10. COUP D'ÉTAT	headache	_____
11. CAUSE CÉLÈBRE	controversy	_____
12. CUL-DE-SAC	dead end	_____
13. BON VIVANT	good sport	_____
14. RÉSUMÉ	curriculum vitae	_____
15. AVANT-GARDE	front-runners	_____

LESSON 2. ADDITIONAL FRENCH BORROWINGS

Here are fifteen more words borrowed from French. Their mastery can put vigor into your vocabulary, especially in writing.

1. **tour de force** (tŏŏr′də fôrs′) an exceptional achievement using the full skill, ingenuity, and resources of a person, country, or group.
2. **connoisseur** (kon′ə sûr′, -sŏŏr′) a person who is especially competent to pass critical judgments in art or in matters of taste.
3. **raconteur** (rak′on tûr′, -tŏŏr′) a person who is skilled in relating anecdotes.
4. **poseur** (pō zûr′) a person who attempts to impress others by assuming or affecting a manner, degree of elegance, etc.
5. **saboteur** (sab′ə tûr′) a person who deliberately destroys property, obstructs services, or undermines a cause.
6. **décolletage** (dā′kol täzh′) the neckline of a dress cut low in the front or back and often across the shoulders.
7. **mêlée** (mā′lā, mā lā′) a confused, general hand-to-hand fight.
8. **tout à fait** (tŏŏ′ tä fā′) entirely.

9. **chauffeur** (shō'fər, shō fûr') a person employed to drive another person's automobile.
10. **fiancé** (fē'än sā', fē än'sā) a man engaged to be married.
11. **protégé** (prō'tə zhā', prō'tə zhā') a person under the patronage or care of someone influential who can further his or her career.
12. **gourmet** (gŏŏr mā', gŏŏr'mā) a connoisseur in the delicacies of the table.
13. **tout de suite** (tŏŏt swēt') at once; immediately.
14. **chic** (shēk) attractive and fashionable in style; stylish.
15. **tout le monde** (tŏŏ'lə mônd') everyone; everybody.

Quiz 3: Defining Words
Define each of the following words.

1. tout à fait _____
2. gourmet _____
3. chauffeur _____
4. tout le monde _____
5. décolletage _____
6. tout de suite _____
7. tour de force _____
8. chic _____
9. protégé _____
10. connoisseur _____
11. raconteur _____
12. mêlée _____
13. saboteur _____
14. poseur _____
15. fiancé _____

Suggested Answers: 1. entirely 2. a connoisseur in the delicacies of the table 3. a person employed to drive another person's automobile 4. everyone; everybody 5. a low-cut neckline or backless dress 6. at once; immediately 7. an exceptional achievement using the full skill, ingenuity, and resources of a person, country, or group 8. attractive and fashionable in style 9. a person under the patronage or care of someone influential who can further his or her career 10. a person who is especially competent to pass critical judgments in art, especially one of the fine arts, or in matters of taste 11. a person who is skilled in relating anecdotes 12. a confused, general hand-to-hand fight 13. a person who destroys property, obstructs services, or subverts a cause 14. a person who attempts to impress others by assuming or affecting a manner, degree of elegance, etc. 15. a man engaged to be married

Quiz 4: Synonyms

Each of the following phrases contains an italicized word. Select the best synonym for each word from the choices provided. Write your answer in the space provided.

1. a daring *décolletage*
   a. low-cut dress   b. dance   c. acrobatics   d. behavior
2. a *chic* hat
   a. French   b. imported   c. expensive   d. stylish
3. the nervous *fiancé*
   a. engaged woman   b. engaged man   c. executive
   d. husband
4. *tout le monde* attended
   a. connoisseurs   b. specialists   c. everyone   d. no one
5. the entertaining *raconteur*
   a. comedian   b. storyteller   c. singer   d. poet
6. an amazing *tour de force*
   a. show of force   b. war victory   c. humiliation
   d. achievement
7. pass the butter *tout de suite*
   a. immediately   b. thank you   c. please   d. later
8. a transparent *poseur*
   a. model   b. prank   c. fraud   d. gag
9. a captured *saboteur*
   a. spy   b. demolisher   c. turncoat   d. revolutionary
10. my *protégé*
    a. mentor   b. tutor   c. child   d. dependent
11. a new *chauffeur*
    a. kitchen helper   b. mentor   c. chef   d. driver
12. a violent *mêlée*
    a. free-for-all   b. storm   c. criminal   d. sea
13. a noted *connoisseur*
    a. expert   b. politician   c. hostess   d. professor
14. completed the job *tout à fait*
    a. quickly   b. sloppily   c. entirely   d. yesterday
15. a famous *gourmet*
    a. driver   b. waitress   c. heavy eater   d. food expert

Lesson 3.

Numerous other languages have left their mark on English as well—including Italian, Spanish, and Latin. We will begin with a group of words borrowed from Italian.

ITALIAN BORROWINGS

1. **alfresco** (al fres′kō) out-of-doors; in the open air.
2. **piazza** (pē az′ə, -ä′zə) a town square.
3. **dilettante** (dil′i tänt′) a person who takes up an art, activity, or subject merely for amusement; dabbler.
4. **fiasco** (fē as′kō) a complete and ignominious failure.
5. **imbroglio** (im brōl′yō) a confused state of affairs; a complicated or difficult situation; bitter misunderstanding.
6. **impresario** (im′pri sär′ē ō′, -sär′-) a person who organizes or manages public entertainments; a manager, director, or the like.
7. **incognito** (in′kog nē′tō, in kog′ni tō′) having one's identity concealed, as under an assumed name, especially to avoid notice.
8. **manifesto** (man′ə fes′tō) a public declaration of intentions, opinions, objectives, or motives, as one issued by a government, a sovereign, or an organization.
9. **replica** (rep′li kə) a copy or reproduction of a work of art.

Quiz 5: Matching Synonyms
Match each of the following numbered words with its closest synonym. Write your answer in the space provided.

1. FIASCO	a. manager	_____
2. IMBROGLIO	b. town square	_____
3. INCOGNITO	c. outdoors	_____
4. IMPRESARIO	d. failure	_____
5. MANIFESTO	e. public declaration	_____
6. PIAZZA	f. confusion	_____
7. REPLICA	g. reproduction	_____
8. ALFRESCO	h. in disguise	_____
9. DILETTANTE	i. dabbler	_____

Quiz 6: Definitions
Each of the following phrases contains an italicized word. From the three choices provided, circle the best definition.

1. an *alfresco* café
   a. open-air   b. expensive   c. famous
2. traveling *incognito*
   a. cheaply   b. under an alias   c. quickly

3. a major *fiasco*
   a. cigar   b. fault   c. failure
4. an important *manifesto*
   a. declaration   b. expansion   c. bond issue
5. a real *dilettante*
   a. expert   b. socialite   c. amateur
6. a horrible *imbroglio*
   a. confusion   b. disgrace   c. conflagration
7. a broad *piazza*
   a. forest   b. error   c. town square
8. an expensive *replica*
   a. request   b. copy   c. machine
9. a famous *impresario*
   a. singer   b. actor   c. manager

LESSON 4. ADDITIONAL ITALIAN BORROWINGS

Italian is often said to be the most musical of the Romance languages. Make sure to practice the pronunciations of the following musical and artistic terms borrowed from Italian. The two quizzes at the end of the lesson will help you reinforce the words and their meanings.

1. **sotto voce** (sot′ō vō′chē) in a low, soft voice, so as not to be overheard.
2. **sonata** (sə nä′tə) a composition for one or two instruments, typically with three or four contrasting movements.
3. **fugue** (fyo͞og) a polyphonic composition based on one, two, or more themes that are enunciated by several voices or parts in turn, and are subject to contrapuntal treatment; in psychiatry, a period in which a patient suffers from loss of memory, often begins a new life, and upon recovery, remembers nothing from the amnesiac period. Borrowed through French from Italian "fuga," literally *a fleeing, flight.*
4. **intermezzo** (in′tər met′sō, -med′zō) a short dramatic, musical, or other entertainment of light character introduced between the acts of a drama or opera.
5. **cantata** (kən tä′tə) a choral composition, either sacred and resembling a short oratorio, or secular, as a drama set to music but not to be acted.
6. **maestro** (mī′strō) an eminent composer, teacher, or conductor of music.

7. **chiaroscuro** (kē är′ə skyŏŏr′ō) the distribution of light and shade in a picture.
8. **villanella** (vil′ə nel′ə) a rustic Italian part-song without accompaniment. The French word "villanelle," meaning *a short poem of fixed form,* was adapted from Italian.

Quiz 7: Defining Words

Define each of the following words.

1. villanella _____
2. chiaroscuro _____
3. sonata _____
4. sotto voce _____
5. maestro _____
6. cantata _____
7. intermezzo _____
8. fugue _____

Suggested Answers: 1. a part-song without accompaniment 2. the distribution of light and shade in a picture 3. a musical composition for one or two instruments, typically with three or four contrasting movements 4. in a low, soft voice 5. an eminent composer, teacher, or conductor of music 6. a choral composition 7. a short, light entertainment offered between the acts of a drama or opera 8. a polyphonic composition based on one or more themes

Quiz 8: True/False

In the space provided, write T if the definition of the numbered word is true or F if it is false.

		T or F
1. MAESTRO	famous musician	_____
2. CHIAROSCURO	shadows	_____
3. INTERMEZZO	musical interlude	_____
4. CANTATA	song	_____
5. SONATA	ballad	_____
6. VILLANELLA	part-song	_____
7. FUGUE	musical instrument	_____
8. SOTTO VOCE	strident voice	_____

LESSON 5. SPANISH BORROWINGS

Our neighbors to the south have also enriched our language with a number of words that reflect the merging of Spanish culture with our own. You may find that you are already familiar with some of the following words but were unaware of their Hispanic ancestry.

1. **desperado** (des′pə rä′dō, -rā′-) a bold, reckless criminal or outlaw.
2. **fiesta** (fē es′tə) in Spain and Latin America, a festival celebrating a religious holiday; any festive celebration.
3. **siesta** (sē es′tə) a midday or afternoon rest or nap, especially as taken in Spain and Latin America.
4. **bonanza** (bə nan′zə, bō-) a rich mass of ore, as found in mining; a spectacular windfall.
5. **pronto** (pron′tō) promptly; quickly.
6. **patio** (pat′ē ō′, pä′tē ō′) a paved outdoor area adjoining a house; courtyard.
7. **bolero** (bə lâr′ō, bō-) a lively Spanish dance in triple meter; a waist-length jacket worn open in front.
8. **bravado** (brə vä′dō) swaggering display of courage.

Quiz 9: True/False

In the space provided, write T if the definition of the numbered word is true or F if it is false.

		T or F
1. SIESTA	nap	_____
2. PATIO	courtyard	_____
3. BOLERO	jacket	_____
4. FIESTA	celebration	_____
5. BRAVADO	applause	_____
6. PRONTO	dappled pony	_____
7. DESPERADO	desperate lover	_____
8. BONANZA	sprawling ranch	_____

Quiz 10: Matching Synonyms

Select the best definition for each numbered word. Write your answer in the space provided.

1. PRONTO	a. great, sudden wealth or luck	_____
2. BRAVADO	b. afternoon nap	_____
3. BONANZA	c. courtyard	_____
4. BOLERO	d. bold outlaw	_____
5. DESPERADO	e. festive celebration	_____
6. SIESTA	f. promptly	

7. PATIO   g. waist-length jacket   _____
8. FIESTA   h. swaggering show of
                         bravery   _____

LESSON 6. ADDITIONAL SPANISH BORROWINGS

Here are some additional Spanish words to spice up your speech and writing. Study the definitions and complete the two quizzes at the end of the lesson to help you reinforce what you have learned.

1. **tango** (tang′gō) a ballroom dance of Spanish-American origin.
2. **arroyo** (ə roi′ō) a small steep-sided watercourse or gulch with a nearly flat floor, usually dry except in heavy rains.
3. **sierra** (sē er′ə) a chain of hills or mountains, the peaks of which suggest the teeth of a saw.
4. **mesa** (mā′sə) a land formation having a flat top and steep rock walls, common in arid and semi-arid parts of the United States and Mexico.
5. **chili con carne** (chil′ē kon kär′nē) a spicy Mexican-American dish of meat, beans, onion, chopped pepper, tomatoes, and seasonings.
6. **guerrilla** (gə ril′ə) a member of a small, independent band of soldiers that harass the enemy by surprise raids, sabotage, etc.
7. **mustang** (mus′tang) a small, hardy horse of the American plains.
8. **caudillo** (kou t͟hē′lyô, -t͟hē′yô) a head of state, especially a military dictator.

Quiz 11: Definitions

For each definition, select the correct vocabulary word. Write your answer in the space provided.

_____   1. a member of a band of independent soldiers who harass the enemy through surprise attacks
           a. quadroon b. arroyo c. mustang d. guerrilla
_____   2. a Mexican-American dish of meat, beans, tomatoes, onion, chopped pepper, and seasonings
           a. sierra b. taco c. chili con carne d. peccadillo

_____ 3. a small, steep-sided watercourse or gulch with a nearly flat floor
   a. arroz con pollo   b. tango   c. arroyo   d. mesa

_____ 4. a small, hardy horse
   a. arroyo   b. mustang   c. mesa   d. caudillo

_____ 5. a military dictator
   a. caudillo   b. mesa   c. sierra   d. arroyo

_____ 6. a ballroom dance of Spanish-American origin
   a. tango   b. waltz   c. quadroon   d. arroyo

_____ 7. a land formation having a flat top and steep rock walls
   a. Sierra Madre   b. tango   c. arroyo   d. mesa

_____ 8. a chain of hills or mountains
   a. quadroon   b. mesa   c. sierra   d. arroyo

Quiz 12: Matching Synonyms

Match each of the numbered words with its closest synonym. Write your answer in the space provided.

1. MESA	a. soldier	_____
2. MUSTANG	b. saw-toothed mountains	_____
3. CAUDILLO	c. ballroom dance	_____
4. ARROYO	d. flat-topped land formation	_____
5. GUERRILLA	e. chief of state	_____
6. TANGO	f. spicy dish of meat and beans	_____
7. CHILI CON CARNE	g. dry gulch	_____
8. SIERRA	h. horse	_____

Lesson 7. Latin Borrowings

We've already encountered a great number of words with Latin roots in previous lessons, but most of them have been transformed over the centuries. Here are eight Latin words and phrases that survived intact when they were incorporated into English. All are words that can add power to your speech and writing. Study the definitions and complete the two quizzes.

1. **decorum** (di kôr′əm) dignified behavior, manners, or appearance.

2. **gratis** (grat′is, grā′tis) without charge or payment; free.
3. **in toto** (in tō′tō) in all; in the whole.
4. **odium** (ō′dē əm) intense hatred or dislike, especially toward something or someone regarded as contemptible, despicable, or repugnant.
5. **per se** (pûr sā′, sē′) by, of, for, or in itself.
6. **pro tempore** prō′ tem′pə rē′, -rā′) temporarily; for the time being.
7. **status quo** (stā′təs kwō′, stat′əs) the existing state or condition; things as they are.
8. **terra firma** (ter′ə fûr′mə) firm or solid earth; dry land.

Quiz 13: Defining Words
Define each of the following words.

1. pro tempore _____
2. odium _____
3. in toto _____
4. per se _____
5. terra firma _____
6. decorum _____
7. gratis _____
8. status quo _____

Suggested Answers: 1. temporarily; for the time being 2. intense hatred or dislike 3. in all; in the whole 4. by, of, for, or in itself 5. firm or solid earth; dry land 6. dignified behavior, manners, or appearance 7. without charge or payment; free 8. the existing state or condition

Quiz 14: True/False
In the space provided, write T if the definition of the numbered word is true or F if it is false.

		T or F
1. STATUS QUO	existing state	_____
2. PRO TEMPORE	for the time being	_____
3. ODIUM	bad odor	_____
4. TERRA FIRMA	solid ground	_____
5. PER SE	amount	_____
6. IN TOTO	with the dog	_____
7. GRATIS	free	_____
8. DECORUM	embellishment	_____

ANSWERS TO QUIZZES IN CHAPTER 13

Answers to Quiz 1

1. e 2. h 3. k 4. m 5. o 6. d 7. n 8. f 9. b 10. j 11. l 12. a 13. g 14. i
15. c

Answers to Quiz 2

1. T 2. T 3. T 4. T 5. T 6. F 7. F 8. F 9. F 10. F 11. T 12. T 13. T
14. T 15. T

Answers to Quiz 4

1. a 2. d 3. b 4. c 5. b 6. d 7. a 8. c 9. b 10. d 11. d 12. a 13. a 14. c
15. d

Answers to Quiz 5

1. d 2. f 3. h 4. a 5. e 6. b 7. g 8. c 9. i

Answers to Quiz 6

1. a 2. b 3. c 4. a 5. c 6. a 7. c 8. b 9. c

Answers to Quiz 8

1. T 2. T 3. T 4. F 5. F 6. T 7. F 8. F

Answers to Quiz 9

1. T 2. T 3. T 4. T 5. F 6. F 7. F 8. F

Answers to Quiz 10

1. f 2. h 3. a 4. g 5. d 6. b 7. c 8. e

Answers to Quiz 11

1. d 2. c 3. c 4. b 5. a 6. a 7. d 8. c

Answers to Quiz 12

1. d 2. h 3. e 4. g 5. a 6. c 7. f 8. b

Answers to Quiz 14

1. T 2. T 3. F 4. T 5. F 6. F 7. T 8. F

14. SPECIAL WORDS

LESSON 1. SLANG

Slang is a very informal use of vocabulary and idiom, typically formed by creative, often clever juxtapositions of images or words. It is characteristically more metaphorical, playful, elliptical, vivid, and ephemeral than ordinary language.

New slang expressions tend to come from subcultures, such as adolescents, ethnic minorities, citizen-band radio broadcasters, sports groups, criminals, and members of established institutions, such as the armed forces or labor unions. If members of the subculture have sufficient contact with the mainstream culture, the slang expression often passes into general use. For instance, "cool" *(fashionable, well-accepted)*, "nitty-gritty" *(the core or crux of some matter)*, and "The Man" *(the law)* all derive from the black culture of New York's Harlem area.

Slang develops just as other levels of language develop. In some instances, words acquire new meanings ("cat" for a *person*); in others, a meaning becomes extended ("fink," at first *a strikebreaker*, now refers to any betrayer). Words become abbreviated ("burger" for "hamburger," "perk" for "percolate"); and acronyms become widely used ("VIP"). Often words are created to deal with social and other innovations (as "tailgating," "yuppie," "hip-hop").

Slang expressions can quickly become passé ("sheik," "skiddoo," "goo-goo eyes," "the cat's pajamas," "hepcat") or standard speech ("hand-me-down" for "second-hand item"). Today, mass communication has greatly speeded up the circulation of slang expressions.

While slang invigorates a language, giving it freshness and energy, it has no place in formal speech and writing. Use it occasionally to flavor your conversation, but be careful to suit your audience and purpose. Also, make sure the words you're using are not stale and out of date.

Quiz 1: Write In

Each of the following sentences contains an italicized slang word or expression that is perfectly appropriate in the context of informal conversation. For each sentence, replace the slang word with a word or phrase that would be better suited to more formal usage and notice the effect of the change. Write your answer in the space provided.

_____   1. He really *bugs* me when he does that.
_____   2. Slow down! *Smokey's* up ahead behind those bushes!
_____   3. That chore was a real *pain in the neck.*
_____   4. Johnny was hit on the *bean* with the softball.
_____   5. I had a lot of *moola* riding on that bet.
_____   6. I *blew* it all at the races.
_____   7. That franchise deal was a *ripoff.*
_____   8. If you keep on drinking like that, you're going to get *plastered.*
_____   9. I wish he'd quit his *bellyaching.*
_____   10. When she's in one of those moods, she's a real *sourpuss.*
_____   11. He *zapped* the figures marching across the screen and defeated his opponent.
_____   12. What's your *beef*?
_____   13. I told him to *bug off.*
_____   14. If he doesn't start studying soon, he's going to *flunk* this course.
_____   15. Mike is *hooked on* video games.

Suggested Answers: 1. annoys, bothers 2. state highway trooper 3. nuisance, bother 4. head 5. money 6. spent, wasted 7. fraud, swindle 8. drunk 9. complaining, grumbling 10. complainer, grumbler, grouch 11. hit, destroyed, demolished 12. complaint 13. leave, depart 14. fail 15. addicted to, obsessed with

LESSON 2. JARGON AND ARGOT

"Get him in here stat," the doctor ordered. "Stat," a word adopted by the medical establishment from Latin "statim," is medical argot for "immediately" and is used when doctors and their assistants want to communicate quickly and efficiently. Both "jargon" and "argot" refer to the vocabulary that is peculiar to a specific group of people and that has been devised for intergroup communication or identification. Its use is also a means of restricting access by the uninitiated and creating a sense of exclusivity among group members. Though the words "jargon" and "argot" are interchangeable, "jargon" has derogatory connotations and one of its common meanings is *gibberish, nonsense*. For that reason we shall use the designation "argot" for specialized terminology.

While some argot does pass into general circulation, most of it remains incomprehensible to the layperson. Argot should be used only within the field to which it belongs; otherwise, it will probably fail to communicate your meaning. Here are some examples of argot drawn from different disciplines.

Legal Argot

on all fours	a legal precedent exactly on the mark
blacklining	marking up a legal document for changes
nit	a small point
conformed copy	a legal document with a printed rather than a signed name
counterparts	identical copies signed by different parties

Publishing Argot

dummy	a mocked-up copy to be checked, as for pagination
proof	a trial impression of composed type taken to correct errors and make alterations
gutter	the white space formed by the inner margins of two facing pages of a book
slush pile	unsolicited manuscripts

Printing Argot

bleed	illustration or printing that extends beyond the trim size of the page
roll size	paper width
live art	the actual art being used
blanket	the rubber sheet in a printing press that transfers the image from the plate to the paper

Theater Argot

angel   a theatrical backer
spot   a spotlight
apron   the part of a stage in front of the curtain
ice   free tickets

Computer Argot

boot up   to start a computer by loading the operating system
crash   a major computer malfunction
debug   to detect and correct errors in a system
interface connection; interaction
on-line   connected to a main computer

Aeronautics Argot

jig   a device in which an airplane part can be held while it is being worked on
BAFO   best and final offer
RFQ   request for quote
CDRL   contract data requirements list

Quiz 2: Matching Synonyms

Below are some examples of baseball argot. See how closely you can match each word or phrase with its meaning. Write your answer in the space provided.

_____ 1. fungo

_____ 2. around the horn

_____ 3. hit for the cycle

_____ 4. can of corn

_____ 5. grand slam

_____ 6. Baltimore chop

a. a high fly ball that's easy to catch

b. batter hits the ball down so it will bounce high

c. a baseball tossed in the air and struck as it comes down

d. a home run with three runners on base

e. to get a single, double, triple, and home run in one game

f. a double play started by the third baseman

LESSON 3. DIALECT AND BRITICISMS

A dialect is a version of language spoken in a particular geographic region or by a specific group of people. Dialects frequently contain words, pronunciations, and grammatical structures that are not accepted as standard English. For example, in the British Yorkshire dialect, "something" would be rendered as "summat."

Although the Americans and the British have little difficulty communicating with each other, each country nevertheless retains a vocabulary of its own. Words used specifically by the British are known as Briticisms. Here are some of the more common ones.

Americanism	*Briticism*
bar	pub
laid off (from a job)	redundant
raincoat	mackintosh
police officer, cop	bobby
guy	bloke
candy store	sweet-shop
crazy	barmy
druggist	chemist
TV	telly
gasoline	petrol
elevator	lift
run (in a stocking)	ladder
sofa	settee
subway	underground
hood (of a car)	bonnet
naked	starkers
napkin	serviette
truck	lorry
call up (on the telephone)	ring up
French-fried potatoes	chips

Quiz 3: Matching Synonyms

Match each Briticism with its American counterpart. Write your answer in the space provided.

1. LIFT	a. napkin	_____
2. UNDERGROUND	b. sofa	_____

3. TELLY   c. hood (of a car)   _____
4. BARMY   d. truck   _____
5. CHIPS   e. guy   _____
6. REDUNDANT   f. elevator   _____
7. SETTEE   g. druggist   _____
8. PETROL   h. TV   _____
9. BLOKE   i. police officer, cop _____
10. BOBBY   j. run (in a stocking) _____
11. LORRY   k. subway   _____
12. CHEMIST   l. crazy   _____
13. RING UP   m. call up   _____
14. MACKINTOSH   n. gasoline   _____
15. SERVIETTE   o. raincoat   _____
16. PUB   p. French fries   _____
17. SWEET-SHOP   q. bar   _____
18. LADDER   r. laid off   _____
19. BONNET   s. candy store   _____
20. STARKERS   t. naked   _____

ANSWERS TO QUIZZES IN CHAPTER 14

Answers to Quiz 2

1. c 2. f 3. e 4. a 5. d 6. b

Answers to Quiz 3

1. f 2. k 3. h 4. l 5. p 6. r 7. b 8. n 9. e 10. i 11. d 12. g 13. m 14. o
15. a 16. q 17. s 18. j 19. c 20. t

15. GUIDE TO GENDER-NEUTRAL LANGUAGE

Word choices and grammatical constructions that ignore or minimize the presence and contributions of one sex in society—at home or school or the workplace, in business or professional spheres, in social or personal relationships—may be considered sexist. Many writers and speakers try to avoid such usages, and they reject as well language that calls attention to the sex of an individual when it is irrelevant to the role or situation under discussion. Here are specific suggestions for using gender-neutral terms, from replacing one term with another to recasting sentences.

1. Replacing *man* or *men*, or words or expressions containing either, when they are clearly intended to refer to a person of either sex or to include members of both sexes.

Instead of	*Consider using*
man	human being, human, person, individual
mankind, man (collectively)	human beings, humans, humankind, humanity, people, human race, human species, society, men and women
man-made	synthetic, artificial
workingman	worker, wage earner
man in the street	average person, ordinary person

2. Using gender-neutral terms wherever possible to designate occupations, positions, roles, etc., rather than terms that specify sex. This dictionary gives neutral equivalents for many gender-specific terms. A full list of nonsexist job

designations can be found in the *Dictionary of Occupational Titles* published by the U.S. Department of Labor.

a.   Avoiding terms ending in *-man* or other gender-specific forms. One approach is to use words ending in *-person*. Some of these terms, like *salesperson* and *spokesperson,* have achieved wide acceptance; others, like *councilperson* and *weatherperson,* still sound awkward to many people. When discussing an individual whose sex is known, gender-specific terms such as *anchorwoman, businessman, saleswoman,* and *salesman* can be used, although in this situation, too, many people still prefer the neutral terms.

Instead of	*Consider using*
anchorman	anchor
bellman, bellboy	bellhop
businessman	businessperson *or more specifically* business executive, manager, business owner, retailer, etc.
cameraman	camera operator, cinematographer
chairman	chair, chairperson
cleaning lady, cleaning woman	housecleaner, office cleaner, housekeeper
clergyman	member of the clergy, cleric *or more specifically* minister, rabbi, priest, pastor, etc.
congressman	representative, member of Congress, legislator
fireman	firefighter
forefather	ancestor
housewife	homemaker
insurance man	insurance agent
layman	layperson, nonspecialist, nonprofessional
mailman, postman	mail carrier, letter carrier
policeman	police officer, law enforcement officer
salesman	salesperson, sales representative

spokesman	spokesperson, representative
stewardess, steward	flight attendant
weatherman	weather reporter, weathercaster, meteorologist
workman	worker

b. Avoiding "feminine" suffixes such as *-ess, -ette, -trix,* and *-enne.* Words with these suffixes are often regarded as implying triviality or inferiority on the part of the person or role involved, as well as making unnecessary reference to the person's sex.

Instead of	*Consider using*
authoress	author
aviatrix	aviator
poetess	poet
proprietress	proprietor
sculptress	sculptor
suffragette	suffragist
usherette	usher

A few such terms, like *actress, heiress,* and *hostess,* remain in active use, though many women prefer the terms *actor, heir,* and *host.* Several substitutions for both *waitress* and *waiter*—*waitperson, waitron,* and *server*—are gaining ground, but none has yet replaced the traditional designations. Legal terms like *executrix* and *testatrix* are still used, but with diminishing frequency.

c. Eliminating as modifiers the words *lady, female, girl, male,* and the like for terms that otherwise have no gender designation, as in *lady doctor, female lawyer, girl athlete,* or *male secretary*, unless they serve to clarify meaning. Such expressions tend to patronize the individual involved by suggesting that the norm for the role is the gender *not* specified, and that for someone of the gender specified to be found in that role is somehow remarkable or peculiar. When it is necessary to point out the female aspect of a person in a given role or occupation, using *female* or *woman* as a modifier is preferable to *lady: My grandmother was the first woman doctor to practice in this town.*

3. Referring to members of both sexes by parallel terms, names, or titles.

Instead of	Consider using
man and wife	husband and wife
men and girls	men and women, boys and girls
men and ladies	men and women, ladies and gentlemen
President Johnson and Mrs. Meir	President Johnson and Prime Minister Meir *or* Mr. Johnson and Mrs. Meir

4. Avoiding the third person singular masculine pronoun when referring to an individual who could be of either sex, as in *When a reporter covers a controversial story, he has a responsibility to present both sides of the issue.* Rephrasing the sentence in any of the following ways will circumvent this situation:

   a. Structuring the sentence in the plural and using the third person plural pronouns *they/their/theirs/them: When reporters cover controversial stories, they have a responsibility* .... (Some people approve the use of a plural pronoun to refer to an indefinite like *everyone* or *anyone,* as in *Everyone packed their own lunch,* but many people do not, at least in formal writing.)

   b. Using either first or second person pronouns—*I/me/my/mine, we/us/our/ours, you/your/yours*—that do not specify sex: *As a reporter covering a controversial story, I have a responsibility* ... or *As reporters covering controversial stories, we have a responsibility* ... or *When you are a reporter covering a controversial story, you have a responsibility* ....

   c. Using the third person *one: As a reporter covering a controversial story, one has a responsibility* .... (Although common in British usage, *one* can seem stilted or excessively formal to Americans. This pronoun is most effective when used sparingly.)

   d. Using both the masculine and feminine singular pronouns: *When a reporter covers a controversial story, he or she* (or *she or he*) *has a responsibility* .... (This approach is the one most likely to produce awkwardness. But if the pronouns are not repeated too often, it may sometimes be the most satisfactory solution.) The abbreviated forms *he/she, his/her, him/her* (and the reverse forms, with the feminine pronoun first) are also available, though they are not widely used in formal writing. The blend *s/he* is also used by some people.

e. Using the passive voice: *When controversial stories are covered, there is a responsibility to present both sides of the issue* (or *both sides of the issue should be presented*).

f. Rephrasing the sentence to avoid any pronoun: *When covering a controversial story, a reporter has a responsibility* . . . .

g. Using nouns, like *person, individual,* or a synonym appropriate to the context, instead of pronouns: *Reporters often cover controversial stories. In such cases the journalist has a responsibility* . . . .

h. Using a relative clause: *A reporter who covers a controversial story has a responsibility* . . . .

Different solutions will work better in different contexts.

5. Avoiding language that disparages, stereotypes, or patronizes either sex.

a. Avoiding reference to an adult female as a *girl;* to women collectively as *the distaff side* or *the fair sex;* to a wife as *the little woman;* to a female college student as a *coed;* to an unmarried woman as a *bachelor girl, spinster,* or *old maid.*

b. Being aware that such generalized phrases as *lawyers/doctors/farmers and their wives* or *a teacher and her students* or *a secretary and her boss* can be taken to exclude an entire sex from even the possibility of occupying a role. It is possible to choose words or forms that specify neither sex or acknowledge both sexes, as in *lawyers . . . and their spouses* (or *families* or *companions*); *a teacher and his or her students* (or *a teacher and students* or *teachers and their students*); *a secretary and his or her boss* (or *a secretary and boss*).

c. Avoiding terms like *womanly, manly, feminine,* or *masculine* in referring to traits stereotypically associated with one sex or the other. English abounds in adjectives that describe such qualities as strength or weakness, nurturing or determination or sensitivity, without intrinsic reference to maleness or femaleness.

16. POWER VOCABULARY OF THE '90S

English vocabulary keeps growing bigger each year. This exuberant growth can be attributed to two factors: (1) The vocabulary explosion that began with the eighteenth-century industrial revolution has continued unabated to this day, thanks largely to scientific and technological innovation; and (2) The many resources available today—from books, magazines, newspapers, specialized glossaries, and electronic databases, not to mention radio and television shows, motion pictures, and plays—popularize and give life to new words.

To help you keep up with many of the new words and meanings that are now part of modern American English, we have put together the following vocabulary quizzes. These quizzes are arranged according to general subjects. How word savvy are you? How many of these new terms are you familiar with?—

Based on what you may have heard in everyday talk, match each of the numbered words with the closest synonym or definition. Write your answer in the space provided.

Quiz 1. General Vocabulary

1. AGITA	a. low-wage job	_____
2. KENBEI	b. wonderful	_____
3. FREQUENT FLIER	c. anxiety	_____
4. DOULA	d. excited	_____
5. MCJOB	e. suburban area	_____
6. HISSY	f. fast route	_____
7. SUPERHIGHWAY	g. midwife	_____
8. PHAT	h. temper tantrum	_____
9. STOKED	i. anti-American sentiment	_____
10. EDGE CITY	j. habitual traveller	_____

Quiz 2. Science, Medicine, and Technology

1. ANYON
2. NECROPSY
3. EXTRACHROMOSOMAL
4. ANTIREJECTION
5. VINCA

a. periwinkle
b. DNA acting independently
c. autopsy
d. elementary particle
e. preventing refusal of transplants

_____
_____
_____
_____
_____

Quiz 3. Computers and Cyberspace

1. CYBER-
2. NEWBIE
3. SNAIL MAIL
4. DONGLE
5. APPLICATION

a. uninitiated Internet user
b. device preventing unauthorized use
c. computer program
d. physical delivery of information
e. pertaining to the Internet

_____
_____
_____
_____
_____

Quiz 4. Business, Economics, and Law

1. BORK
2. EU
3. QUANT
4. STOCKIST
5. MAQUILADORA

a. European Community
b. U.S. company in Mexico
c. attack through media
d. place stocking merchandise
e. numbers expert

_____
_____
_____
_____
_____

Quiz 5. Sensitivity and Religion

1. ABLEISM
2. ROSHI
3. CHALLENGED
4. VERTICALLY CHALLENGED
5. SUPERCHURCH

a. leader of a Zen order
b. inhibited
c. large congregations with facilities
d. short
e. discrimination against the disabled

_____
_____
_____
_____
_____

Quiz 6. Music, Art, and the Media

1. MOSH
2. RAVE
3. HIP-HOP
4. METAFICTION

5. SHOCK JOCK

a. raucous dance _____
b. rap music _____
c. bold radio personality _____
d. fiction that analyzes
   another work of
   fiction _____
e. rowdy dance party

Quiz 7. Fashion and Food

1. BREWSKI
2. BASMATI
3. LATTE
4. KENTE

5. SPOKESMODEL

a. espresso with milk _____
b. Ghanaian cloth _____
c. Indian rice _____
d. glamourous
   spokesperson _____
e. beer _____

Quiz 8. Sports and Games

1. UNDERCARD

2. ZAMBONI™
3. CRUCIVERBALIST

4. MOONBALL

5. HAIL MARY

a. supporting event to a
   feature event _____
b. high lob in tennis _____
c. long pass of
   desperation _____
d. designer of crossword
   puzzles _____
e. ice-smoothening
   vehicle _____

ANSWERS TO QUIZZES IN CHAPTER 16

Answers to Quiz 1

1. c 2. i 3. j 4. g 5. a 6. h 7. f 8. b 9. d 10. e

Answers to Quiz 2

1. d 2. c 3. b 4. b 5. a

Answers to Quiz 3

1. e 2. a 3. d 4. b 5. c

Answers to Quiz 4

1. c 2. a 3. e 4. d 5. b

Answers to Quiz 5

1. e 2. a 3. b 4. d 5. c

Answers to Quiz 6

1. a 2. e 3. b 4. d 5. c

Answers to Quiz 7

1. e 2. c 3. a 4. b 5. d

Answers to Quiz 8

1. a 2. e 3. d 4. b 5. c

17. BRUSH UP ON BASIC USAGE

Language and the way it is used change constantly. This glossary provides a concise guide to contemporary English usage. It will show you how certain words and phrases are used and why certain usage is unacceptable.

"Informal" indicates that a word or phrase is often used in everyday speech but should generally be avoided in formal discourse. "Nonstandard" means that the word or phrase is not suitable for everyday speech and writing or in formal discourse. The glossary also covers many frequently confused words and homonyms.

a/an In both spoken and written English, an is used before words beginning with a vowel sound *(He carried an umbrella. The Nobel is an honor)* and when the consonants *f, h, l, m, n, r, s,* and *x* are pronounced by name *(The renovations created an L-shaped room. Miles received an F in physics)*. Use a before words beginning with a consonant sound *(What a fish! I bought a computer)* and words that start with vowels but are pronounced as consonants *(A union can be dissolved. They live in a one-room apartment)*. Also use a with words that start with consonant letters not listed above and with the vowel *u* *(She earned a C in French. He made a U-turn)*.

For words that begin with *h,* if the initial *h* is not pronounced, the word is preceded by an *(It will take an hour)*. Adjectives such as *historic, historical, heroic,* and *habitual* are commonly preceded by an, especially in British English, but the use of a is common in both writing and speech *(She read a historical novel)*. When the *h* is strongly pronounced, as in a stressed first syllable, the word is preceded by a *(I bought a history of Long Island)*.

above Above can be used as an adjective *(The above entry is incomplete)* or as a noun *(First, please read the above)* in referring to what has been previously mentioned in a passage. Both uses are standard in formal writing.

accept/except Accept is a verb meaning "to receive": *Please accept a gift.* Except is usually a preposition or a conjunction meaning "other than" or "but for": *He was willing to accept an apology from everyone except me.*

259

When except is used as a verb, it means "to leave out": *He was excepted from the new regulations.*

accidentally/accidently The correct adverb is accidentally, from the root word accidental, not accident (*Russel accidentally slipped on the icy sidewalk*). Accidently is a misspelling.

adoptive/adopted Adoptive refers to the parent: *He resembles his adoptive father.* Adopted refers to the child: *Their adopted daughter wants to adopt a child herself.*

adverse/averse Both words are adjectives, and both mean "opposed" or "hostile." Averse, however, is used to describe a subject's opposition to something (*The minister was averse to the new trends developing in the country*), whereas adverse describes something opposed to the subject (*The adverse comments affected his self-esteem*).

advice/advise Advice, a noun, means "suggestion or suggestions": *Here's some good advice.* Advise, a verb, means "to offer ideas or suggestions": *Act as we advise you.*

affect/effect Most often, affect is a verb, meaning "to influence," and effect is a noun meaning "the result of an action": *His speech affected my mother very deeply, but had no effect on my sister at all.* Affect is also used as a noun in psychology and psychiatry to mean "emotion": *We can learn much about affect from performance.* In this usage, it is pronounced with the stress on the first syllable. Effect is also used as a verb meaning "to bring about": *His letter effected a change in their relationship.*

aggravate/annoy In informal speech and writing, aggravate can be used as a synonym for annoy. However, in formal discourse the words mean different things and should be used in this way: *Her back condition was aggravated by lifting the child, but the child's crying annoyed her more than the pain.*

agree to/agree with Agree to means "to consent to, to accept" (usually with a plan or idea). Agree with means "to be in accord with" (usually with a person or group): *I can't believe they will agree to start a business together when they don't agree with each other on anything.*

ain't The term is nonstandard for "am not," "isn't," or "aren't." It is used in formal speech and writing only for humorous effect, usually in dialogue.

aisle/isle Aisle means "a passageway between sections of seats": *It was impossible to pass through the airplane aisle during the meal service.* Isle means "island": *I would like to be on a desert isle on such a dreary morning.*

all ready/already All ready, a pronoun and an adjective, means "entirely prepared"; already, an adverb, means "so soon" or "previously": *I was all ready to leave when I noticed that it was already dinnertime.*

all right/alright All right is always written as two words; alright is a misspelling: *Betsy said that it was all right to use her car that afternoon.*

allusion/illusion An allusion is a reference or hint: *He made an allusion to the past.* An illusion is a deceptive appearance: *The canals on Mars are an illusion.*

almost/most Almost, an adverb, means "nearly"; most, an adjective, means "the greatest part of" something. Most is not synonymous with almost, as the following example shows: *During our vacation we shop at that store almost every day and buy most of the available snack foods.*

In informal speech, *most* (as a shortened form of *almost*) is used as an adverb. It occurs before such pronouns as *all, anyone, anybody, everyone,* and *everybody;* the adjectives *all, any,* and *every;* and the adverbs *anywhere* and *everywhere.* For example: *Most everyone around here is related.* The use of *most* as an adverb is nonstandard and is uncommon in formal writing except when used to represent speech.

a lot/alot/allot *A lot* is always written as two words. It is used informally to mean "many": *The unrelenting heat frustrated a lot of people. Allot* is a verb meaning "to divide" or "to set aside": *We allot a portion of the yard for a garden.* Alot is not a word.

altogether/all together *Altogether* means "completely" or "totally"; *all together* means "all at one time" or "gathered together": *It is altogether proper that we recite the Pledge all together.*

allude/elude Both words are verbs. *Allude* means "to mention briefly or accidentally": *During our conversation, he alluded to his vacation plans. Elude* means "to avoid or escape": *The thief has successfully eluded capture for six months.*

altar/alter *Altar* is a noun meaning "a sacred place or platform": *The couple approached the altar for the wedding ceremony. Alter* is a verb meaning "to make different; to change": *He altered his appearance by losing fifty pounds, growing a beard, and getting a new wardrobe.*

A.M., P.M./a.m., p.m. These abbreviations for time are most frequently restricted to use with figures: *The ceremony begins at 10:00 A.M. (not ten thirty A.M.)*

among/between *Among* is used to indicate relationships involving more than two people or things, while *between* is used to show relationships involving two people or things, or to compare one thing to a group to which it belongs: *The three quarreled among themselves because she had to choose between two of them. Between* is also used to express relationships of persons or things considered individually, no matter how many: *Between holding public office, teaching, and raising a family, she has little free time.*

amount/number *Amount* refers to quantity that cannot be counted: *The amount of work accomplished before a major holiday is always negligible. Number,* in contrast, refers to things that can be counted: *He has held a number of jobs in the past five months.* But some concepts, like time, can use either *amount* or *number,* depending how the elements are identified in the specific sentence: *We were surprised by the amount of time it took us to settle into our new surroundings. The number of hours it took to repair the sink pleased us.*

and etc. Since *etc.* means "and all the rest," *and etc.* is redundant; the "and" is not needed. Many prefer to use "and so forth" or "and the like" as a substitute for the abbreviation.

and/or The combination *and/or* is used mainly in legal and business writing. Its use should be avoided in general writing, as in *He spends his weekends watching television and/or snacking.* In such writing, either one or the other word is sufficient. If you mean either, use or; if you mean both, use and. To make a greater distinction, revise the phrasing: *He spends his weekends watching television, snacking, or both.*

and which/and who "And" is unnecessary when "which" or "who" is used to open a relative clause. Use and which or and who only to open a second clause starting with the same relative pronoun: *Elizabeth is my neighbor who goes shopping every morning and who calls me every afternoon to tell me about the sales.*

a number/the number As a subject, a number is most often plural and the number is singular: *A number of choices are available. The number of choices is limited.* As with many agreement questions, this guideline is followed more often in formal discourse than in speech and informal writing.

ante-/anti- The prefix ante- means "before" *(antecedent, antechamber, antediluvian);* the prefix anti- means against *(antigravity, antifreeze).* Anti- takes a hyphen before an *i* or a capital letter: *anti-Marxist, anti-inflationary.*

anxious/eager Traditionally, anxious means "nervous" or "worried" and consequently describes negative feelings. In addition, it is usually followed by the word "about": *I'm anxious about my exam.* Eager means "looking forward" or "anticipating enthusiastically" and consequently describes positive feelings. It is usually followed by "to": *I'm eager to get it over with.* Today, however, it is standard usage for anxious to mean "eager": *They are anxious to see their new home.*

anybody, any body/anyone, any one Anybody and anyone are pronouns; any body is a noun modified by "any" and any one is a pronoun or adjective modified by "any." They are used as follows: *Was anybody able to find any body in the debris? Will anyone help me? I have more cleaning than any one person can ever do.*

any more/anymore Any more means "no more"; anymore, an adverb, means "nowadays" or "any longer": *We don't want any more trouble. We won't go there anymore.*

anyplace Anyplace is an informal expression for "anywhere." It occurs in speech and informal writing but is best avoided in formal prose.

anyways/anyway; anywheres/anywhere Anyways is nonstandard for anyway; anywheres is nonstandard for anywhere.

apt/likely Apt is standard in all speech and writing as a synonym for "likely" in suggesting chance without inclination: *They are apt to call any moment now.* Likely, meaning "probably," is frequently preceded by a qualifying word: *The new school budget will very likely raise taxes.* However, likely without the qualifying word is standard in all varieties of English: *The new school budget will likely raise taxes.*

as Do not use as in place of *whether: We're not sure whether (not "as") you should do that.* Also avoid using as as a substitute for *because, since, while, whether,* or *who,* where its use may create confusion. In the following sentence, for example, as may mean "while" or "because": *As they were driving to California, they decided to see the Grand Canyon.*

as/because/since While all three words can function as subordinating conjunctions, they carry slightly different shades of meaning. As establishes a time relationship and can be used interchangeably with when or while. Because and since, in contrast, describe causes and effects: *As we brought out the food, it began to drizzle. Because (since) Nancy goes skiing infrequently, she prefers to rent skis.*

as/like When as functions as a preposition, the distinction between as and like depends on meaning: As suggests that the subject is equivalent to the description: *He was employed as a teacher.* Like, in contrast, suggests similarity but not equivalence: *Speakers like her excel in front of large groups.*

ascent/assent Ascent is a noun that means "a move upward or a climb": *Their ascent up Mount Ranier was especially dangerous because of the recent rock slides.* Assent can be a noun or a verb. As a verb, assent means "to concur, to express agreement": *The union representative assented to the agreement.* As a noun, assent means "an agreement": *The assent was not reached peacefully.*

assistance/assistants Assistance is a noun that means "help, support": *Please give us your assistance here for a moment.* Assistants is a plural noun that means "helpers": *Since the assistants were late, we found ourselves running behind schedule.*

assure, ensure, insure Assure is a verb that means "to promise": *The plumber assured us that the sink would not clog again.* Ensure and insure are both verbs that mean "to make certain," although some writers use insure solely for legal and financial writing and ensure for more widespread usage: *Since it is hard to insure yourself against mudslide, we did not buy the house on the hill. We left late to ensure that we would not get caught in traffic.*

at Avoid using at after "where": *Where are you seeing her (not "at")?* Whether used as an adverb or as a preposition, "where" contains the preposition "at" in its definition.

at this point in time Although the term at this point in time is widely used (especially in politics), many consider it verbose and stuffy. Instead, use "now" or "at this time": *We are not now ready to discuss the new budget.*

awful/awfully Avoid using awful or awfully to mean "very" in formal discourse: *We had an awfully busy time at the amusement park.* Although the use of awful to mean "terrible" (rather than "inspiring awe") has permeated all levels of writing and speech, consider using in its place a word that more closely matches your intended meaning: *We had an unpleasant (not "awful") time because the park was hot, noisy, and crowded.*

awhile/a while Awhile is an adverb and is always spelled as one word: *We visited awhile.* A while is a noun phrase (an article and a noun) and is used after a preposition: *We visited for a while.*

backward/backwards In formal discourse, backward is preferred: *This stroke is easier if you use a backward motion* (adjective). *Counting backward from 100 can be an effective way to induce sleep* (adverb).

bad/badly Bad, an adjective, is used to describe a noun or pronoun. Badly, an adverb, is used to describe a verb, adjective, or another adverb. Thus: *She felt bad because her broken leg throbbed badly.*

bare/bear Bare is an adjective or a verb. As an adjective, bare means "naked, unadorned": *The wall looked bare without the picture.* As a verb, bare means "to reveal": *He bared his soul.* Bear is a noun or a verb. As a noun, bear refers to the animal: *The teddy bear was named after Theodore Roosevelt.* As a verb, bear means to carry: *He bears a heavy burden.*

because/due to the fact that/since Because or since are preferred over the wordy phrase due to the fact that: *He wrote the report longhand because (not "due to the fact") his computer was broken.*

before/prior to Prior to is used most often in a legal sense: *Prior to settling the claim, the Smiths spent a week calling the attorney general's office.* Use before in almost all other cases: *Before we go grocery shopping, we sort the coupons we have clipped from the newspaper.*

being as/being that Avoid both being as and being that in formal writing. Instead, use "since" or "because." For example: *Since you asked, I'll be glad to help.*

beside/besides Although both words can function as prepositions, they have different shades of meaning: beside means "next to"; besides means "in addition to" or "except": *Besides, Richard would prefer not to sit beside the dog. There is no one here besides John and me.* Besides is also an adverb meaning "in addition": *Other people besides you feel the same way about the dog.*

better/had better The verb "had" is necessary in the phrase had better and should be retained: *She had better return the lawn mower today.*

between you and I Pronouns that function as objects of prepositions are traditionally used in the objective case: *Please keep this between you and me. I would appreciate it if you could keep this between her and them.*

bi- Many words that refer to periods of time through the prefix bi- are potentially confusing. Ambiguity is avoided by using the prefix semi-, meaning "twice each" *(semiweekly; semimonthly; semiannual)* or by using the appropriate phrases *(twice a week; twice each month; every two months; every two years).*

bias/prejudice Generally, a distinction is made between bias and prejudice. Although both words imply "a preconceived opinion" or a "subjective point of view" in favor of something or against it, prejudice is generally used to express unfavorable feelings.

blonde/blond A blonde indicates a woman or girl with fair hair and skin. Blond, as an adjective, refers to either sex *(My three blond children. He is a cute blond boy),* but blonde, as an adjective, still applies to women: *The blonde actress and her companion made the front page of the tabloid.*

borrow/lend Borrow means "to take with the intention of returning": *The book you borrow from the library today is due back in seven days.* Lend means "to give with the intention of getting back": *I will lend you the rake, but I need it back by Saturday.* The two terms are not interchangeable.

borrow off/borrow from Borrow off, considered slang, is not used in formal speech and writing; borrow from is the preferred expression.

bottom line This overworked term is frequently used as a synonym for "outcome" or "the final result": *The bottom line is that we have to reduce inven-*

tory to maintain profits. Careful writers and speakers eschew it for less shopworn descriptions.

brake/break The most common meaning of brake as a noun is a device for slowing a vehicle: *The car's new brakes held on the steep incline.* Brake can also mean "a thicket" or "a species of fern." Break, a verb, means "to crack or make useless": *Please be especially careful that you don't break that vase.*

breath/breathe Breath, a noun, is the air taken in during respiration: *Her breath looked like fog in the frosty morning air.* Breathe, a verb, refers to the process of inhaling and exhaling air: *"Please breathe deeply,"* the doctor said to the patient.

bring/take Bring is to carry toward the speaker: *She brings it to me.* Take is to carry away from the speaker: *She takes it away.*

bunch Use the noun bunch in formal writing only to refer to clusters of things grouped together, such as grapes or bananas: *That bunch of grapes looks better than the other one.* In formal writing, use *group* or *crowd* to refer to gatherings of people; bunch is used to refer to groups of people or items only in speech and informal writing.

burst, bursted/bust, busted Burst is a verb meaning "to come apart suddenly." The word busted is not acceptable in either speech or writing. The verb bust and adjective busted are both informal or slang terms; as such, they should not be used in formal writing.

but however/but yet There is no reason to combine but with another conjunction: *She said she was leaving, yet (not "but yet") she poured another cup of coffee.*

but that/but what As with the previous example, there is no reason to add the word but to either that or what: *We don't doubt that (not "but that") you will win this hand.*

buy/by Buy, a verb, means to "acquire goods at a price": *We have to buy a new dresser.* By can be a preposition, an adverb, or an adjective. As a preposition, by means "next to": *I pass by the office building every day.* As an adverb, by means "near, at hand": *The office is close by.* As an adjective, by means "situated to one side": *They came down on a by passage.*

calculate/figure/reckon None of these words is an acceptable substitute for *expect* or *imagine* in formal writing, although they are used in speech and informal prose.

can/may Traditionally, may is used in formal writing to convey permission; can, ability or capacity. In speech, however, the terms are used interchangeably to mean permission: *Can (May) I borrow your hedge clippers?* Can and may are frequently but not always interchangeable when used to mean possibility: *A blizzard can (or may) occur any time during February.* In negative constructions, can't is more common than mayn't, the latter being rare: *You can't eat that taco in the den.*

cannot/can not Cannot is occasionally spelled can not. The one-word spelling is by far the more common. The contraction can't is used mainly in speech and informal writing.

can't help but Can't help but, as in *You can't help but like her,* is a double negative. This idiom can be replaced by the informal can't help or the formal cannot but where each is appropriate: *She can't help wishing that it was spring. I cannot but wish things had turned out differently.* While can't help but is common in all types of speech, avoid using it in formal writing.

canvas/canvass Canvas, a noun, refers to a heavy cloth: *The boat's sails are made of canvas.* Canvass, a verb, means "to solicit votes": *The candidate's representatives canvass the neighborhood seeking support.*

capital/Capitol Capital is the city or town that is the seat of government: *Paris is the capital of France.* Capitol refers to the building in Washington, D.C., in which the U.S. Congress meets: *When I was a child, we went for a visit to the Capitol building.* When used with a lowercase letter, capitol is the building of a state legislature. Capital also means "a sum of money": *After the sale of their home, they had a great deal of capital.* As an adjective, capital means "foremost" or "first-rate": *He was a capital fellow.*

cause of . . . on account of/due to The phrases on account of and due to are unnecessary with cause of. Omit the phrases or revise the entire sentence: *One cause of physical and psychological problems is due to too much stress.* Change the sentence to: *Too much stress causes physical and psychological problems.*

censor/censure Although both words are verbs, they have different meanings. To censor is to remove something from public view on moral or other grounds, and to censure is to give a formal reprimand: *The committee censored the offending passages from the book and censured the librarian for placing it on the shelves.*

center around/center on Although both phrases are often criticized for being illogical, they have been used in writing for more than a hundred years to express the notion of collecting or gathering as if around a center point. The phrase *revolve around* is often suggested as an alternative, and the prepositions *at, in,* and *on* are considered acceptable with center in the following sense: *Their problems centered on their lack of expertise.*

chair/chairperson Chairperson is used widely in academic and governmental circles as an alternative to "chairman" or "chairwoman." While some reject the term chairperson as clumsy and unnecessary and use the term chair for any presiding officer, regardless of sex, chairperson is still standard in all types of writing and speech.

choose/chose Choose is a verb that means "to select one thing in preference to another": *Why choose tomatoes when they are out of season?* Chose is the past tense of "to choose": *I chose tomatoes over cucumbers at the salad bar.*

cite/sight/site To cite means to "quote a passage": *The scholar often cited passages from noted authorities to back up his opinions.* Sight is a noun that means "vision": *With her new glasses, her sight was once again perfect.* Site is a noun that means "place or location": *They picked out a beautiful site overlooking a lake for their new home.*

climatic/climactic The word climatic comes from the word "climate" and refers to weather: *This summer's brutal heat may indicate a climatic change.* Climactic, in contrast, comes from the word "climax" and refers to a point of high drama: *In the climactic last scene the hideous creature takes over the world.*

clothes/cloths Clothes are garments: *For his birthday, John got some handsome new clothes.* Cloths are pieces of fabric: *Use these cloths to clean the car.*

coarse/course Coarse, an adjective, means "rough or common": *The horsehair fabric was too coarse to be made into a pillow. Although he's a little coarse around the edges, he has a heart of gold.* Course, a noun, means "a path" or "a prescribed number of classes": *They followed the bicycle course through the woods. My courses include English, math, and science.*

complement/compliment Both words can function as either a noun or a verb. The noun complement means "that which completes or makes perfect": *The rich chocolate mousse was a perfect complement to the light meal.* The verb complement means "to complete": *The oak door complemented the new siding and windows.* The noun compliment means "an expression of praise or admiration": *The mayor paid the visiting officials the compliment of escorting them around town personally.* The verb compliment means "to pay a compliment to": *Everyone complimented her after the presentation.*

complementary/complimentary Complementary is an adjective that means "forming a complement, completing": *The complementary colors suited the mood of the room.* Complimentary is an adjective that means "expressing a compliment": *The complimentary reviews ensured the play a long run.* Complimentary also means "free": *We thanked them for the complimentary tickets.*

conformity to/conformity with Although the word conformity can be followed by either "to" or "with," conformity to is generally used when the idea of obedience is implied: *The new commissioner issued a demand for conformity to health regulation.* Conformity with is used to imply agreement or correspondence: *This is an idea in conformity with previous planning.*

consensus/consensus of The expression consensus of *(consensus of opinion)* is considered redundant, and the preferred usage is the single plural noun consensus, meaning "general agreement or concord": *Since the consensus was overwhelming, the city planners moved ahead with the proposal.* The phrase *general consensus* is also considered redundant. Increasingly, the word consensus is widely used attributively, as in the phrase *consensus politics.*

contact The word is both a verb and a noun. As a verb, it is frequently used imprecisely to mean "to communicate" when a more exact word *(telephone, write to, consult)* would better communicate the idea. Contact as a noun meaning "a person through whom one can obtain information" is now standard usage: *He is my contact in the state department.*

continual/continuous Use continual to mean "intermittent, repeated often" and continuous to mean "uninterrupted, without stopping": *We suffered continual losses of electricity during the hurricane. They had continuous phone service during the hurricane.* Continuous and continual are never interchangeable with regard to spatial relationships: *a continuous series of passages.*

corps/corpse Both words are nouns. A corps is a group of people acting together; the word is often used in a military context: *The officers' corps assembled before dawn for the drill.* A corpse is a dead body: *The corpse was in the morgue.*

counsel/council Counsel is a verb meaning "to give advice": *They counsel recovering gamblers.* Council is a noun meaning "a group of advisers": *The trade union council meets in Ward Hall every Thursday.*

couple/couple of Both phrases are informally used to mean "two" or "several": *I need a couple more cans of spackle. I took a couple of aspirins for my headache.* The expression a couple of is used in standard English, especially in referring to distance, money, or time: *He is a couple of feet away. I have a couple of thousand dollars in the bank. The store will open in a couple of weeks.* Couple may be treated as either a singular or plural noun.

credible/creditable/credulous These three adjectives are often confused. Credible means "believable": *The tale is unusual, but seems credible to us.* Creditable means "worthy": *Sandra sang a creditable version of the song.* Credulous means "gullible": *The credulous Marsha believed that the movie was true.*

criteria/criterion Criteria is the plural of criterion (a standard for judgment). For example: *Of all their criteria for evaluating job performance, customer satisfaction was the most important criterion.*

data/datum Data is the plural of datum (fact). Although data is often used as a singular, it should still be treated as plural in formal speech and writing: *The data pertain (not "pertains") to the first half of the experiment.* To avoid awkward constructions, most writers prefer to use a more commonplace term such as "fact" or "figure" in place of datum.

descent/dissent Descent, a noun, means "downward movement": *Much to their surprise, their descent down the mountain was harder than their ascent had been.* Dissent, a verb, means "to disagree": *The town council strongly dissented with the proposed measure.* Dissent as a noun means "difference in sentiment or opinion": *Dissent over the new proposal caused a rift between colleagues.*

desert/dessert Desert as a verb means to abandon; as a noun, an arid region: *People deserted in the desert rarely survive.* Dessert, a noun, refers to the sweet served as the final course of a meal: *My sister's favorite dessert is strawberry shortcake.*

device/devise Device is a noun meaning "invention or contrivance": *Do you think that device will really save us time?* Devise is a verb meaning "to contrive or plan": *Did he devise some device for repairing the ancient pump assembly?*

die/dye Die, as a verb, means "to cease to live": *The frog will die if released from his aquarium into the pond.* Dye as a verb means "to color or stain something": *I dye the drapes to cover the stains.*

differ from/differ with Differ from means "to be unlike"; differ with means "to disagree with": *The sisters differ from each other in appearance. We differ with you on this matter.*

different from/different than Although different from is the preferred usage

(His attitude is different from mine), different than is widely accepted when a clause follows, especially when the word "from" would create an awkward sentence. Example: *The stream followed a different course than the map showed.*

discreet/discrete Discreet means "tactful;" discrete, "separate." For example: *Do you have a discreet way of refusing the invitation? The mosaic is made of hundreds of discrete pieces of tile.*

disinterested/uninterested Disinterested is used to mean "without prejudice, impartial" *(He is a disinterested judge)* and uninterested to mean "bored" or "lacking interest." *(They are completely uninterested in sports).*

dominant/dominate Dominant, an adjective, means "ruling, controlling": *Social scientists have long argued over the dominant motives for human behavior.* Dominate, a verb, means "to control": *Advice columnists often preach that no one can dominate you unless you allow them to.*

don't/does not Don't is the contraction for "do not," not for does not, as in *I don't care, she doesn't (not don't) care.*

done Using done as an adjective to mean "through, finished" is standard. Originally, done was used attributively *(The pact between them was a done thing),* but it has become more common as a compliment: *Are your pictures done yet? When we were done with the power saw, we removed the blade.*

double negatives Although the use of double negatives *(They never paid no dues)* was standard for many years in English, today certain uses of the double negative are universally considered unacceptable: *He didn't have nothing to do,* for example. In educated speech and writing, "anything" would be used in place of "nothing."

doubt that/doubt whether/doubt if Doubt that is used to express conviction *(I doubt that they intended to hurt your feelings);* doubt whether and doubt if are used to indicate uncertainty: *I doubt whether (or if) anyone really listened to the speaker.*

due to In formal discourse, due to is acceptable only after a form of the verb "to be": *Her aching back was due to poor posture.* Due to is not acceptable as a preposition meaning "because of" or "owing to": *Because of (not "due to") the poor weather, the bus was late.*

each When each is used as a pronoun, it takes a singular verb *(Each was born in Europe),* although plurals are increasingly used in formal speech and writing in an attempt to avoid using "he" or "his" for sentences that include females or do not specify sex: *(Each of them had their (rather than "his") own agenda.* More and more, the same pattern of pronoun agreement is being used with the singular pronouns *anyone, anybody, everyone, everybody, no one, someone,* and *somebody.* When the pronoun each is followed by an "of" phrase containing a plural noun or pronoun, usage guides suggest that the verb be singular, but the plural is used often even in formal writing: *Each of the children has (or "have") had a school physical.*

When the adjective each follows a plural subject, the verb agrees with the subject: *The rooms each have separate thermostats.*

each and every Use "each" or "every" in place of the phrase each and every, generally considered wordy: *Each of us enjoyed the concert. Every one of us stayed until the end of the performance.*

each other/one another Each other is traditionally used to indicate two members; one another for three or more: *The two children trade lunches with each other. The guests greeted one another fondly.* In standard practice, though, these distinctions are not observed in either speech or writing.

elicit/illicit Elicit, a verb, means "call forth;" illicit, an adjective, means "against the law": *The assault elicited a protest against illicit handguns.*

emigrate/immigrate Emigrate means "to leave one's own country to settle in another": *She emigrated from France.* Immigrate means "to enter a different country and settle there": *My father immigrated to America when he was nine years old.*

eminent/imminent Eminent means "distinguished": *Marie Curie was an eminent scientist in the final years of her life.* Imminent means "about to happen": *The thundershower seemed imminent.*

enthused/enthusiastic The word enthused is used informally to mean "showing enthusiasm." For formal writing and speech, use the adjective enthusiastic: *The team was enthusiastic about the quarterback's winning play.*

envelop/envelope Envelop is a verb that means "to surround": *The music envelops him in a soothing atmosphere.* Envelope, a noun, is a flat paper container, usually for a letter: *Be sure to put a stamp on the envelope before you mail that letter.*

especially/specially The two words are not interchangeable: especially means "particularly;" specially means "for a specific reason." For example: *I especially value my wedding ring; it was made specially for me.*

-ess/-or/-er The suffix -ess has often been used to denote feminine nouns. While many such words are still in use, English is moving increasingly toward nouns that do not denote sex differences. The most widely observed guideline today is that if the sex of the performer is not relevant to the performance of the task or function, the neutral ending -or or -er should be used in place of -ess. Thus, words such as *ambassadress, ancestress, authoress, poetess, proprietress, sculptress* are no longer used; and the airlines, for example, have replaced both *steward* and *stewardess* with *flight attendant.*

et al. Et al., the Latin abbreviation for "and other people," is fully standard for use in a citation to refer to works with more than three authors: *Harris et al.*

etc. Since etc. (et cetera) is the Latin abbreviation for "and other things," it should not be used to refer to people. In general, it should be avoided in formal writing as imprecise. In its place, provide the entire list of items or use "and so on."

-ette English nouns whose -ette ending signifies a feminine role or identity are passing out of usage. *Farmerette, suffragette, usherette,* for example, have been replaced by *farmer, suffragist,* and *usher,* respectively.

ever so often/every so often Ever so often means happening very often and every so often means happening occasionally.

everybody, every body/everyone, every one Everybody and everyone are indefinite pronouns: *Everybody likes William, and everyone enjoys his company.* Every body is a noun modified by "every" and every one is a pronoun modified by "every;" both refer to a person in a specific group and are usually followed by "of": *Every body of water in our area is polluted; every one of our ponds is covered in debris.*

everyday/every day Everyday is an adjective that means "used daily, typical, ordinary"; every day is made up of a noun modified by the adjective "every" and means "each day": *Every day they had to deal with the everyday business of life.*

everywheres/everywhere Everywheres is a nonstandard term for everywhere and should be avoided in speech and writing.

exam/examination Exam should be reserved for everyday speech and examination for formal writing: *The College Board examinations are scheduled for this Saturday morning at 9:00.*

except for the fact that/except that Use except that in place of the verbose phrase except for the fact that: *Except that (not "except for the fact that") the button is missing, this is a lovely skirt.*

explicit/implicit Explicit means "stated plainly;" implicit means "understood," "implied": *You know we have an implicit understanding that you are not allowed to watch any television shows that contain explicit sex.*

fair/fare Fair as an adjective means "free from bias," "ample," "unblemished," "of light hue," or "attractive." As an adverb, it means "favorably." It is used informally to mean "honest." Fare as a noun means "the price charged for transporting a person" or "food."

farther/further Traditionally, farther is used to indicate physical distance *(Is it much farther to the hotel?)* and further is used to refer to additional time, amount, or abstract ideas *(Your mother does not want to talk about this any further).*

fewer/less Traditionally, fewer, a plural noun, has most often been used to refer to individual units that can be counted: *There are fewer buttons on this shirt. No fewer than forty of the fifty voters supported the measure.* Less, a singular noun, is used to refer to uncountable quantities: *She eats less every day. I have less patience than I used to.*

Standard English does not usually reflect these distinctions, however. When followed by "than," less is used as often as fewer to indicate plural nouns that refer to items that can be counted: *There were no less than eight million people. No less than forty of the fifty voters supported the measure.*

figuratively/literally Figuratively, meaning "involving a figure of speech," usually implies that the statement is not true. Literally, meaning "actually, without exaggeration," implies that the statement is true: *The poet Robert Frost once figuratively described writing poetry without regular meter and rhyme as playing tennis with the net down. My sister literally passed out when she saw what had happened to her new car.*

Literally is commonly used as an intensifier meaning "in effect, virtually": *The state representative was literally buried alive in the caucus.* This usage should be avoided in formal discourse.

fix The verb fix, meaning "to repair," is fully accepted in all areas of speech and writing. The noun fix, meaning "repair" or "adjustment," is used informally.

fixing to/intend to Use intend to in place of the colloquial term fixing to: *The community intends to (not "is fixing to") raise money to help the victims of the recent fire.*

flaunt/flout Flaunt means "to show off;" flout, "to ignore or treat with disdain." For example: *They flouted convention when they flaunted their wealth.*

flunk/fail Use the standard term fail in speech and writing; flunk is a colloquial substitute.

former/latter Former is used to refer to the first of two items; latter, the second: *We enjoy both gardening and painting, the former during the summer and the latter during the winter.* When dealing with three or more items, use "first" and "last" rather than former and latter: *We enjoy gardening, painting, and skiing, but the last is very costly.*

formally/formerly Both words are adverbs. Formally means "in a formal manner": *The minister addressed the king and queen formally.* Formerly means "previously": *Formerly, he worked as a chauffeur; now, he is employed as a guard.*

forth/fourth Forth is an adverb meaning "going forward or away": *From that day forth, they lived happily ever after.* Fourth is most often used as an adjective that means "next after the third": *Mitchell was the fourth in line.*

fortuitous Fortuitous means "happening accidentally": *A fortuitous meeting with a former acquaintance led to a change in plans.* It is also used sometimes as a synonym for "lucky" or "fortunate."

from whence Although the phrase from whence is sometimes criticized on the grounds that "from" is redundant because it is included in the meaning of "whence," the idiom is nonetheless standard in both speech and writing: *She finally moved to Kansas, from whence she began to build a new life.*

fulsome Originally, fulsome meant "abundant," but for hundreds of years the word has been used to mean "offensive, disgusting, or excessively lavish." While the word still maintains the connotations of "excessive" or "offensive," it has also come to be used in the original sense as well: *Compare the severe furniture of the living room to the fulsome decorations in the den.*

fun Fun should not be used as an adjective in formal writing. Instead, substitute a word such as "happy," "pleasant," or "entertaining": *They had a pleasant (not "fun") afternoon at the park.*

gentleman Once used only to refer to men of high social rank, the term gentleman now also specifies a man of courtesy and consideration: *He behaves like a gentleman.* It is also used as a term of polite reference and address in the singular and plural: *This gentleman is waiting to be served. Are we ready to begin, gentlemen?*

get The verb get is used in many slang and colloquial phrases as a substitute for forms of "to be." For example: *They won't get accepted with that attitude.* In American English, an alternative past participle is gotten, espe-

cially in the sense of "received" and "acquired": *I have gotten (or "got")
all I ever wanted.*

    Both have and has got (meaning "must") are occasionally criticized as
being redundant, but are nonetheless fully standard in all varieties of
speech and writing: *You have got to carry your driver's licence at all times.*

good/well Good, an adjective, should be used to describe someone or something: *Joe is a good student.* Well, when used as an adverb, should describe
an action: *She and Laura play well together on the swing set.* Well, when
used as an adjective after "look," "feel" or other linking verbs, often refers
to good health: *You're looking well.*

good and/very Avoid using good and as a substitute for very: *I was very (not
"good and") hungry.*

graduate The passive form, once considered the only correct usage, is seldom
used today: *I was graduated from the Merchant Marine Academy last May.*
Although some critics condemn the use of graduate as a transitive verb
meaning "to receive a degree or diploma from," its use is increasing in
both speech and writing: *She graduated from elementary school in Cleveland.*

great The word great has been overused in informal writing and speech as a
synonym for "enthusiastic," "good," or "clever": *She was really great at
making people feel at home.*

had drank/had drunk According to some authorities, had drank is acceptable
usage: *I had drank a gallon of milk.* Had drunk, though, is fully standard
and the preferred usage.

has/have; has got/have got The word "got" is unnecessary; simply use has or
have: *Jessica has a mild case of chicken pox.*

had ought/ought Had ought is considered wordy; the preferred usage is ought:
She ought (not "had ought") to heed her mother's advice.

half/a half a/a half Use either half *or* a half; a half a is considered wordy:
Please give me a half (not "a half a") piece. I'd like half that slice, please.

hanged/hung Although both words are past-tense forms of "to hang," hanged
is used to refer to executions *(Billy Budd was hanged)* and hung is used for
all other meanings: *The stockings were hung by the chimney with care.*

have/of Use have rather than of after helping verbs like "could," "should,"
"would," "may," and "might": *They should have (not "of") let me know of
their decision earlier.*

healthy/healthful Healthy means "possessing health;" healthful means
"bringing about health": *They believed that they were healthy people because they ate healthful food.*

he, she; he/she The pronouns he and she refer to male and female antecedents,
respectively. Traditionally, when an antecedent in singular form could be
either female or male, "he" was always used to refer to either sex: *A child is
often apprehensive when he first begins school.* Today, however, various ap-
proaches have been developed to avoid the all-purpose "he." Many people
find the construction *he/she* (or *he or she*) awkward: *A child is often apprehensive when he/she first begins school.* The blended form *s/he* has not been

widely adopted, probably because of confusion over pronunciation. Most people now favor either rephrasing the sentence entirely to omit the pronoun or reconstructing the sentence in the third-person plural: *Children are often apprehensive when they first begin school.*

hopefully Hopefully means "with hope": *They waited hopefully for a look at the astronaut.* In formal writing and speech, avoid using hopefully to mean "it is to be hoped": *We hope (not "Hopefully") Captain Smith will come out of the hangar soon.*

how come/why How come is used informally in speech to substitute for why.

human/humane Both words are adjectives. Human means "pertaining to humanity": *The subject of the documentary is the human race.* Humane means "tender, compassionate, or sympathetic": *Many of her patients believed that her humane care speeded their recovery.*

idea/ideal Idea means "thought," while ideal means "a model of perfection" or "goal." The two words are not interchangeable. They should be used as follows: *The idea behind the blood drive is that our ideals often move us to help others.*

if/whether Use whether rather than if to begin a subordinate clause when the clause states a choice: *I don't know whether (not "if") I should stay until the end or leave right after the opening ceremony.*

impact Both the noun and verb impact are used to indicate forceful contact: *I cannot overstate the impact of the new policy on productivity.* Some speakers and writers avoid using impact as a verb to mean "to have an effect," as in *Our work here impacts on every division in the firm.*

imply/infer Imply means "to suggest without stating": *The message on Karen's postcard implies that her vacation has not turned out as she wished.* Infer means "to reach a conclusion based on understood evidence": *From her message I infer that she wishes she had stayed home.* When used in this manner, the two words describe two sides of the same process.

in Several phrases beginning with in are verbose and should be avoided in formal writing. Refer to the following chart:

Replace the phrase . . .
in this day and age

With . . .
now

Replace the phrase . . .
in spite of the fact that

With . . .
although *or* even though

Replace the phrase . . .
in the neighborhood of

With . . .
approximately *or* about

Replace the phrase . . .
in the event that

> With . . .
> if

The following phrases can be omitted entirely: *in a very real sense, in number, in nature, in reality, in terms of,* and *in the case of.*

in/into In is used to indicate condition or location, "positioned within": *She was in labor. The raccoon was in the woodpile.* Into, in contrast, indicates movement or a change in condition "from the outside to the inside": *The raccoon went into the shed. He went into cardiac arrest.* Into is also used as a slang expression for "involved with" or "interested in": *They are really into health foods.*

inferior than Inferior to and worse than are the generally preferred forms: *This wine is inferior to (not "inferior than") the burgundy we had last night.*

incredible/incredulous Incredible means "cannot be believed;" incredulous means "unbelieving": *The teacher was incredulous when she heard the pupil's incredible story about the fate of his term project.*

individual/person/party Individual should be used to stress uniqueness or to refer to a single human being as contrasted to a group of people: *The rights of the individual should not supersede the rights of a group.* Person is the preferred word in other contexts: *What person wouldn't want to have a chance to sail around the world?* Party is used to refer to a group: *Send the party of five this way, please.* Party is also used to refer to an individual mentioned in a legal document.

ingenious/ingenuous Ingenious means "resourceful, clever": *My sister is ingenious when it comes to turning leftovers into something delicious.* Ingenuous means "frank, artless": *The child's ingenuous manner is surprising considering her fame.*

in regards to/with regards to Both terms are considered nonstandard terms for "regarding," "in regard to," "with regard to," and "as regards." *As regards (not "in regards to") your request of April 1, we have traced your shipment and it will be delivered tomorrow.*

inside/outside; inside of/outside of When the words inside and outside are used as prepositions, the word of is not included: *Stay inside the house. The authorization is outside my department.* Inside of is used informally to refer to time *(I'll be there inside of an hour)*, but in formal speech or writing within is the preferred usage: *The dump was cleaned up within a month.*

insignia Insignia was originally the plural of the Latin word "insigne." The plural term insignias has been standard usage since the eighteenth century.

irregardless/regardless Regardless is the standard term; avoid irregardless in both speech and writing.

is when/is where Both phrases are unacceptable and are to be avoided.

its/it's/its' Its is the possessive form if *it: The shrub is losing its blossoms.* It's is the contraction for *it is: It's a nice day.* The two are often confused because possessives are most frequently formed with -'s. Its' is nonstandard usage.

It's me/It's I The traditional rule is that personal pronouns after the verb "to be" take the nominative case *(I, she, he, we, they).* Today, however, such usage as *it's me, that's him, it must be them* are almost universal in informal speech. The objective forms have also replaced the nominative forms in informal speech in such constructions as *me neither, who, them?* In formal discourse, however, the nominative forms are still used: *it's I, that is he.*

-ize/-wise Use the suffix -ize to change a noun or adjective into a verb: *categorize.* Use the suffix -wise to change a noun or adjective into an adverb: *otherwise.*

kind of/sort of/type of Avoid using either kind of, sort of, or type of as synonyms for "somewhat" in formal speech and writing. Instead, use rather: *She was rather (not "kind of") slender.* It is acceptable to use the three terms only when the word kind, sort, or type is stressed: *This kind of cheese is hard to digest.* Do not add "a": *I don't know what kind of (not "kind of a") cheese that is.* When the word kind, sort, or type is not stressed, omit the phrase entirely: *That's an unusual (not "unusual kind of") car. She's a pleasant (not "pleasant sort of a") person.*

later/latter Later is used to refer to time; latter, the second of two items named: *It is later than you think. Of the two shirts I just purchased, I prefer the latter.* See also former/latter.

lay/lie Lay is a transitive verb that means "to put down" or "to place." It takes a direct object: *Please lay the soup spoon next to the teaspoon.* Lie is an intransitive verb that means "to be in a horizontal position" or "be situated." It does not take a direct object: *The puppy lies down where the old dog had always lain. The hotel lies on the outskirts of town.* The confusion arises over lay, which is the present tense of the verb lay and the past tense of the verb lie.

> To lie (recline)
>
> Present: *Spot lies (is lying) down.*
>
> Future: *Spot will lie down.*
>
> Past: *Spot lay down.*
>
> Perfect: *Spot has (had, will have) lain down.*
>
> To lay (put down)
>
> Present: *He lays (is laying) his dice down.*
>
> Future: *He will lay his dice down.*
>
> Past: *He laid his dice down.*
>
> Perfect: *He has (had, will have) laid his dice down.*

Although lie and lay tend to be used interchangeably in all but the most careful, formal speech, the following phrases are generally considered nonstandard and are avoided in written English: *Lay down, dears. The dog laid in the sun. Abandoned cars were laying in the junkyard. The reports have laid in the mailbox for a week.*

lead/led Lead as a verb means "to take or conduct on the way": *I plan to lead a quiet afternoon.* Led is the past tense: *He led his followers through the dangerous underbrush.* Lead, as a noun, means "a type of metal": *Pipes are made of lead.*

learn/teach Learn is to acquire knowledge: *He learned fast.* Teach is to impart knowledge: *She taught well.*

leave/let Leave and let are interchangeable only when followed by the word "alone": *Leave him alone. Let him alone.* In other instances, leave means "to depart" or "permit to remain in the same place": *If you leave, please turn off the copier. Leave the extra paper on the shelf.* Let means "to allow": *Let him work with the assistant, if he wants.*

lessen/lesson Lessen is a verb meaning "to decrease": *To lessen the pain of a burn, apply ice to the injured area.* Lesson is most often used as a noun meaning "material assigned for study": *Today, the lesson will be on electricity.*

let's Let's is often used as a word in its own right rather than as the contraction of "let us." As such, it is often used in informal speech and writing with redundant or appositional pronouns: *Let's us take in a movie. Let's you and me go for a walk.* Usage guides suggest avoiding let's us in formal speech and writing, although both *let's you and me* and *let's you and I* occur in the everyday speech of educated speakers. While the former conforms to the traditional rules of grammar, the latter, nevertheless, occurs more frequently.

lightening/lightning Lightening is a form of the verb that means "to brighten": *The cheerful new drapes and bunches of flowers went a long way in lightening the room's somber mood.* Lightning is most often used as a noun to mean "flashes of light generated during a storm": *The thunder and lightning frightened the child.*

like/such as Use like to compare an example to the thing mentioned and such as to show that the example is representative of the thing mentioned: *Judy wants to be a famous clothing designer like John Weitz, Liz Claiborne, and Yves St. Laurent. Judy has samples of many fine articles such as evening dresses, suits, and jackets.*

Many writers favor not separating such and as with an intervening word: *samples of many fine articles such as* rather than *samples of such fine articles as.*

loose/lose Loose is an adjective meaning "free and unattached": *The dog was loose again.* Loose can also be a verb meaning "let loose": *The hunters loose the dogs as soon as the ducks fall.* Lose is a verb meaning "to part with unintentionally": *He will lose his keys if he leaves them on the countertop.*

lots/lots of Both terms are used in informal speech and writing as a substitute for "a great many," "very many," or "much."

mad/angry Traditionally, mad has been used to mean "insane;" angry, "full of ire." While mad can be used to mean "enraged, angry," in informal usage, you should replace mad with angry in formal discourse: *The president is angry at Congress for overriding his veto.*

man The use of the term man as a synonym for "human being," both by itself and in compounds *(mankind),* is declining. Terms such as *human being(s), human race, humankind, humanity, people,* and, when necessary, *men and women* or *women and men* are widely accepted in formal usage.

-man/-person The use of the term man as the last element in compound words referring to a person of either sex who performs some function *(anchorman, chairman, spokesman)* has declined in recent years. Now such compound words are only widely used if the word refers to a male. The sex-neutral word person is otherwise substituted for man *(anchorperson, chairperson, spokesperson)*. In other instances, a form without a suffix *(anchor, chair)*, or a word that does not denote gender *(speaker)*, is used.

The compound words *freshman, lowerclassmen, underclassmen* are still generally used in schools, and *freshman* is used in the U.S. Congress as well. These terms are applied to members of both sexes. As a modifier, *freshman* is used with both singular and plural nouns: *freshman athlete, freshman legislators.* See also chair/chairperson.

maybe/may be Maybe, an adverb, means "perhaps": *Maybe the newspapers can be recycled with the plastic and glass.* May be, a verb, means "could be": *It may be too difficult, however.*

me and Me and is considered nonstandard usage when part of a compound subject: *Bob and I (not "Me and Bob") decided to fly to Boston.*

media Media, the plural of medium, is used with a plural verb: *Increasingly, the radio and television media seem to be stressing sensational news.*

mighty Mighty is used informally for "very" or "extremely": *He is a mighty big fighter.*

moral/morale As a noun, moral means "ethical lesson": *Each of Aesop's fables has a clear moral.* Morale means "state of mind" or "spirit": *Her morale was lifted by her colleague's good wishes.*

more important/more importantly Both phrases are acceptable in standard English: *My donations of clothing were tax deductible; more important(ly), the clothes were given to homeless people.*

Ms. (or Ms) The title Ms. is widely used in business and professional circles as an alternative to "Mrs." and "Miss," both of which reveal a woman's marital status. Some women prefer "Mrs.," where appropriate, or the traditional "Miss," which is still fully standard for an unmarried woman or a woman whose marital status is unknown. Since Ms. is not an abbreviation, some sources spell it without a period; others use a period to parallel "Mr." It is correctly used before a woman's name but not before her husband's name: *Ms. Leslie Taubman* or *Ms. Taubman (not "Ms. Steven Taubman").*

much/many Use many rather than much to modify plural nouns: *They had many (not "much") dogs. There were too many (not "much") facts to absorb.*

Muslim/Moslem Muslim is now the preferred form for an adherent of Islam, though Moslem, the traditional form, is still in use.

mutual One current meaning of mutual is "reciprocal": *Employers and employees sometimes suffer from a mutual misunderstanding.* Mutual can also mean "held in common; shared": *Their mutual goal is clearly understood.*

myself; herself; himself; yourself The -self pronouns are intensive or reflexive, intensifying or referring to an antecedent: *Kerri herself said so. Mike and I did it ourselves.* Questions are raised when the -self forms are used instead of personal pronouns (I, me, etc.) as subjects, objects, or complements.

This use of the -self forms is especially common in informal speech and writing: *Many came to welcome my wife and myself back from China.* All these forms are also used, alone or with other nouns or pronouns, after "as," "than," or "but" in all varieties of speech and writing: *Letters have arrived for everyone but the counselors and yourselves.* Although there is ample precedent in both British and American usage for the expanded uses of the -self constructions, the -self pronouns should be used in formal speech and writing only with the nouns and pronouns to which they refer: *No one except me (not "myself") saw the movie.*

nauseous/nauseated Nauseated is generally preferred in formal writing over nauseous: *The wild ride on the roller coaster made Wanda feel nauseated.*

neither . . . nor When used as a correlative, neither is almost always followed by nor: *neither Caitlyn nor her father . . .* The subjects connected by neither . . . nor take a singular verb when both subjects are singular *(Neither Caitlyn nor her father is going to watch the program)* and a plural verb when both are plural *(Neither the rabbits nor the sheep have been fed yet today).* When a singular and a plural subject are joined by these correlatives, the verb should agree with the nearer noun or pronoun: *Neither the mayor nor the council members have yielded. Neither the council members nor the mayor has yielded.*

nohow The word nohow, nonstandard usage for "in no way" or "in any way," should be avoided in speech and writing.

none None can be treated as either singular or plural depending on its meaning in a sentence. When the sense is "not any persons or things," the plural is more common: *The rescue party searched for survivors, but none were found.* When none is clearly intended to mean "not one" or "not any," it is followed by a singular verb: *Of all the ailments I have diagnosed during my career, none has been stranger than yours.*

no . . . nor/no . . . or Use no . . . or in compound phrases: *We had no milk or eggs in the house.*

nothing like, nowhere near Both phrases are used in informal speech and writing, but they should be avoided in formal discourse. Instead, use "not nearly": *The congealed pudding found in the back of the refrigerator is not nearly as old as the stale bread on the second shelf.*

nowheres/nowhere The word nowheres, nonstandard usage for nowhere, should be avoided in speech and writing.

of Avoid using of with descriptive adjectives after the adverbs "how" or "too" in formal speech and writing. This usage is largely restricted to informal discourse: *How long of a ride will it be? It's too cold of a day for swimming.*

off of/off Off of is redundant and awkward; use off: *The cat jumped off the sofa.*

OK/O.K./okay All three spellings are considered acceptable, but the phrases are generally reserved for informal speech and writing.

on account of/because of Since it is less wordy, because of is the preferred phrase: *Because of her headache, they decided to go straight home.*

on the one hand/on the other hand These two transitions should be used together: *On the one hand, we hoped for fair weather. On the other hand, we knew the rain was needed for the crops.* This usage, though, can be wordy. Effective substitutes include "in contrast," "but," "however," and "yet": *We hoped for fair weather, yet we knew the rain was needed for the crops.*

only The placement of only as a modifier is more a matter of style and clarity than of grammatical rule. In strict, formal usage, only should be placed as close as possible *before* the word it modifies. In the following sentence, for example, the placement of the word only suggests that no one but the children was examined: *The doctor examined only the children.* In the next sentence, the placement of only says that no one but the doctor did the examining: *Only the doctor examined the children.* Nonetheless, in all types of speech and writing, people often place only before the verb regardless of what it modifies. In spoken discourse, speakers may convey their intended meaning by stressing the word or construction to which only applies.

owing to the fact that "Because" is generally accepted as a less wordy substitute for owing to the fact that.

pair/pairs When modified by a number, the plural of pair is commonly pairs, especially when referring to persons: *The three pairs of costumed children led off Halloween parade.* The plural pair is used mainly in reference to inanimate objects or nonhumans: *There are four pair (or "pairs") of shoelaces. We have two pair (or "pairs") of rabbits.*

passed/past Passed is a form of the verb meaning "to go by": *Bernie passed the same buildings on his way to work each day.* Past can function as a noun, adjective, adverb, or preposition. As a noun, past means "the history of a nation, person, etc.": *The lessons of the past should not be forgotten.* As an adjective, past means "gone by or elapsed in time": *John is worried about his past deeds.* As an adverb, past means "so as to pass by": *The fire engine raced past the parked cars.* As a preposition, past means "beyond in time": *It's past noon already.*

patience/patients Patience, a noun, means "endurance": *Chrissy's patience makes her an ideal baby-sitter.* Patients are people under medical treatment: *The patients must remain in the hospital for another week.*

peace/piece Peace is "freedom from discord": *The negotiators hoped that the new treaty would bring about lasting peace.* Piece is "a portion of a whole" or "a short musical arrangement": *I would like just a small piece of cake, please. The piece in E flat is especially beautiful.*

people/persons In formal usage, people is most often included to refer to a general group, emphasizing anonymity: *We the people of the United States . . .* Use persons to indicate any unnamed individuals within the group: *Will the persons who left their folders on the table please pick them up at their earliest convenience?* Except when individuals are being emphasized, people is generally suggested for use rather than persons.

per; a/an Per, meaning "for each," occurs mainly in technical or statistical contexts: *This new engine averages fifty miles per hour. Americans eat fifty pounds of chicken per person per year.* It is also frequently used in sports commentary: *He scored an average of two runs per game.* A or an is often considered more suitable in nontechnical use: *The silk costs ten dollars a yard. How many miles an hour can you walk?*

percent/per cent Percent comes from the English *per cent.*, an abbreviation of the Latin *per centum.* It almost always follows a number: *I made 12 percent interest by investing my money in that new account.* In formal writing, use the word rather than the symbol (%). The use of the two-word form per cent is diminishing.

percent/percentage Percent is used with a number, percentage with a modifier. Percentage is used most often after an adjective: *A high percentage of your earnings this year is tax deductible.*

personal/personnel Personal means "private": *The lock on her journal showed that it was clearly personal.* Personnel refers to employees: *Attention all personnel!* The use of personnel as a plural has become standard in business and government: *The personnel were dispatched to the Chicago office.*

phenomena Like words such as criteria and media, phenomena is a plural form (of "phenomenon"), meaning "an observable fact, occurrence, or circumstance": *The official explained that the disturbing phenomena we had seen for the past three evenings were nothing more than routine aircraft maneuvers.*

plain/plane Plain as an adjective means "easily understood," "undistinguished," or "unadorned": *His meaning was plain to all. The plain dress suited the gravity of the occasion.* As an adverb, plain means "clearly and simply": *She's just plain foolish.* As a noun, plain is a flat area of land: *The vast plain seemed to go on forever.* As a noun, plane has a number of different meanings. It most commonly refers to an airplane, but is also used in mathematics and fine arts and is a tool used to shave wood.

plenty As a noun, plenty is acceptable in standard usage: *I have plenty of money.* In informal speech and writing plenty is often a substitute for "very": *She was traveling plenty fast down the freeway.*

plus Plus is a preposition meaning "in addition to": *My salary plus overtime is enough to allow us a gracious lifestyle.* Recently, plus has been used as a conjunctive adverb in informal speech and writing: *It's safe, plus it's economical.* This usage is still considered nonstandard.

practicable/practical Practicable means "capable of being done": *My decorating plans were too difficult to be practicable.* Practical means "pertaining to practice or action": *It was just not practical to paint the floor white.*

practically Use practically as a synonym for "in effect," or "virtually." It is also considered correct to use it in place of "nearly" in all varieties of speech and writing.

precede/proceed Although both words are verbs, they have different meanings. Precede means "to go before": *Morning precedes afternoon.* Proceed means "to move forward": *Proceed to the exit in an orderly fashion.*

presence/presents Presence is used chiefly to mean "attendance; close proximity": *Your presence at the ceremony will be greatly appreciated.* Presents are gifts: *Thank you for giving us such generous presents.*

previous to/prior to "Before" is generally preferred in place of either expression: *Before (not "previous to" or "prior to") repairing the tire, you should check to see if there are any other leaks.*

principal/principle Principal can be a noun or an adjective. As a noun, principal means "chief or head official" *(The principal decided to close school early on Tuesday)* or "sum of capital" *(Invest only the interest, never the principal).* As an adjective, principal means "first or highest": *The principal ingredient is sugar.* Principle is a noun only, meaning "rule" or "general truth": *Regardless of what others said, she stood by her principles.*

providing/provided Both forms can serve as subordinating conjunctions meaning "on the condition that": *Provided (Providing) that we get the contract in time, we will be able to begin work by the first of the month.* While some critics feel that provided is more acceptable in formal discourse, both are correct.

question of whether/question as to whether Both phrases are wordy substitutes for "whether": *Whether (not "the question of whether" or "the question as to whether") it rains or not, we are planning to go on the hike.*

quiet/quite Quiet, as an adjective, means "free from noise": *When the master of ceremonies spoke, the room became quiet.* Quite, an adverb, means "completely, wholly": *By the late afternoon, the children were quite exhausted.*

quotation/quote Quotation, a noun, means "a passage quoted from a speech or book": *The speaker read a quotation of twenty-five lines to the audience.* Quote, a verb, means "to repeat a passage from a speech, etc.": *Marci often quotes from popular novels.* Quote and quotation are often used interchangeably in speech; in formal writing, however, a distinction is still observed between the two words.

rain/reign/rein As a noun, rain means "water that falls from the atmosphere to earth." As a verb, rain means "to send down; to give abundantly": *The crushed piñata rained candy on the eager children.* As a noun, reign means "royal rule;" as a verb, "to have supreme control": *The monarch's reign was marked by social unrest.* As a noun, rein means "a leather strap used to guide an animal;" as a verb, "to control or guide": *He used the rein to control the frisky colt.*

raise/rise/raze Raise, a transitive verb, means "to elevate": *How can I raise the cost of my house?* Rise, an intransitive verb, means "to go up, to get up": *Will housing costs rise this year?* Raze is a transitive verb meaning "to tear down, demolish": *The wrecking crew was ready to raze the condemned building.*

rarely ever/rarely/hardly The term rarely ever is used informally in speech and writing. For formal discourse, use either rarely or hardly in place of rarely ever: *She rarely calls her mother. She hardly calls her mother.*

real/really In formal usage, real (an adjective meaning "genuine") should not be used in place of really (an adverb meaning "actually"): *The platypus hardly looked real. How did it really happen?*

reason is because/reason is since Although both expressions are commonly used in informal speech and writing, formal usage requires a clause beginning with "that" after "reason is": *The reason the pool is empty is that (not* *"because"* or *"since"*) *the town recently imposed a water restriction.* Another alternative is to recast the sentence: *The pool is empty because the town recently imposed a water restriction.*

regarding/in regard to/with regard to/relating to/relative to/with respect to/respecting All the above expressions are wordy substitutes for "about," "concerning," or "on": *Janet spoke about (not "relative to," etc.) the PTA's plans for the September fund drive.*

relate to The phrase *relate to* is used informally to mean "understand" or "respond in a favorable manner": *I don't relate to chemistry.* It is rarely used in formal writing or speech.

repeat it/repeat it again *Repeat it* is the expression to use to indicate someone should say something for a second time: *I did not hear your name; please repeat it. Repeat it again* indicates the answer is to be said a third time. In the majority of instances, *repeat it* is the desired phrase; *again,* an unnecessary addition.

respectful/respective *Respectful* means "showing (or full of) respect": *If you are respectful toward others, they will treat you with consideration as well. Respective* means "in the order given": *The respective remarks were made by executive board members Joshua Whittles, Kevin McCarthy, and Warren Richmond.*

reverend/reverent As an adjective (usually capitalized), *Reverend* is an epithet of respect given to a clergyman: *The Reverend Mr. Jones gave the sermon.* As a noun, a *reverend* is "a clergyman": *In our church, the reverend opens the service with a prayer. Reverent* is an adjective meaning "showing deep respect": *The speaker began his remarks with a reverent greeting.*

right/rite/write *Right* as an adjective means "proper, correct" and "as opposed to left;" as a noun it means "claims or titles;" as an adverb it means "in a straight line, directly;" as a verb it means "to restore to an upright position." *Rite* is a noun meaning "a solemn ritual": *The religious leader performed the necessary rites. Write* is a verb meaning "to form characters on a surface": *The child liked to write her name over and over.*

says/said Use *said* rather than *says* after a verb in the past tense: *At the public meeting, he stood up and said (not "says"), "The bond issue cannot pass."*

seldom ever/seldom *Seldom* is the preferred form in formal discourse: *They seldom (not "seldom ever") visit the beach.*

sensual/sensuous *Sensual* carries sexual overtones: *The massage was a sensual experience. Sensuous* means "pertaining to the senses": *The sensuous aroma of freshly baked bread wafted through the house.*

set/sit *Set,* a transitive verb, describes something a person does to an object: *She set the book down on the table. Sit,* an intransitive verb, describes a person resting: *Marvin sits on the straight-backed chair.*

shall/will Today, *shall* is used for first-person questions requesting consent or opinion: *Shall we go for a drive? Shall I buy this dress or that?* *Shall* can also be used in the first person to create an elevated tone: *We shall call on you at six o'clock.* It is sometimes used with the second or third person to state a speaker's resolution: *You shall obey me.*

Traditionally, *will* was used for the second and third persons: *Will you attend the party? Will he and she go as well?* It is now widely used in speech and writing as the future-tense helping verb for all three persons: *I will drive, you will drive, they will drive.*

should/would Rules similar to those for choosing between "shall" and "will" have long been advanced for should and would. In current American usage, use of would far outweighs that of should. Should is chiefly used to state obligation: *I should repair the faucet. You should get the parts we need.* Would, in contrast, is used to express a hypothetical situation or a wish: *I would like to go. Would you?*

since Since is an adverb meaning "from then until now": *She was appointed in May and has been supervisor ever since.* It is also used as an adverb meaning "between a particular past time and the present, subsequently": *They had at first refused to cooperate, but have since agreed to volunteer.* As a preposition, since means "continuously from": *It has been rainy since June.* It is also used as a preposition meaning "between a past time or event and the present": *There have been many changes since the merger.* As a conjunction, since means "in the period following the time when": *He has called since he changed jobs.* Since is also used as a synonym for "because": *Since you're here early, let's begin.*

situation The word situation is often added unnecessarily to a sentence: *The situation is that we must get the painting done by the weekend.* In such instances, consider revising the sentence to pare excess words: *We must get the painting done by the weekend.*

slow/slowly Today slow is used chiefly in spoken imperative constructions with short verbs that express motion, such as "drive," "walk," "swim," and "run." For example: *Drive slow, Don't walk so slow.* Slow is also combined with present participles to form adjectives: *He was slow-moving. It was a slow-burning fire.* Slowly is found commonly in formal writing and is used in both speech and writing before a verb *(He slowly walked through the hills)* as well as after a verb *(He walked slowly through the hills).*

so Many writers object to so being used as an intensifier, noting that in such usage it is often vague: *They were so happy.* So followed by "that" and a clause usually eliminates the vagueness: *They were so happy that they had been invited to the exclusive party.*

so/so that So that, rather than so, is most often used in formal writing to avoid the possibility of ambiguity: *He visited Aunt Lucia so that he could help her clear the basement.*

some Some is often used in informal speech and writing as an adjective meaning "exceptional, unusual" and as an adverb meaning "somewhat." In more formal instances, use "somewhat" in place of some as an adverb or a more precise word such as "remarkable" in place of some as an adjective: *Those are unusual (not "some") shoes. My sister and brother-in-law are going to have to rush somewhat (not "some") to get here in time for dinner.*

somebody/some body Somebody is an indefinite pronoun: *Somebody recommended this restaurant.* Some body is a noun modified by an adjective: *I have a new spray that will give my limp hair some body.*

someone/some one Someone is an indefinite pronoun: *Someone who ate here* *said the pasta was delicious.* Some one is a pronoun adjective modified by "some": *Please pick some one magazine that you would like to read.*

someplace/somewhere Someplace should be used only in informal writing and speech; use somewhere for formal discourse.

sometime/sometimes/some time Traditionally, these three words have carried different meanings. Sometime means "at an unspecified time in the future": *Why not plan to visit Niagara Falls sometime?* Sometimes means "occasionally": *I visit my former college roommate sometimes.* Some time means "a span of time": *I need some time to make up my mind about what you have said.*

somewheres Somewheres is not accepted in formal writing or speech; use the standard "somewhere": *She would like to go somewhere (not "somewheres") special to celebrate New Year's Eve.*

split infinitive There is a longstanding convention that prohibits placing a word between "to" and the verb: *To understand fully another culture, you have to live among its people for many years.* This convention is based on an analogy with Latin, in which an infinitive is only one word and therefore cannot be divided. Criticism of the split infinitive was especially strong when the modeling of English on Latin was especially popular, as it was in the nineteenth century. Today many note that a split infinitive sometimes creates a less awkward sentence: *Many American companies expect to more than double their overseas investments in the next decade.*

stationary/stationery Although these two words sound alike, they have very different meanings. *Stationary* means "staying in one place": *From this distance, the satellite appeared to be stationary.* Stationery means "writing paper": *A hotel often provides stationery with its name preprinted.*

straight/strait Straight is most often used as an adjective meaning "unbending": *The path cut straight through the woods.* Strait, a noun, is "a narrow passage of water connecting two large bodies of water" or "distress, dilemma": *He was in dire financial straits.*

subsequently/consequently Subsequently means "occurring later, afterward": *We went to a new French restaurant for dinner; subsequently, we heard that everyone who had eaten the Caesar salad became ill.* Consequently means "therefore, as a result": *The temperature was above 90 degrees for a week; consequently, all the tomatoes burst on the vine.*

suppose to/supposed to; use to/used to Both suppose to and use to are incorrect. The preferred usage is supposed to or used to: *I was supposed to (not "suppose to") get up early this morning to go hiking in the mountains. I used to (not "use to") enjoy the seashore, but now I prefer the mountains.*

sure/surely When used as an adverb meaning surely, sure is considered inappropriate for formal discourse. A qualifier like "certainly" should be used instead of sure: *My neighbors were certainly right about it.* It is widely used, however, in speech and informal writing: *They were sure right about that car.*

sure and/sure to; try and/try to Sure to and try to are the preferred forms for formal discourse: *Be sure to (not "sure and") come home early tonight. Try to (not "try and") avoid the traffic on the interstate.*

taught/taut Taught is the past tense of "to teach": *My English teachers taught especially well.* Taut is "tightly drawn": *Pull the knot taut or it will not hold.*

than/then Than, a conjunction, is used in comparisons: *Robert is taller than Michael.* Then, an adverb, is used to indicate time: *We knew then that there was little to be gained by further discussion.*

that The conjunction that is occasionally omitted, especially after verbs of thinking, saying, believing, and so forth: *She said (that) they would come by train.* The omission of the conjunction almost always occurs when the dependent clause begins with a personal pronoun or a proper name. The omission is most frequent in informal speech and writing.

that/which Traditionally, that is used to introduce a restrictive clause: *They should buy the cookies that the neighbor's child is selling.* Which, in contrast, is used to introduce nonrestrictive clauses: *The cookies, which are covered in chocolate, would make a nice evening snack.* This distinction is maintained far more often in formal writing than in everyday speech, where voice can often distinguish restrictive from nonrestrictive clauses.

that/which/who That is used to refer to animals, things, and people: *That's my dog. I like that pen. Is that your mother?* In accepted usage, who is used to refer only to people: *Who is the man over there?* Which is used to refer only to inanimate objects and animals: *Which pen do you prefer? Which dog is the one that you would like to buy?*

their/there/they're Although these three words sound alike, they have very different meanings. Their, the possessive form of "they," means "belonging to them": *Their house is new.* There can point out place *(There is the picture I was telling you about)* or function as an expletive *(There is a mouse behind you!).* They're is a contraction for "they are": *They're not at home right now.*

them/those Them is nonstandard when used as an adjective: *I enjoyed those (not "them") apples a great deal.*

this here/these here/that there/them there Each of these phrases is nonstandard: this here for "this;" these here for "these;" that there for "that;" them there for "those."

threw/thru/through Threw, the past tense of the verb "throw," means "to hurl an object": *He threw the ball at the batter.* Through means "from one end to the other" or "by way of": *They walked through the museum all afternoon.* Through should be used in formal writing in place of thru, a colloquial spelling.

thusly/thus Thusly is a pointless synonym for thus. Speakers and writers often use thusly only for a deliberately humorous effect.

till/until/'til Till and until are used interchangeably in speech and writing; 'til, a shortened form of until, is rarely used.

time period The expression time period is redundant, since "period" is a period of time. *The local ambulance squad reported three emergency calls in a one-week period (not "time period").*

to/too/two Although the words sound alike, they are different parts of speech and have different meanings. To is a preposition indicating direction or part of an infinitive; too is an adverb meaning "also" or "in extreme;" and two is a number: *I have to go to the store to buy two items. Do you want to come too?*

too Be careful when using too as an intensifier in speech and writing: *The dog is too mean.* Adding an explanation of the excessive quality makes the sentence more logical: *The dog is too mean to trust alone with children.*

toward/towards The two words are used interchangeably in both formal and informal speech and writing.

track/tract Track, as a noun, is a path or course: *The railroad track in the Omaha station has recently been electrified.* Track as a verb, is "to follow": *Sophisticated guidance control systems are used to track the space shuttles.* Tract is "an expanse of land" or "a brief treatise": *Jonathan Swift wrote many tracts on the political problems of his day.*

try and/try to While try to is the preferred form for informal speech and writing, both phrases occur in all types of speech and writing.

type/type of In written English, type of is the preferred construction: *This is an unusual type of flower.* In informal speech and writing, it is acceptable to use type immediately before a noun: *I like this type car.*

unexceptional/unexceptionable Although both unexceptional and unexceptionable are adjectives, they have different meanings and are not interchangeable. Unexceptional means "commonplace, ordinary": *Despite the glowing reviews the new restaurant had received, we found it offered unexceptional meals and services.* Unexceptionable means "not offering any basis for exception or objection; beyond criticism": *We could not dispute his argument because it was unexceptionable.*

unique Since unique is an absolute adjective meaning "one of a kind," it cannot sensibly be used with a modifier such as "very," "most," or "extremely": *That is a unique (not "very unique" or "most unique") outfit.*

usage/use Usage is a noun that refers to the generally accepted way of doing something. The word refers especially to the conventions of language: *"Most unique" is considered incorrect usage.* Use can be either a noun or a verb. As a noun, use means "the act of employing or putting into service": *In the adult education course, I learned the correct use of tools.* Usage is often misused in place of the noun use: *Effective use (not "usage") of your time results in greater personal satisfaction.*

use/utilize/utilization Utilize means "to make use of": *They should utilize the new profit-sharing plan to decrease taxable income.* Utilization is the noun form of utilize. In most instances, however, use is preferred to either utilize or utilization as less overly formal and stilted: *They should use the new profit-sharing plan to decrease taxable income.*

used to could/used to be able to The phrase used to could is nonstandard for used to be able to: *I used to be able to (not "used to could") touch my toes.*

very The adverb very is sometimes used unnecessarily, especially in modifying an absolute adjective: *It was a very unique experience.* In such instances, it clearly should be omitted. Further, very has become overworked and has lost much of its power. Use more precise modifiers such as "extremely" and "especially."

want in/want out Both phrases are informal: want in for "want to enter;"

want out for "want to leave": *The dog wants to enter (not "wants in"). The cat wants to leave (not "wants out").*

way/ways Way is the preferred usage for formal speech and writing; ways is used colloquially: *They have a little way (not "ways") to go before they reach the campground.*

when/where Where and when are not interchangeable: *Weekends are occasions when (not "where") we have a chance to spend time with the family.*

where at/where to Both phrases are generally considered to be too informal to be acceptable in good writing and speech: *Where is John? (not "Where is John at?") Where is Mike going? (not "Where is Mike going to?")*

where/that Where and that are not interchangeable: *We see by the memo that (not "where") overtime has been discontinued.*

which/witch Which is a pronoun meaning "what one": *Which desk is yours?* Witch is a noun meaning "a person who practices magic": *The superstitious villagers accused her of being a witch.*

who/whoever; whom/whomever Traditionally, who/whoever is used as a subject (the nominative case) and whom/whomever as an object (the objective case). In informal speech and writing, however, since who and whom often occur at the beginning of a sentence, people usually select who, regardless of grammatical function.

without/unless Without as a conjunction is a dialectical or regional use of unless.

with regards to/with regard to/as regards/regarding Use with regard to, regarding, or as regards in place of with regards to in formal speech and writing: *As regards your inquiry, we have asked our shipping department to hold the merchandise until Monday.*

who's/whose Who's is the contraction for "who is" or "who has": *Who's the person in charge here? Who's got the money?* Whose is the possessive form of who: *Whose book is this?*

would have Do not use the phrase would have in place of had in clauses that begin with "if" and express a state contrary to fact: *If the driver had (not "would have") been wearing his seat belt, he would have escaped without injury.*

would of/could of There is no such expression as would of or could of: *He would have (not "would of") gone.* Also, of is not a substitute for " 've,": *She would've (not "would of") left earlier.*

you was You was is nonstandard for you were: *You were (not "you was") late on Thursday.*

your/you're Your is the possessive form of "you": *Your book is overdue at the library.* You're is the contraction of "you are": *You're just the person we need for this job.*

18. Vocabulary-Building Puzzles

It's no surprise that people who love to solve word puzzles have superior vocabularies. Here are a number of different puzzles designed to add to *your* word power. There are three different types of puzzles to tease your brain and augment your vocabulary. Have fun!

Puzzle 1. Super Six

Most of the words in this puzzle have six letters; two of them have five. Your job is to fit each word listed below in its proper place in the puzzle. To help you get started, we've filled in one word, "mantra."

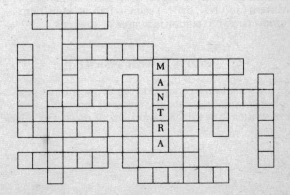

Word List

1. **cabal** (kə bal′) a small group of conspirators, especially one plotting against a government
2. **fecund** (fē′kund, fek′und) prolific, fertile, fruitful
3. **bisque** (bisk) a heavy cream soup of puréed shellfish or vegetables; ice cream made with powdered macaroons or nuts
4. **drivel** (driv′əl) nonsense
5. **bungle** (bung′gəl) to do clumsily or awkwardly; botch
6. **wimple** (wim′pəl) a woman's headcloth drawn in folds under the chin, formerly worn out of doors, and still in use by nuns
7. **morose** (mə rōs′) gloomy, depressed
8. **balsam** (bôl′səm) a fragrant resin exuded from certain trees
9. **demean** (di mēn′) to lower in dignity or standing; debase
10. **petard** (pi tärd′) an engine of war or an explosive device formerly used to blow in a door or gate, form a breach in a wall, etc.
11. **mantra** (man′trə, män′-) a word or formula to be recited or sung
12. **feisty** (fī′stē) animated, energetic, spirited, plucky
13. **welter** (wel′tər) to roll, toss, or heave, as waves; to wallow or become deeply involved
14. **supine** (sōō pīn′) lying on the back
15. **beadle** (bēd′l) in British universities, an official who supervises and leads processions; macebearer; a parish officer who keeps order during services, waits on the clergy, etc.
16. **duress** (dŏŏ res′, dyŏŏ-) coercion, force, constraint
17. **sinew** (sin′yŏŏ) tendon; a source of strength

Puzzle 2. Word Find #1

There are seventeen words hidden in this word-find puzzle. To complete the puzzle, locate and circle all the words. The words may be written forward, backward, up, or down. Good luck!

```
C A T A F A L Q U E D
R D N U C I B U R T E
U E P O I L L A C A T
C S C A R A B G D G A
I O Z O B E R M I E C
B E L B U A B I C N I
L E Z A R A S R U B T
E F O N T A N E L A S
B S A T U R N A L I A
M S I P O R P A L A M
```

Word List:

1. **malapropism** (mal′ə prop iz′əm) the act or habit of misusing words ridiculously

2. **rubicund** (rōō′bi kund′) red or reddish

3. **saturnalia** (sat′ər nā′lē ə) unrestrained revelry; orgy

4. **catafalque** (kat′ə fôk′, -fôlk′, -falk′) a raised structure on which the body of a deceased person lies in state

5. **quagmire** (kwag′mī³r′, kwog′-) an area of miry or boggy ground

6. **lucid** (lōō′sid) crystal-clear

7. **bauble** (bô′bəl) a cheap piece of ornamentation; gewgaw

8. **masticated** (mas′ti kā′tid) chewed

9. **calliope** (kə lī′ə pē′) a musical instrument consisting of a set of harsh-sounding steam whistles that are activated by a keyboard

10. **rebozo** (ri bō′sō, -zō) a long woven scarf, worn over the head and shoulders, especially by Mexican women

11. **rubric** (rōō′brik) a title, heading, direction, or the like, in a book, written or printed in red or otherwise distinguished from the rest of the text

12. **fontanel** (fon′tn el′) one of the spaces, covered by a membrane, between the bones of the fetal or young skull

13. **raze** (rāz) to wreck, demolish

14. **scarab** (skar′əb) a beetle regarded as sacred by the ancient Egyptians; a representation or image of a beetle, much used by the ancient Egyptians

15. **abnegate** (ab′ni gāt′) to surrender or renounce (rights, conveniences, etc.); deny oneself
16. **bursar** (bûr′sər, -sär) a treasurer or business officer, especially of a college or university
17. **crucible** (krōō′sə bəl) a vessel of metal or refractory material employed for heating substances to a high temperature

PUZZLE 3. ACROSTIC #1

First unscramble each of the seven vocabulary words so that it matches its definition. Then use the words to fill in the appropriate spaces on the correspondingly numbered lines. When you have completed the entire puzzle, another vocabulary word will read vertically in the first spaces.

1. PONILANER having no equal
2. YOGLUE a speech or writing in praise of a person
3. MERRYPUT nonsense
4. REESIO an evening party or social gathering
5. HUNRIC a mischievous child
6. SIKKO an open pavilion
7. TEARRA errors in writing or printing

1. __ __ __ __ __ __ __ __ __ __
2. __ __ __ __ __ __
3. __ __ __ __ __ __ __ __
4. __ __ __ __ __ __
5. __ __ __ __ __ __
6. __ __ __ __ __
7. __ __ __ __ __ __

Word List:

soirée   errata   nonpareil
eulogy   trumpery   kiosk
urchin

PUZZLE 4. WORD FIND #2

There are eighteen words hidden in this word find puzzle. To complete the puzzle, locate and circle all the words. The words may be written forward, backward, up, or down. Good luck!

```
N O N S E Q U I T U R
E B G A D F L Y B O E
T A U T O L O G Y E M
T L D U E U R O D N O
L U A R P U R L O I N
E S M N A C L O Y T S
S T S I J S U X E N T
O R O N E C N O N O R
M A N E M L O D B T A
E D S O D E N R U O T
P E J O R A T I V E E
```

Word List:

1. **nonce** (nons) the present; the immediate occasion or purpose
2. **damson** (dam′zən, -sən) the small dark-blue or purple fruit of a plum
3. **nexus** (nek′səs) a means of connecting; tie; link
4. **jape** (jāp) to jest; joke; jibe
5. **tontine** (ton′tēn, ton tēn′) an annuity-scheme in which subscribers share a common fund with the benefit of survivorship, the survivors' shares being increased as the subscribers die, until the whole goes to the last survivor
6. **balustrade** (bal′ə strād′, bal′ə strād′) a railing
7. **doxology** (dok sol′ə jē) a hymn or form of words containing an ascription of praise to God
8. **non sequitur** (non sek′wi tər, -tŏŏr′) an inference or conclusion that does not follow from the premises
9. **purloin** (pər loin′, pûr′loin) to take dishonestly; steal
10. **dolmen** (dōl′men, -mən, dol′-) a structure, usually regarded as a tomb, consisting of two or more large, upright stones set with a space between and capped by a horizontal stone
11. **doyen** (doi en′, doi′ən) the senior member, as in age or rank, of a group
12. **remonstrate** (ri mon′strāt) to protest
13. **nettlesome** (net′l səm) annoying; disturbing

14. **tautology** (tô tol′ə jē) needless repetition of an idea in different words, as in "widow woman"
15. **rue** (rōō) to deplore; mourn; regret
16. **gadfly** (gad′flī′) a person who repeatedly and persistently annoys or stirs up others with provocative criticism
17. **pejorative** (pə jôr′ə tiv, -jor′-) having a disparaging, derogatory, or belittling effect or force
18. **saturnine** (sat′ər nīn′) having or showing a sluggish, gloomy temperament

Puzzle 5. Acrostic #2

First unscramble each of the seven vocabulary words so that it matches its definition. Then use the words to fill in the appropriate spaces on the correspondingly numbered lines. When you have completed the entire puzzle, another vocabulary word will read vertically in the first spaces.

1. RACEUSA a break, usually in the middle of a verse
2. ORAMIRE a large wardrobe
3. BAMNELT moving lightly over a surface
4. SOURIOUX doting upon or submissive to one's wife
5. CANDIMENT a beggar
6. MYPONE a person, real or imaginary, from whom something, as a tribe, nation, or place, takes its name
7. FITFIN a light lunch (British usage)

1. __ __ __ __ __ __ __
2. __ __ __ __ __ __ __
3. __ __ __ __ __ __ __
4. __ __ __ __ __ __ __ __
5. __ __ __ __ __ __ __ __
6. __ __ __ __ __ __
7. __ __ __ __ __ __

Word List:

tiffin	lambent	mendicant
eponym	caesura	armoire
uxorious		

PUZZLE 6. WORD FIND #3

There are fourteen words hidden in this word-find puzzle. To complete the puzzle, locate and circle all the words. The words may be written forward, backward, up, or down. Good luck!

```
D  N  U  B  R  E  M  M  U  C
U  N  A  M  S  D  U  B  M  O
L  C  O  B  E  Z  A  G  A  M
C  O  A  L  E  S  C  E  H  P
I  I  M  Y  R  I  A  D  O  O
M  F  E  Y  N  E  E  R  U  T
E  T  I  O  L  O  G  Y  T  E
R  O  U  S  T  A  B  O  U  T
```

Word List:

1. **gazebo** (gə zā′bō, -zē′-) a structure, as a summerhouse or pavilion, built on a site affording a pleasant view
2. **roustabout** (roust′ə bout′) a wharf laborer or deck hand; a circus laborer
3. **compote** (kom′pōt) fruit stewed or cooked in syrup
4. **coif** (kwäf, koif) a hairstyle
5. **cummerbund** (kum′ər bund′) a wide sash worn as a waist-band, especially one with horizontal pleats worn beneath a dinner jacket
6. **seer** (sēr) a prophet; mystic
7. **ombudsman** (om′bədz mən, -man′, -bŏŏdz-, ôm′-) a commissioner appointed by a legislature to hear and investigate complaints by private citizens against government officials and agencies
8. **mahout** (mə hout′) the keeper or driver of an elephant
9. **tureen** (tŏŏ rēn′, tyŏŏ-) a large, deep covered dish for serving soup or stew
10. **coalesce** (kō′ə les′) to blend; join
11. **fey** (fā) fairylike; whimsical or strange; supernatural, enchanted; in unnaturally high spirits

12. **etiology** (ē′tē ol′ə jē) the study of the causes of diseases
13. **dulcimer** (dul′sə mər) a trapezoidal zither with metal strings that are struck with light hammers
14. **myriad** (mir′ē əd) many; innumerable

Puzzle 7. The "P" Patch

Each of the words in this puzzle begins with the letter "p." Your job is to fit each of the words listed below in its proper place in the puzzle. To help you get started, we've filled in one word, "pimpernel."

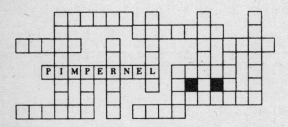

Word List:

1. **patois** (pat′wä, pä′twä, pa twä′) a rural or provincial form of speech, especially of French
2. **parse** (pärs, pärz) to describe (a word or series of words) grammatically, telling the parts of speech, inflectional forms, etc.
3. **poteen** (pə tēn′, -chēn′) illicitly distilled whiskey
4. **pimpernel** (pim′pər nel′, -nl) a plant of the primrose family, having scarlet, purplish, or white flowers that close at the approach of bad weather
5. **piebald** (pī′bôld′) having patches of black and white or of other colors
6. **paean** (pē′ən) any song of praise, joy, or thanksgiving
7. **prosody** (pros′ə dē) the science or study of poetic meters and versification
8. **pica** (pī′kə) a type size measuring twelve points
9. **pout** (pout) to sulk; look sullen
10. **pastiche** (pa stēsh′, pä-) a literary, musical, or artistic piece consisting wholly or chiefly of motifs or techniques borrowed from one or more sources

11. **pariah** (pə rī′ə) an outcast
12. **piddle** (pid′l) to waste time; dawdle
13. **placebo** (plə sē′bō) a substance having no pharmacological effect but given to a patient or subject of an experiment who supposes it to be a medicine
14. **paucity** (pô′si tē) scarcity; meagerness or scantiness
15. **peon** (pē′ən, -on) an unskilled laborer; drudge; person of low social status
16. **pupa** (pyōō′pə) an insect in the nonfeeding, usually immobile, transformation stage between the larva and the imago
17. **pinto** (pin′tō, pēn′-) piebald; mottled; spotted; a pinto horse

PUZZLE 8. WORD FIND #4

There are twenty words hidden in this word-find puzzle. To complete the puzzle, locate and circle all the words. The words may be written forward, backward, up, or down. Good luck!

```
T S I T A M S I M U N B
C A C H E P O T U O L F
A P F E R A L R S E E R
L X R A M S A I M R N E
L U D D I T E A O T G N
O A Z Y A I K G I U I E
U F A D O C H E R O O T
S S C A T H A R S I S I
C A S E M E N T Y O L C
```

Word List:

1. **triage** (trē äzh′) the process of sorting victims, as of a battle or disaster, to determine priority of medical treatment
2. **cachepot** (kash′pot′, -pō′) an ornamental container for holding or concealing a flowerpot
3. **frenetic** (frə net′ik) highly excited
4. **callous** (kal′əs) unfeeling
5. **miasma** (mī az′mə, mē-) noxious exhalations from putrescent matter
6. **outré** (ōō trā′) beyond the bounds of what is usual or considered proper

7. **cheroot** (shə rōōt′) a cigar having open, untapered ends
8. **feral** (fēr′əl, fer′-) wild, primitive
9. **flout** (flout) to treat with disdain, scorn, or contempt; scoff at
10. **catharsis** (kə thär′sis) purging of the emotions, especially through a work of art
11. **Luddite** (lud′īt) a member of any of various bands of English workers (1811–1816) who destroyed industrial machinery in the belief that its use diminished employment; any opponent of new technologies
12. **faux** pas (fō pä′) a social gaffe; error
13. **soigné** (swän yā′) carefully or elegantly done; well-groomed
14. **seer** (sēr) a prophet; mystic
15. **numismatist** (nōō miz′mə tist, -mis′-, nyōō-) a person who collects coins
16. **pastiche** (pa stēsh′, pä-) a literary, musical, or artistic piece consisting wholly or chiefly of motifs or techniques borrowed from one or more sources
17. **heady** (hed′ē) intoxicating; exciting
18. **coda** (kō′də) a passage concluding a musical composition
19. **cloy** (kloi) to weary by excess, as of food, sweetness, or pleasure; surfeit or sate
20. **casement** (kās′mənt) a window sash opening on hinges

PUZZLE 9. ACROSTIC #3

First unscramble each of the seven vocabulary words so that it matches its definition. Then use the words to fill in the appropriate spaces on the correspondingly numbered lines. When you have completed the entire puzzle, another vocabulary word will read vertically in the first spaces.

1. ZIMZUNE a crier who calls Muslims to prayer
2. NEXUPGE to erase
3. DAILYRAP the art of cutting and polishing gems; highly exact and refined in style
4. PARTIFIE a small alcoholic drink taken before dinner
5. COCARMENNY black magic; conjuration
6. TIGMEL a small tool; a cocktail
7. WESHEC to shun; avoid

1. __ __ __ __ __ __ __
2. __ __ __ __ __ __ __

3. __ __ __ __ __ __ __ __

4. __ __ __ __ __ __ __ __

5. __ __ __ __ __ __ __ __ __ __

6. __ __ __ __ __ __ __ __

7. __ __ __ __ __ __

Word List:

eschew	necromancy	lapidary
gimlet	muezzin	apéritif
expunge		

PUZZLE 10. WORD FIND #5

There are thirteen words hidden in this word-find puzzle. To complete the puzzle, locate and circle all the words. The words may be written forward, backward, up, or down. Good luck!

```
S L U M G U L L I O N S M
C I T C E L C E N B O R I
A N E D E M A N A V R I N
B A H E G E M O N Y O X A
R E C A N T E D E R M I R
O A A E P I P H A N Y L E
U P C E T A U N E T X E T
S A N C T I M O N I O U S
```

Word List:

1. **slumgullion** (slum gul′yən, slum′gul′-) a stew of meat, potatoes, and vegetables
2. **oxymoron** (ok′si môr′on) a figure of speech in which a locution produces an effect by seeming self-contradictory, as in "cruel kindness" or "to make haste slowly"
3. **paean** (pē′ən) any song of praise, joy, or thanksgiving
4. **minarets** (min′ə rets′, min′ə rets′) slender towers or turrets that are attached to a mosque and from which a muezzin calls the people to prayer
5. **sanctimonious** (sangk′tə mō′nē əs) insincere, hypocritical
6. **hegemony** (hi jem′ə nē, hej′ə mō′nē) leadership or predominant influence

7. **inane** (i nān′) pointless, silly
8. **extenuate** (ik sten′yo͞o āt′) to make or try to make seem less serious, especially by offering excuses
9. **nirvana** (nir vä′nə, -van′ə, nər-) in Buddhism, freedom from the endless cycle of personal reincarnations, with their consequent suffering, as a result of the extinction of individual passion, hatred, and delusion
10. **recanted** (ri kan′tid) retracted; denied
11. **edema** (i dē′mə) abnormal accumulation of fluids in body tissues, causing swelling
12. **epiphany** (i pif′ə nē) an appearance or manifestation, especially of a deity
13. **eclectic** (i klek′tik) selecting; choosing from various sources

Puzzle 11. Spectacular Seven

Each of the words in this puzzle has seven letters. Your job is to fit each of the words listed below in its proper place in the puzzle. To help you get started, we've filled in one word, "heinous," which means *reprehensible* or *evil*.

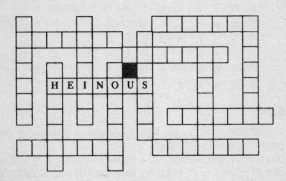

Word List:

1. **acolyte** (ak′ə līt′) an altar boy
2. **pismire** (pis′mī°r′, piz′-) an ant
3. **shoguns** (shō′gənz, -gunz) the chief Japanese military commanders from the eighth to twelfth centuries, or the hereditary officials who governed Japan, with the emperor as nominal ruler, until 1868

4. **panacea** (pan´ə sē´ə) a remedy for all ills; cure-all
5. **pooh-bah** (pōō´bä´) a person who holds several positions, especially ones that give him importance; a pompous person
6. **hirsute** (hûr´sōōt, hûr sōōt´) hairy
7. **foibles** (foi´bəlz) minor weaknesses or failings of character
8. **debacle** (də bä´kəl, -bak´əl, dā-) a general breakup or dispersion; sudden collapse
9. **carping** (kär´ping) fault-finding; critical
10. **cuckold** (kuk´əld) the husband of an unfaithful wife
11. **distaff** (dis´taf) a staff with a cleft end for holding wool, flax, etc., from which the thread is drawn in spinning by hand; the female sex; woman's work
12. **palfrey** (pôl´frē) a riding horse, as distinguished from a war horse; a woman's horse
13. **winsome** (win´səm) cute, charming

PUZZLE 12. WORD FIND #6

There are nineteen words hidden in this word-find puzzle. To complete the puzzle, locate and circle all the words. The words may be written forward, backward, up, or down. Good luck!

```
P  R  E  L  A  P  S  A  R  I  A  N
E  E  M  E  T  I  E  R  V  U  E  O
I  M  B  R  O  G  L  I  O  B  H  I
G  O  D  H  A  R  M  A  O  G  C  T
N  T  E  S  P  O  U  S  E  H  U  A
O  I  B  T  I  B  M  A  G  E  A  R
I  P  A  N  D  E  M  I  C  R  G  O
R  E  C  A  F  F  E  F  A  K  I  R
R  S  A  V  O  I  R  F  A  I  R  E
T  N  A  C  I  R  Y  G  E  N  A  P
```

Word List:

1. **peroration** (per´ə rā´shən) the concluding part of a speech or discourse
2. **oeuvre** (ûrv, ûrv´rə) the works of a writer, painter, or the like, taken as a whole

3. **prelapsarian** (prē'lap sâr'ē ən) pertaining to conditions existing before the fall of humankind

4. **mummery** (mum'ə rē) an empty or ostentatious performance

5. **gherkin** (gûr'kin) a pickle

6. **fakir** (fə kēr', fā'kər) a Muslim or Hindu religious ascetic or mendicant monk commonly considered a wonder worker

7. **métier** (mā'tyā, mā tyā') an occupation

8. **peignoir** (pān wär', pen-, pān'wär, pen'-) a woman's dressing gown

9. **pandemic** (pan dem'ik) (of a disease) prevalent throughout an entire country or continent or the whole world

10. **savoir faire** (sav'wär fâr') a knowledge of just what to do in any situation; tact

11. **gauche** (gōsh) uncouth; awkward

12. **imbroglio** (im brōl'yō) a confused state of affairs

13. **panegyric** (pan'i jir'ik, -jī'rik) an oration, discourse, or writing in praise of a person or thing

14. **dharma** (där'mə, dur'-) in Buddhism, the essential quality or nature, as of the cosmos or one's own character

15. **efface** (i fās') to wipe out; cancel or obliterate; make (oneself) inconspicuous

16. **espouse** (i spouz', i spous') to advocate or support; marry

17. **epitome** (i pit'ə mē) a person or thing that is typical of or possesses to a high degree the features of a whole class; embodiment

18. **gambit** (gam'bit) in chess, an opening in which a player seeks by sacrificing a pawn or piece to obtain some advantage; any maneuver by which one seeks to gain an advantage

19. **cant** (kant) deceit; insincerity or hypocrisy; the private language of a group, class, or profession; singsong or whining speech

ANSWERS TO PUZZLES

Answers to Puzzle 1

```
  C A B A L
  I
F   S U P I N E
E Q                 M O R O S E
C U         D       A         I   F
U   W E L T E R     N   B U N G L E
N I         E       T     E   E   I
D E M E A N         I     A   W   S
  P         V       P E T A R D   T
B A L S A M         L     L
  E             D U R E S S
```

Answers to Puzzle 2

(word search grid — Puzzle 2)

Answers to Puzzle 3

nonpareil	having no equal
eulogy	a speech or writing in praise of a person
trumpery	nonsense
soirée	an evening party or social gathering
urchin	a mischievous child
kiosk	an open pavilion
errata	errors in writing or printing

(netsuke (net'skē, -skä) in Japanese art, a small carved figure, originally used as a buttonlike fixture on a man's sash)

Answers to Puzzle 4

(word search grid — Puzzle 4)

Answers to Puzzle 5

caesura	a break, usually in the middle of a verse
armoire	a large wardrobe
lambent	moving lightly over a surface
uxorious	doting upon or submissive to one's wife
mendicant	a beggar
eponym	a person, real or imaginary, from whom something, as a tribe, nation, or place, takes its name
tiffin	a light lunch (British usage)

Answers to Puzzle 6

(word search grid — Puzzle 6)

Answers to Puzzle 7

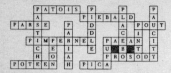

Answers to Puzzle 8

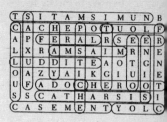

Answers to Puzzle 9

muezzin	a crier who calls Muslims to prayer
expunge	to erase
lapidary	the art of cutting and polishing gems; highly exact and refined in style
apéritif	a small alcoholic drink taken before dinner
necromancy	black magic; conjuration
gimlet	a small tool; a cocktail
eschew	to shun; avoid

(mélange (mā länzh′, -länj′) a mixture or medley)

Answers to Puzzle 10

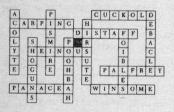

Answers to Puzzle 11

Answers to Puzzle 12

TIPS FOR FURTHER STUDY

Random House Webster's College Dictionary, Newly Revised and Updated. Random House, Inc. © 1996. One of America's best general dictionaries. It is especially strong in its coverage of new words. Definitions are clear and easy to understand.

Webster's New World College Dictionary, Third College Edition, Revised and Updated. Macmillan, © 1995. One of America's best dictionaries, *Webster's New World* features extremely clear definitions and labels.

Random House Unabridged Electronic Dictionary, CD-ROM, Version 2.0 for Windows 95. The first and only unabridged dictionary available as a Windows 95 and Windows 3.1 CD-ROM—featuring over 115,000 pronunciations and 2,200 graphic images.

Grow Your Vocabulary, Rob Schleifer. Random House, Inc. © 1995. In an inviting format, this book combines a practical vocabulary-building program with a fascinating study of word origins. Each highlighted English word root is accompanied by a selection of words derived from that root.

30 Days to a More Powerful Vocabulary, Dr. Wilfred Funk & Norman Lewis. Pocket Books, © 1970. The most widely used manual of its kind, this book shows how to acquire a larger, more effective vocabulary in one month by studying 15 minutes a day.

INDEX